Lure of the Lone Trail

Lure of the Lone Trail

Writings from the North Woods

Glen Sheppard

Momentum Books Ltd.
Ann Arbor, Michigan

Manufactured in the United States of America

1995 1994 1993   5 4 3 2 1

Momentum Books Ltd.
210 Collingwood, Suite 106
Ann Arbor, Michigan 48103
U.S.A.

ISBN 1-879094-20-7

Library of Congress Cataloging-in-Publication Data

Sheppard, Glen, 1936-
    Lure of the lone trail : writings from the North Woods / by Glen
Sheppard ; illustrations by Doug Parrish.
        p.   cm.
    ISBN 1-879094-20-7 (paper) : $15.95
    1. Charlevoix County (Mich.) — Description and travel. 2. Outdoor
life — Michigan — Charlevoix County. 3. Natural History — Michigan
— Charlevoix County — Outdoor books. 4. Au Sable River Region
(Mich.) — Description and travel. 5. Outdoor life — Michigan — Au
Sable River Region. 6. Natural history — Michigan — Au Sable River
Region — Outdoor books.   I. Title.
F572.C4S54 1993
917.74'860443 — dc20   92-30391
                                                           CIP

Dedicated to Dave Smethurst, George and Robin Buchner, Art Neumann, Carl T. Johnson, Ken Ide, Tom Opre, Rip VanWinkle, Myrl Keller, Ford Kellum, Jack Lockwood, Warren Shapton, Tom Washington, Ralph MacMullan, Gene Gazlay, John Spencer, Bill Rustem, Ned Caveney, John Tanton, John MacGregor, Pete Petoskey, Charlie Welch, Gordon Guyer, Nels Johnson, Gary Schnicke, Ralph Bailey, Chuck Harris, Bud Jones, Bill Bullen, Rusty Gates, and hundreds of others who left the trenches to lead the charge for Michigan conservation, including the dauntless ranks of conservation officers who have risked their lives to shepherd our natural heritage.

Contents

From the Publisher

There's a poet at work in northern Michigan. Only he's not writing rhymes. He's writing the kind of easy-to-read stories that make you laugh and cry and want to read passages out loud to someone. Actually, Glen Sheppard feels rather than writes. And he transmits those feelings with an economy of words reminiscent of the young Ernest Hemingway. There must be something in the northern Michigan waters!

These are stories not so much about people as they are about the land they inhabit, and its wildlife. They are told from the point of view of a man who has spent his life in the north, living and loving it with a passion. What makes it all seem like poetry is the respectful way he captures the smells and sounds of the north country. You can see the morning fog. You can hear the soft tread of a ten-point buck, and the splash of a trout. You can taste the early frost that turns his landscapes into magical scenes.

Nearly thirty years ago Glen Sheppard bought the *North Woods Call*, a small northern Michigan newspaper that specialized in outdoor news. That gave him license to write a column about anything he wanted to. Fortunately, he chose to immortalize the land he lives on. This book is a selection of Shep's finest columns, grouped by season. If you've been lucky enough to smell the pines in northern Michigan and wondered whether that scent could ever be captured, it has been — on these pages. If you've never experienced the magnificence of the north, these stories will transport you there, heart and soul.

Foreword

Though I hadn't met Glen Sheppard when I was appointed to the Michigan Natural Resources Commission in 1986, like all serious Michigan conservationists I knew him and his newspaper, the *North Woods Call*, by reputation. I soon met Shep and concluded that reputation may be understated. The *Call* and Shep are a single entity. They have been one of the most stable, predictable defenders of Michigan's natural resources for decades. A few months later, I agreed to serve as interim director of the Michigan Department of Natural Resources. By that time, Shep and I had become friends. I soon learned that his first allegiance is to his north woods (coming in second, I suspect, is wife Mary Lou, followed by his dogs).

He never hesitated to tell the world when he thought I was on the wrong course. But through it all we remained friends, he, I believe, respecting my sincerity and me his. I also discovered there is much I could learn about Michigan conservation and its people from this blunt, sometimes snarling, creature of swamps and trout streams. Though we might disagree on intensity, Shep never once gave me a bum steer on a conservation issue. On the editorial page in each issue is a bold-faced statement telling you where Shep stands. It announces that the *Call* is "An admittedly biased newspaper. Dedicated to the proposition that there is only one side in any issue involving natural resources ... NATURE'S!" Make no mistake, Shep means it.

Some say he is a rogue. I've never seen him care enough to dispute those who attack his character. I once heard him say, "Hell, he won't be in this business long enough to matter," about a public official who had slammed him in one of the state's largest papers. (And, sure enough, that official wasn't around long.)

It is said his news and editorial writing is rapier sharp. Also that it bludgeons like a sledge hammer. Whatever, you instantly grasp the message. Shep likes to remind cautious, indecisive public officials that "the guy who penned the line 'discretion is the better part of valor' was a damned discreet coward." I have yet to hear anyone accuse Shep of being overly circumspect.

Gordon Guyer
President
Michigan State University

Postscript: I can't leave this without pitching a commercial for Michigan's natural resources and the *North Woods Call*. As well as the *Call* serves Michigan conservation, its shortcoming is that not enough of the people who care about the things Shep writes about in these columns read it. *Call* readers become Michigan's best informed (and often most motivated) conservationists. We need more of them. For subscription details write to the *North Woods Call*, 00509 Turkey Run, Charlevoix, MI 49720.

Introduction

*D*etroit *Free Press* columnist Hugh McDiarmid sat at our table a bit ago, sipping our Scotch and scanning the galley proofs for this book. "Where is the introduction?" he demanded. "Every author has to write an introduction giving his wife credit for his work!" Hugh barked. (If you know him you'll understand.)

Well, the last thing I consider myself, or want to be, is an author. But Hugh is right. Writing these columns, and far more so putting out the *North Woods Call*, would long ago have become an unbearable grind if Mary Lou were not my partner in this exercise and virtually all of the experiences and emotions related here.

Over the years, many *North Woods Call* readers have urged us to assemble the *Ramblings* columns in a book. It just never interested me. So, in reality, this book is far more a creation of Ed and Judy McGlinn than of Glen Sheppard. Ed insisted the book be published. He found a publisher, selected the columns printed here from hundreds that have appeared in the *Call*. Then he and Judy edited them and nursed them to the final product.

Several dogs, especially Toots and Call, also contributed to the depth of joy I find in the out-of-doors. I cannot imagine life without a dog by my side, in the field or at the hearth and fly-tying bench.

Dad — William L. Sheppard — planted and nurtured the seed, then some military experiences honed a lust to forever recapture, nourish and protect the appreciation for nature, quiet, solitude and life you may find expressed here.

There's a postcard I've kept on my desk for 15 years. I don't know who sent it. It is postmarked from Saginaw. It arrived after I wrote a *Ramblings* column about the magic, the wonder, of the places where brook trout and mayflies live, suggesting they are God's favorite creations. It reads: "I really liked the *North Woods Ramble* part of the 7/24 issue of the *Call*. Yes, brook trout country is closer to where I am. Hope you make it back soon." It is signed: "G."

I know He didn't send it. But, I want to believe He really does agree.

Hope you do too.

G.L.S.
October 1992

The Lone Trail

The trails of the world be countless,
and most of the trails be tried;
you tread on the heels of the many,
till you come where the ways divide;
and one lies safe in the sunlight,
and the other is dreary and wan.
Yet you look aslant at the Lone Trail,
and the Lone Trail lures you on.
And somehow you're sick of the highway,
with its noise and its easy needs.
And you seek the risk of the by–way,
and you reck not where it leads.

Robert Service

SPRING

Favorite Mayflies
March 25, 1987

Which is the most beautiful, most fascinating mayfly on Michigan trout streams?

Absurd question? You've got more important things to ponder, you say — like your bank account or who's going to be the next president. You gotta be kidding. No one is that important. (Or really, that self-important.)

Lots of wondrous things live along and in trout streams. Trout can't be the most intriguing. Heck, if you've been at it for enough decades you've spent more time pondering the wonders of pine cones, mosses, currents, otters, kingfishers, and especially, mayflies than you have trout.

As a guy who since toddler stage has spent hundreds of hours on his belly and butt staring through eyes, that even at their best a half century ago weren't very darn good, at things like the first little green curl of a baby fern and again, most especially, at mayflies, I've sorta earned my stripes and rockers as an expert on the trivia of trout streams.

But I still haven't resolved which is the most wondrous of the mayflies. I have, however, decided that in trout country there is nothing comparable to mayflies.

The first time I recall posing the question to someone was a July morning in the mid-1950s. The night had been hot and humid, followed by a ponderous hatch of what we now know are Tricorythodes (white-winged black) mayflies — about size 24 — sometime between 6:00 and 7:00 a.m.

Back then we lumped them all into the same category: blue duns. You fished them from size 12 to 18. No one — at least no one we knew — fished anything smaller than a size 18 fly. And even that was considered sorta weird.

A 5X leader tippet in those days had the strength of an 8X today.

Most of us had read Ray Bergman's *Trout*. So we knew something about mayflies — but still not nearly as much as a beginning twelve-year-old does today.

Well, anyway, we were sitting on the bank of the South Branch, just inside what today is the no-kill water. My companion was an electrician at a GM plant down by Saginaw or Flint. I'd run into him trying to fish "my" hole for caddis flies several nights. He was a polite, neat guy. He fished the big caddis — Hex-hatch — dry and the rest of the time fished streamers. I was on a purist kick: nothing but dry flies.

Expecting the Tricorythodes hatch, I'd left my camp at Canoe Harbor about 7:00 a.m.

By 8:00 a.m. a cold front swept in. The air was full of the little mayflies. But the cold kept them from mating and dropping to the river (spinning) to lay their eggs. Thus, no trout were rising.

The guy from GM — probably fifteen or twenty years my senior — came trudging down the bank with a big streamer on his leader. I was brewing river-water tea on one of those old Army Sterno stoves. He sat down to share a cup.

One of the little flies — about the size of this O — fluttered to the water. I waded out, submerged my hand and lifted it, returning to the bank with the creature sitting, wings cocked like an emperor's crown, in my palm.

Digging a magnifying glass out of my vest, we took turns marveling at its perfection: the legs, the tail, the wings.

Unlike some important folks, an electrician and a young newsman instantly recognized that they could never "own" anything so precious. That this creation was far too magical to be anyone's property.

But he sorta half heartedly — because the fishing was lousy — suggested that Hendrickson mayflies are a bit more perfect than Trics. The discussion got pretty deep. (Fog was starting to roll up the river by then and we were on our second cup of tea.)

You can, of course, make an overwhelming argument in favor of any of the mayflies. Another favorite is the Hexagenia recurvata — Red Hex. It's about the size of the more common Hexagenia limbata — giant Michigan mayfly — but more colorful and much rarer. A few fishermen on the Jordan, Big Creek, Upper Manistee, Black and some other streams know it. They love it.

And sure, not even bluebirds, peregrine falcons and cardinals compare to the gray drake or brown drake. There's also an olive-colored mayfly, about size 14 and 16, that used to frequent the Jordan — before lamprey chemicals and sand — that has to rate with the best of them. (I've never identified it in the literature.) I've seen gossamer-winged, fairy-tailed mayflies on Antrim County's Cedar River that entomologists have yet to describe.

Ahh. Pre-trout season vapors can lead to an old fly flinger's memories down many paths — all rich, all worth exploring again.

And one truth persists: if mayflies survive there, God still claims it.

Munscong Bay
May 25, 1983

The trails of the world be countless,
and most of the trails be tried;
you tread on the heels of the many,
till you come where the ways divide;
and one lies safe in the sunlight,
and the other is dreary and wan.
Yet you look aslant at the Lone Trail,
and the Lone Trail lures you on.
And somehow you're sick of the highway,
with its noise and its easy needs.
And you seek the risk of the by-way,
and you reck not where it leads.

Robert Service

Joe Johnston looks back on it now, at where the trail divided for him and admits, wearily, that he had "the best of all worlds."

Yet he has no regrets for casting off on his own trail. It is long, some days it seems endless, with no sign of progress after fifteen or twenty hours of sheer gut labor. But it is his, and he's gonna make it work. He's gonna stick to it, even when it seems forsaken.

Here at Johnston's fishing camp on the flat muddy waters of Munscong, the work is never done. There may never be a real profit. The kind you put in the bank and watch interest grow on. At thirty-four, Joe isn't ready to accept that when morning breaks. But when the sun starts down over the waterfowl flooding and all he sees is another day, another month, another year of trying to catch up, he has to wonder.

Not that Joe is unique. The hunting and fishing world — the world of outdoorsmen — is loaded with those who chose the Lone Trail, with the ensuing risks and sacrifice, to do their thing. They want to be closer to the water, the woods, the swamp, the open air, despite the aching muscles, the gut-blinding fear that the next check will bounce, and the nagging guilt as they question if they have taken too much for themselves and can give too little to their families.

Joe threw security to the winds of Munscong in mid-1981, when he made a deal to take over the bankrupt Cole's fishing camp, seven miles east of Pickford, on the south shore of Munscong.

Others hadn't been able to hack it. The bank had it back. The cabins were, literally, under water — their floors rotten. The docks were worthless. The old camp store a shambles. The water, sewer, and electric system needed rebuilding.

But Joe Johnston knew he could make it. He made a modest down payment and went to work. There was no money to hire a carpenter, electrician, or plumber. There was only his own sweat and the skills learned during a lifetime on the farm and doing for himself.

He lay on his back in the mud to jack the cabins up, put modest foundations under them and replaced the floors. The dock pilings demanded hours of solo driving — then the ice tore them out this spring. There were yards of wiring to lay, ditches to dig, and plumbing to install.

It is nowhere near done. So Joe works from dawn to dusk. If there's an extra dollar or two he buys more material. If there isn't, he patches his way through the next day.

The good times are starting right now. The fishermen are coming to Munscong after its fabulous walleyes. Usually they limit out. Some cheat and limit out as many as three times a day.

"You can't keep 'em away from here," he says, his bent shoulders suddenly no longer hunched, his eyes and arm sweeping the bay. "Once they find out about it, they never get enough."

That's the way it was for Joe. He and his brother came here when they were in high school. They'd trapped their limit of beaver in Clare County, but could each trap ten more here. Fishermen were taking walleyes "hand over hand in three to four feet of water... I had to come back. I couldn't stay away. Then it got so I couldn't leave."

And when the ducks fly in the fall it is the same way. Joe and a brother own nine hundred decoys. Working decoys.

The best times are the guiding. Many camp patrons insist Joe go fishing with them. In the fall he guides duck hunters.

Those are the hours when the brute labor and endless list of unfinished chores are forgotten. He now is a part of the Munscong. Temporarily — not just a slave to it.

The cabins, the campground, the store, the docks are all spartan. The cabins have chairs, tables, stoves, space heaters, full bathrooms and beds. No TVs. No luxuries.

"The people who come here come to fish and hunt. They are up early and fish hard. When they quit they just want a place to cook their fish, take a shower, get warm, play a few cards, rig their tackle for tomorrow and sack out," Joe says.

"They're not here to loaf on the beach and get a tan, raise hell at a night club, or gawk in honky-tonk gift shops." (Good thing. There are no beaches on Munscong's clay shores and the honky-tonks are down or up the road, in Cedarville and the Soo.)

Tell Joe Johnston he's bucking the odds, that they are against him, and his eyes lose the dreary somberness of a day with his back bent to the shovel. He looks around the camp.

"It isn't much. But it was a lot less when I got here. You just wait until the lawn starts growing (where the mud is now) ... 'till I get some new paint on those cabins, ... 'till ..."

He'll probably make it, too. Those who choose the Lone Trail sometimes do, but it takes a cussed tough soul with a lot of poetry.

There's a lot of sinew and poetry in Joe Johnston — and in Munscong.

The Way It Was
March 23, 1988

Pondering the array of dry flies in the boxes bulging the fishing vest on the gun cabinet door all winter ignited flashbacks to simpler, maybe gentler, times on Michigan trout streams.

In one such recall, mammoth Hersch Campbell, an Au Sable South Branch river guide and pioneer canoe livery owner, is in the bow of my canoe casting that monstrous eleven-foot bamboo rod he was so proud of. As I recall, some "sport" had given it to him after returning from an Atlantic Salmon trip. Though you could probably hoist a canoe out of the river with it, Hersch thought it was just right for the South Branch's brook and brown trout.

All of the rods used on our rivers were more powerful then. Nine-foot cane rods, throwing eight- and nine-weight lines (we had letters for them then) were common. You could buy a pretty good cane rod at the discount drug stores (Kresge's or Cunningham's, I think) for just a few bucks.

Though many people didn't understand it, fly rods were extremely practical and versatile. Even the best level-wind plug reels required more skill than it took to pitch an acceptable fly cast. Spinning reels hadn't yet arrived on these shores.

We used our fly rods for everything from trout dry flies to four-inch bass minnows.

The old fly lines and leaders were a curse. The lines required constant care. They wore out fast and were expensive. Leaders were heavy and unpredictable. You tied your own and kept them between water-dampened felts in a little round tin thing. (I still have a couple somewhere.)

Waders were probably the most expensive thing in a fly fisherman's trunk. They were heavy, awkward, hot and unreliable. And you never went anywhere without your patching kit.

We learned to fly cast by holding a book between our elbow and side, so we wouldn't be able to use our upper arm. You counted "Mississippi one" for your backcast, then "Mississippi two" for the forward cast. Yeah, that's the way we did it. The trip to the trout streams was always an adventure. The roads were a nightmare if there had been rain. It seems that I recall an hours-long trip from Chase Bridge to highway M-72, and down to the old Smith Bridge, before the new bridge was built. Even portions of old highway M-18 below Houghton Lake weren't much better.

And cars! While most of what pass for cars today would be for-ever mired in the roads, the cars of that era were designed for them. It wasn't until about the 1950s that Detroit started putting out trust-worthy cars for a trip of a couple hundred miles. No matter how faithful you were with maintenance, something could, and often did, happen.

Savvy fishermen studied the garages in their favorite fishing areas. They tried to decide which had the best mechanics, kept the best inventory of parts and had the longest hours. You knew you were going to need them. You patronized "your garage" faithfully to cultivate the operator's friendship.

Reliable cars were the death knell for the full-service garage, where there was usually a card game you could get into if the weath-er turned foul.

In that time you could "make" a road just about anywhere in the barrens left by the pine loggers. All you had to do was drive in the straightest line from point A to B, possibly by evading some stumps and avoiding places where the second growth was too much. But it was very common to look at a map and decide to drive to this bend on the river — which could also get you in big trouble. If you made your own road you had to find it to get back after dark.

Though the details are sketchy at best, there is a memory of returning to the car one night and finding the lights wouldn't work. So while Dad drove, I stumbled along with a flashlight in front try-ing to find the bent grass from a few hours earlier with a flashlight. (Most younger fishermen have never had both lights on their car suddenly go bonkers. Things like that were almost routine back then.)

Of course, there were more miles of good trout streams. Streams like the Jordan, Pere Marquette, upper Manistee, Pine, Sturgeon, and many others had not yet been suffocated by sand or poisoned by lamprey chemicals. Canoes were friends. They brought fishermen and nature lovers — not screeching idiots — to the streams.

The Au Sable's Holy Water wasn't a solid strip of fertilized lawns and almost wall-to-wall porches. Campgrounds were quiet places — places of canvas and waders hanging in trees. Places where the noise and campfires were doused shortly after dusk.

A truly startling difference was in the fly boxes. Fly fishermen were nowhere near as complicated. Ray Bergman's *Trout* was our only bible. Simple — straightforward. No need to know Latin or carry a magnifying glass to verify the genus of fly that was hatching.

In our dry fly boxes, the major flies were Adams, blue dun, black gnat and a downwing grasshopper pattern. We messed around with others. But these were about all many guys bothered with, except during caddis time.

I was also fond of a bee imitation. All I can recall about it is that the body was a spiraled combination of yellow and black yarn. It had wings and hackle, but they are lost to memory. I'd fish it both wet and dry and take some nice fish.

Black gnats were just that — all black. Except I favored a short red hackle tail. I recall taking a sixteen-inch brown at mid-day, when the temperature was in the nineties, from the South Branch on a black gnat.

Dry flies were giants. A size 14 was considered small. Most fishermen thought you were a real nut if you fished a 16.

There were a few guys back then — most of them riverboat fishermen — who used tiny flies; 18s and 20s. They caught a lot of fish. We knew that they switched to worms when no one was looking.

Though I went on a tangent every few years tying up the colorful salmon streamers shown in *Trout*, the most deadly in my fly book was a Mickey Finn. One evening, a giant trout lunged out of a deep hole, under a sweeper, below the High Banks. When I struck, he rolled on the surface for a brief moment. He was an "easy three feet."

I went into shock. Bit my tongue and lost my Mickey Finn. All in about a second. It took me a half hour, or so, to get my breath back.

Since then I've landed many fish — salmon and steelhead — as big as that brown really was on flies. But it ain't the same. Never will be again.

And I've never since tasted a Vernor's ginger ale as good as those that came dripping water from the old red coolers at the gas station in Rose City. What daring ecstasy to stand there, looking at all the choices and trying to decide how to spend your nickel. Or was it three cents?

North Woods Spring
May 8, 1985

They say it is paradise. But if you get up on Whitefish Bay in mid-spring you'll learn it is for the birds.

Everyone in the Birch Hill Cafe (the only eatery open the first weekend in May) and at Curley's Motel is there for the birds. The birds, that is, that make Whitefish Point their jumping off point for the trek across Lake Superior.

Even the business folks are for the birds. The bird watchers and counters who travel to Paradise in late April and early May bring the only outside money that's around from the end of snowmobiling to Memorial Day.

Of course, all of the north country is a paradise as spring begins to finally claim the land.

Snow is still holding out in patches along the Tahquammenon River. The falls are, somehow, more powerful, more personal before the crowds arrive. There seems to be more freedom to be engulfed by their throbbing thunder, and to fantasize over their wonder.

The trilliums hadn't made it yet to Tahquammenon Country. A few leeks, and small swatches of green along roadsides, but the smell and sound of spring (especially tree sparrows and warblers) flooded ears and nostrils.

Somewhere west on the Shelldrake River a grouse's wings squeezed cymbal-like crashes out of the air. Oh what a grand and arrogant cock bird he must be.

With drizzly skies cleared by morning, you find Moran is kind of a breaking point. Things are suddenly green.

Back at Matchett Lake and elsewhere, the popples and birches are nearly leafed out. The frogs are plunging into the pond as you sneak around trying to grab one. The feel of the first frog in the hand in the spring is grand. Polliwogs wiggle through last year's cattail stalks. In a few days they'll be hidden by new-grown weeds.

The woodcock chicks, you discover, are about the size of two .22 long rifle shell boxes. And doing well. Both nests. But there's a painful, sinking feeling; without Toots it ain't the same. Damn!

A few caddis were hatching the other day; not a trout fed. The kingfisher cackles its haughty bray at your futile efforts.

To the south, on the warmer, richer Au Sable, Manistee, Pere Marquette and other rivers, the mayfly hatches have been heavy and the trout feeding — you are told. But who wants to share spring with all those humans?

Bluegills, too, are being a tease. If you catch them at the peak of the heat on a warm late afternoon they're just at the edge of the shallows. They nip at the nymph. But even the largest you are quick enough to hook are still numb from the long, mean winter.

Maybe the best is walking in the woods. Only now and in the late fall, can you see your boots as you scuff through the duff. Every living and dead thing is visible.

You walk consciously trying to avoid the *hepatica*, Dutchman's Breeches, trilliums, and other May flowers. They seem so fragile — miracles after more than three feet of snow. You silently scold yourself for stepping on two while trying to miss one.

The fungi in the swamp and on the decaying maples, popples, and beeches is surely a treasure. You can't resist chuckling at the folks you see bent over tulip beds. How much more magnificent these little wild things of the woods!

You've heard reports that the jack-in-the-pulpits are up. You look. Not here. Good excuse to return tomorrow.

Swallows clack and screech, threatening you with their swooping attacks, as you check the nesting boxes. The bluebirds are singing in the morning, but the swallows seem to have claimed nearly all of the more than two dozen boxes. Making more won't help, there isn't room for them.

Oh, that life was full of such dilemmas. That life was always spring in the north woods.

Anticipating Summer
June 1, 1988

The eight-and-a-half-foot Bob Summer's graphite rod strained slightly to hurl the shapeless blob of deer hair some forty feet against a lazy breeze. The day had been hot and muggy — up to ninety degrees in the sun. The breeze and drooping sun brought some relief.

Extreme drought has also brought relief from mosquitoes but not from blackflies. The first dragonflies of the season warmed their sparkling wings in the sun. The just over sixty-degree water was a refreshing and welcome coolness felt through the waders.

A few days before, when they were not legal, bass had eagerly taken nymphs cast for bluegills. Now, though none would be killed, they were legal targets for the deer hair bug.

The long, light rod is sorta small caliber for hefty largemouth bass. It has the spunk to turn a bass bug over, but not enough to turn a largemouth that dives for the weeds. A fair compromise.

In the stretching shadows, it was easy to imagine you could see the hulking forms of big fish with dark stripes down their side sliding over the bottom that lily pads will soon shade.

The first strike came after less than a dozen casts. Feeling the hook it turned to dive, changed its mind and spurted to the top, boiling at the surface twice before slicing off to the south. The rod arched deep into the butt section before it turned the bass. Maybe a minute later, pliers twisted the hook from its jaw. About thirteen or fourteen inches long.

Not a bad start.

To the north, a squawk gave away a goose with a string of fluffy youngsters rounding a bend. They circled a couple of times and then turned back into the little bay.

On more and more of these little lakes between the drumlins where there were no geese five or so years ago, there have been a pair nesting for the past several years and this year there are two pairs. They must compete with themselves and, in too many cases, with nesting mute swans.

On one lake a lone swan returned this year, without its mate. It cries a mournful song and repeatedly flies low, scanning the country for its lost lover. (The kind of thing that sends shivers down a goose hunter's spine.)

Bluegills started attacking the bass bug several times on every cast. They couldn't take the big hook and were only a nuisance. Wading farther down the shore got rid of the bluegills and with some patience, earned three bass in a row — the biggest, maybe twelve inches.

A swirl up against the bank, in no more than six inches of water, induced strain on the shoulder and rod. The line reached out to a good fifty feet and the bug dropped on the edge of the bank; it then plopped into the lake.

After letting it sit motionless for a few seconds, I twitched the rod slightly. The bug slid a few inches. I saw the fish's back before he opened his maw and inhaled the bug.

Hoo! This was gonna be fun.

He raced down the shore as I striped line off the old Marlin spring-powered fly reel. Then spun back at me. Zing! The auto reel paid for itself again, instantly retrieving slack line.

Then the fish dove. There isn't more than three or four feet of water there. He felt like he was burrowing in the mud. Sulking, he tested the rod and the six-pound-test leader tippet, sometimes shaking his head. No way the rod could lift him, as we played tug-of-war.

Bolting for the surface, his tail fluttered as he vaulted clear of the water and twisted for re-entry. The lowered rod tip came up and the line tightened under my palm.

Ha, threw him off balance. A good seventeen inches — maybe more.

Now he circled, still powerful, but without direction. He jumped again and again, but these were more like lazy circles with his head just out of water.

By the time I got him beside me and the pliers on the hook, he had grown to at least nineteen inches. A bullfrog heralded his release.

Continued casting to the bank brought three more bass — none over thirteen inches — to the hook.

Now the frogs and bugs were going crazy. An owl wailed somewhere up in the hardwoods. Tiny fawns with still wobbly legs would be coming to the lake soon to drink with their mothers.

Hello summer! Welcome back to the north woods. Linger as long as you can.

Au Sable Cannon
May 18, 1988

Slumping on the bank of the Au Sable's North Branch, wadered feet dangling in the river, squinting through clouded eyes at hatching Hendrickson and mahogany dun mayflies, something got to puzzling me.

Someone said time is not a factor in a perfect work. Yet they say God had only seven days to make heaven, earth, et cetera. Now, that's a mighty short deadline for making things as perfect as a northern Michigan trout stream, jillions of mayflies and May flowers, spring warblers, and lots of other perfect things that can be found in the north woods in the spring.

After stumbling and gawking around these hallowed places for decades, this department is still of the opinion that mayflies are the most perfect magnificent creatures. From the graceful wings, body, and tails of the tiny white-winged blacks to the giant Hexes, nothing else is shaped as right.

They are also a vital element in the life of such wondrous creatures as brook, brown trout, and grayling. And then stir in the fact that these things all live in trout streams and, surely, it took more than seven days just to come up with the idea, let alone make it happen.

It is nearly as mind-numbing that mere human beings can weave and twist imitations of these gossamer beings onto a hook and send life-like copies flitting through the air and down to the water to snare trout. That, with no depreciation of any other human endeavor, has to be an ultimate art.

And it had been a supreme afternoon. More than a half dozen brown trout had hooked themselves on the number 14 Quill Gordon fly cast into the riffles above Kellogg's Bridge. No longer being able to see the fly on the water or the trout's rise, it has to be a majestic day to hook that many.

It was necessary to fight the urge to slumber — as the afternoon sun warmed a bald head. Mary Lou had me scheduled to barbecue something — I forgot what — on the grill. A splash of Scotch was timely.

But I was almost asleep when the damn cannons started pounding.

Geezus!

Stumbling up the steep bank to the cabin, shoulders bent and a guttural growl rumbling from deep in the fly vest, the whole perfect afternoon was swept away.

The cabin has been here since 1903. Veterans from more than four wars have fled to it to rinse the agony from their minds and bodies. In those holes in Africa, France, Germany, the Philippines, Korea, and Vietnam, they had found the strength from their comrades and the promise of this rustic log retreat under the pines and beside the rippling water to hold out for just another minute, another hour, maybe, another night.

Here they have washed away the baseness that had bent their minds and souls and become whole men again. Here, where God made perfection, they had found the peace they had fought for.

No more. As the guns cracked and whined, a window pane fell to the floor in the upper story. Shattered.

Shattered just as thoroughly as the essence of the Au Sable and its promise of peace. And the reason to seek that peace.

Senseless. Here in Au Sable Country? Here in the paragon land where people will go to war because they know that back home there is something worth preserving, and returning to?

Here we make war!

But apparently, even Guardsmen (for whom we hold no disrespect) must have their supper.

The (aha, yeah, remember now) Platte Bay brown trout fillet Jean and Jerry Rakoczy had parted with, came off the grill as flaky and sweet as dessert. The tea and a round of cribbage passed. Then a second cup of tea watching the sun fall behind the artillery range.

Quiet has returned to Au Sable Country.

Time to blend some wood duck flank feathers, fur and hackles into rusty Hendricksons.

Three down, the wings just going on the fourth and — blaamm!

I turn up the volume on the Interlochen public radio station. Not even that will help.

If men must prepare for war, it has to be done in earnest. It has to be done at night.

How could the same God who created mayflies have created this madness? This insanity? This perversity?

Certainly He did. Or didn't He?

If He did, He should have had more than seven days to get His priorities figured out.

Saying Good-by To Denali
May 31, 1989

For sure, bird dogs don't always have something to do with life-changing decisions.

It started a long time before the other morning. It would have turned out this way even if the young English setter hadn't taken to stabbing her nose into mine about 5:00 a.m. to declare that the first chickadees were celebrating a new day in the hardwoods on this drumlin.

Rip, maybe, made it easier to accept. He'd called to say thanks for earlier comments on his fiftieth-plus opening day at his cabin on the Au Sable. This past April, he disclosed, with a deep tinge of regret in his voice, was the last.

Heading toward his ninetieth year, Rip has closed the cabin. He said the time comes when you have to accept that things are no longer what they were. For him, that means the young will and muscle to keep a fishing camp on the hallowed Au Sable are no longer there. He wasn't ready to accept that reality in April. But by early May he knew the time had come. That part of life that began when World War II was still only a fearful threat, when the Depression was still a time bomb that jeopardized our great country, was ending.

It was that way this morning.

Nails had declared it a new day. It was time to haul myself out of bed. There are a couple chipmunks she feels bound to greet in that half hour before dawn.

The usual drill calls for brewing coffee, fetching the morning *Free Press* from the box out by the road, and sitting there for a half hour, unwinding the cobwebs in my mind.

This morning was different. A kind of haze hung over the drumlins. There was no stopping at the paper box. The legs didn't feel inspired, so the old Suburban roared lazily. Nails stuck her nose into the back of my neck and whined as we kept going down the road toward the big lake.

At the little township park, she kept her place in the seat even when the door was opened for her; not interested in the chance to romp down to the beach.

Maybe she understood that the lake was in an unusual mood. If you've been wooing Lake Michigan's moods for more than a quarter century, you've seldom known her as she was this morning. The fog bank stretched to eternity, but hovered maybe fifty to a hundred feet over the water. Below, it was clear.

Eerie. Not a ripple.

Planting the sole of a boot within an eighth of an inch of the water's edge, I stood hypnotized by the absolute lack of movement. Maybe no more than a half dozen times had I seen the lake so utterly docile.

There was nothing above. It was tempting to believe there was nothing below — that Nature had locked the water into a vast sheet of solid mass.

Nails cautiously ambled down from the car to the edge of the lake. Even she sensed something special — something different. I waited for her to poke her nose into it, showing that it was still — well, water — that she could break the mirror. She didn't. She sat and waited for my next move.

Somehow, that solidified the decision Mary Lou and I had been teetering back and forth on since last fall. Our time for exploring the big lakes' farthest secrets is over. Denali — the twenty-seven-foot wooden wonder — is out for adoption. She is too much for folks our age. Time to admit the lakes and their islands have taken our measure. That we've measured their magic and will now leave them to younger folks.

Like Rip and his retreat on the Au Sable, Denali now deserves someone who can look over her bow as she cuts her wake toward a water-filled horizon without feeling the gnaw in aging joints. Without having to crawl on hands and knees to secure dock lines.

Maybe Nails understood. It took me several minutes to lock the decision into finality. When I lifted the boot from its depression in the sand, she was back in the car, sitting there on the seat — patient, waiting to go home. A chapter in our life was ended.

With Mary Lou still in bed, I dug out some pictures over a fresh cup of coffee. There was Nails, her puppy nose poking out of the hatch in Denali's bow as she swung at anchor off High Island. Another picture showed her, only about three months old, snuggled up with Mary Lou in the bed on a mid-summer morning at the old steamer dock on Lime Island. And another caught her on my lap, her nose over my shoulder, as the old dame churned past Lansing Shoal light house in the Straits.

Later, hoping I suppose, that she'd give it a reprieve, I announced the decision.

"You sure?" she asked. The question hung there. No challenge. Just — is this really it? Is it, really, that time?

Later that day, I caught her in the barn. Her eyes were kinda misty. She said she'd been looking for something for the garden.
I noticed a hand-sized streak through the light dust on Denali's otherwise glistening stern varnish.

I haven't been able to say goodbye with that kind of finality. Earlier, we'd taken the easy way out. Decided to just leave her in the barn for a year or two. Maybe we tried to fool ourselves — that the pain that racks Mary Lou's joints and the other torments would go away. But they won't. Crawling on and off a boat with a cane and pain is no fun.

Denali deserves more. She's in at least as good shape as she was when she first felt Lake Michigan's kiss at Harbor Springs in 1960.

Somewhere, we will try to find her a lover who will keep those magnificent lakes embracing her for another thirty years, just as our memories of her and the quiet, lonely places she took us will always be treasured.

Improvements
May 6, 1987

Times change — sometimes painfully. Often the change is so great you sorta wish you didn't find out.

Last fall, the Department of Natural Resources cut a hiking-skiing trail through the eleven miles of the Mason Tract on the South Branch of the Au Sable. With about a half century of wandering the tract in pursuit of peace, fish, mayflies, ruffed grouse, woodcock, quiet, wildflowers, gnarled cedars, et cetera, the trail idea sounded good to me. I helped sell others on supporting it.

After all, how can anything but good come from hacking out a little underbrush and tacking a few blue trail marker signs on trees? The good, essentially, would be making more people aware of this priceless treasure — thus gaining their support to protect it from the crass commercialism of rental canoeing.

Ah, yes. Naive! Out of step with the times.

Turns out you don't send someone in with a machete, some nails, and a hammer to brush out and mark what the DNR now calls a "hiking and skiing pathway."

Nope. You send in several guys with a bulldozer. They grade a four-foot-wide scar through the pines, popples, oaks and swamps. They build a long wooden bridge over Thayer Creek. They put metal mats in the swamp so hikers won't get their feet damp.

It looks like hell this spring. It is inviting more people to formerly difficult-to-reach fishing holes. It is, certainly, a siren song for all-terrain vehicle users.

But, it really isn't all that bad. Or won't be if DNR lawmen lay on the bikers and ATVers.

The best part of it is that it created the first chance Mio district forester Bill Mittig and I have had to get in the woods together in years. Bill and I are old pals. One of the finest resource managers, conservationists and humans I know.

An auto accident confined Bill to a wheelchair some years ago — shortly after that he transferred from Boyne City to Mio. But he gets around. Still fishes and bow hunts. But, obviously, we don't go wandering around the Jordan Valley together.

Bill started hearing complaints about the Mason Tract trail last fall. He decided that he and I should get a first hand look. How? It ain't designed for a wheel chair. And eleven miles is too far in one day for a gimpy, but still mostly whole, leg.

Easy. He conscripted two DNR four-wheel all-terrain vehicles.

When I got to the trail's launching pad, just downstream from Canoe Harbor, here's Bill, strapped to this whirring red thing, buzzing around the parking lot and grinning like a kid.

Me? I was afraid to get on it. And I could jump off and walk away any time I wanted to. Not Bill. If something happened five miles down the trail he was stuck there — with his damned machine. (We took a two-way radio along just in case.)

The trail, we discovered, offers hikers a grand experience. It snakes through some truly wild areas, with fantastic views of the river. There are pine lands, upland hardwoods, and swamp. It traverses some grand bluffs over the South Branch. Try it this spring, summer or fall. You'll cherish the memories.

You may also do some cussing. The bulldozer left some long, ugly swaths. Why a bulldozer?

Ahh, that's the stuff old guffers didn't know about.

Seems that if you are building a cross country ski trail it must be level. You know, flat — so one ski isn't higher or lower than the next. If you don't build them that way some novice skier may get hurt. If they get hurt, and convince a jury it was because the trail wasn't properly built they will win thousands of dollars in damages from the state.

That's the way it is today. Live, learn and snarl. But it won't change.

They even "cut" ski-width grooves in the trail so folks can slip and slide along them without getting straddle-legged. Egads! (Whatever happened to the four- or five-inch wide wooden slats we skied the real north with?)

Hindsight being 20/20, I wish they'd been satisfied with sending in a guy with a machete and a tack hammer. Or, if they couldn't buy into that, that they'd just forgotten it.

It really isn't that bad, however. Bill sent in a crew with fast-growing seed the day after we were there. By mid-summer most people won't even see the scars. If they can keep the off-road vehicle users off the trail, it will look almost natural come next spring.

The trail is part of a hard-won management plan for the Mason Tract — the first ever. The plan will close some trail roads, protect the Castle site, and close Daisy Bend to canoeists.

Most important, the plan allowed the first logging in fifty or so

years. Last winter 413 acres were logged. The biggest cutting is thirteen acres. Unfortunately, the next logging is ten years down the calendar. Hundreds more acres of pine and aspen need immediate logging to benefit wildlife.

When Dad started taking his oldest son to the Mason Tract, even
a toddler could see over miles of brushland by crawling up and
standing on a pine stump. Today it is a maze of over-mature second
growth popple and oak and Civilian Conservation Corps-planted
jackpine. The grouse hunting that was superb just twenty years ago
is only mediocre.

Pathway hikers who take a break at the edge of several of these
new openings along the trail should be rewarded with a diversity of
songbirds and plants. As soon as this fall they will attract grouse,
woodcock and deer.

I'll wait until mid-summer, when the fair weather fishermen
have left and see if any of those old codgers who only appear when
you're daydreaming with your back to a stump and your face to a
sweeper have anything to say about the hiking trail. I suspect they'll
tell me times change. That they never were what we thought they
were. If one tenth of those hikers and skiers take time to appreciate
the Mason Tract's magic, conservation will be enriched.

Conservation always needs recruits. Even if recruitment costs
weigh heavily on antique memories.

Eulogy For Toots
April 25, 1985

Toots is now on point. Forever. Do you see her — there? There between the tool shed and apple tree, in the feral orchard over by the lake. It is October 1975. She's four months old. It's her first hunt; it's a setup.

I've been watching this bird come to the orchard between 4:00 and 4:30 p.m. daily to feed on apples under the tree.

We skulked through the orchard and around the tottering shed. The bird's ten or twelve feet from her when she clears the shed.

She's on point. Wow! I step up. The bird flushes and dies three to five feet in the air.

"Fetch!"

She doesn't move — still on point. Breaking the gun to slip in another shell, I move up behind to give her a shove in the fanny. "Fetch!" She can see the dead bird, but won't budge.

Frustration mounts, but then two more birds explode from the tree. Snapping the little 20-gauge shut I bust one with the only shot in the chamber. It is only crippled and can be heard thrashing on the side of a pine-covered hill.

"Fetch!" She's down the hill and back with the crippled bird. She drops it on command and sits. "Fetch!" She snaps up the first bird.

She thinks I'm nuts, sitting on the ground hugging her and laughing like a lunatic. What a dog! Can't believe it.

Sure, it wasn't always like that over the next ten years. She gnawed the tip off a favorite fly rod once and tried to eat the drapes in a motel another time. But she was always almost instantly obedient and vied to please. For instance, I once put her on heel, walked to a motel bar from our room and then put her on sit at the table while we had a couple of drinks. Not a quiver, except for her tail swishing across the carpet. She just looked me in the eyes, happy to be there.

Later in that first October, after a wet spell, we had hunted all the upland cover without moving a bird. Rather than take the ridges home we dropped into the crick bottom. Within minutes we both were soaked. Still not a feather was touched.

Finding a place to cross the creek, I was halfway across before I realized she wasn't with me. I called and called. Then, I reluctantly waded back through nearly knee-deep water to find her.

She was on point. The grouse flushed. I shot it. Still on point, she turned to the south. I moved in ahead of her. A woodcock flushed and died. My first mixed double.

Largely because I let her off the hook, she gave up fetching. But if you forced the issue, with some stern talk, she'd go sit on a downed bird for you. Two instances come to mind.

It was the first day of the season a couple years ago. Coming up on a bramble patch, she went on point. Before I could reach her a bird went out wild far ahead of her. I missed a snap shot. Moving in close, a young bird flushed and dropped. Holding point, another went out and died. She moved, in a crouching point, several yards and another bird went down. Enough dead birds, but we played out the brood, her shifting point a few feet and me flushing several more birds.

When I went back to pick them up I couldn't find the third bird, but was certain where it died. She went and sat down by the creek, far from where the bird had dropped, refusing to move and I became more and more angry as she ignored my orders to fetch.

Finally, feeling like a fool and tyrant, I went over to apologize. Hell, she was sitting on the bird.

Another time we're hunting the edge between a cornfield and cedar swamp and she goes on point maybe fifty yards ahead of me. Almost running to get there, I flushed a bird wild and shot it on the move, thinking it was the bird she had pinned.

The shot flushed the bird she had and I only wounded it at the edge of the cedars, but thought I'd dropped it there. After much fruitless searching and demanding that she fetch, I found her nearly a hundred yards into the swamp, sitting on the still live bird.

She was only four weeks old when we picked her up from Jack Jorgensen in Escanaba. The litter was so large they were already being weaned and we didn't want to spend ten hours on the road in another three weeks. She whimpered and whined the first night in the camper bed with us.

By the next morning her pattern was set. For the next three months she'd snuggle down between us and sleep until she had a potty call. Then she'd wiggle and whimper until we'd take her out. She slept by the bed the rest of her life — at home, in tents, the camper, and motels.

Toots loved the water and fishing. She'd sit in the bow of the boat, watching every cast and following it in. If a fish struck she stood up until it was landed. If I tried to leave her on shore she'd swim out to the boat, once nearly drowning herself.

Fly fishing was her favorite. She'd sit on the bank then try to attack a fish when it struck. This nearly lost me several nice trout, and again, her life. I was fishing just above and into a large sweeper, where the river narrows and the current surges. Suddenly I saw her swim by me and get swept up in the current. She hit the sweeper in about a second and started to go under. Flinging the rod on a sand-bar across the river I dove for her, frantically trying to get hold of something and finally getting her mane, then collar. She was out of sight under the logs before I found something to get enough leverage on to pull her out.

Waders filled, I plopped on the bank and cried, I was so angry and happy.

Apparently she thought filling my waders was fun.

A year or so later, she was sitting on the bank of the river with Mary Lou when I came around a bend in fairly deep water. She raced up to me and leapt from the bank right onto my chest, knocking me down. Then she wanted me to stay in the water and play.

At this time of year her special delights were woodcock nests and checking for the first frogs in the pond outside the office window. If you stood there with her, she would point a woodcock nest all day — I think.

She'd spend hours in the pond, feathers flaring as she stalked frogs then pounced at them. (Lord, I can see her down there now.) I caught her one once. She couldn't stand the taste of it in her mouth. Just wanted to play with them.

If someone tells you she's buried in that fresh grave on the side of the drumlin overlooking the pond and our favorite bird woods, beside the juniper, don't believe 'em.

In a minute I may get up the courage to open the gun cabinet and pull out the little double. I'm sure she'll be there, bounding onto my shoulders, licking my face, her tail throbbing like drumming grouse wings.

Or maybe, she's already down there at the edge of the swamp, pointing a woodcock nest. (Lord, forgive me, but right now I think the body bags were easier to handle.)

The Martin Blue Chip
June 14, 1989

For the first time in almost forever, I purposely raised the butt of the rod to eyeball level and took a good look at the tan colored reel. "Martin Blue Chip" it declares in the center, appropriately, on a blue circle about the size of a quarter.

The memories flashed. Don't know if they even make them anymore. But geez, forty or so years ago Martin Blue Chip was the premier automatic (spring wound) fly reel. Country kids, who were into fly fishing, pawed catalogs and outdoor magazine ads, yearning for the impossible goal of someday being rich enough to own a Blue Chip.

Your own Blue Chip! Boy! If you ever got there life would be Easy Street from then on. Oh yeah? Some fifteen or twenty years ago, Martin offered a deal to writers: Blue Chips at a loose change price.

So I've taken it for granted all these years. Not much for serious fishing. Tie into a true trophy and it wouldn't hold up. Line capacity is lacking without room for backing, even with the five weight shooting head fly line.

But like the catalogs and old ads said, one trustworthy beast. Perfect for pitching bugs at bluegills with the gutsy graphite rod Bob Summers puts together. Yet standing there waist deep in waders, with the sun just below the crowns of the maples, birches, and skeletons of the elms on the west shore of the little private lake, there was the feeling that somehow I was richer when I was still so poor I could only aspire to things like the Blue Chip reels I now neglect.

If that didn't make a lot of sense, it still gnawed at me as I knotted a floating nymph-like fly to the 3X leader and pitched it, maybe forty feet into the spreading pink and yellow on the flat water.

Old eyes that have spent too long glaring over the top of a typewriter no longer tell me where the fly lands. It is a kinda guessing game. So you strip in line until you think the slack is gone. Despite the temptation, you don't respond by lifting the rod, or jerking the line, when you see a bulge out there where the fly should be.

If it is a good strike, the bluegill will hook itself.

And, wow! did they. Not every cast hooked a fish. But the ratio was more than one for every other cast. And nice bluegills too. Most ran to at least seven inches. Some to eight inches. Maybe three or four to more than eight inches.

Yeah, there are folks who will tell you about all of the nine- to eleven-inch bluegills they caught last night. But, you know: it isn't Bond Street they've been smoking in their pipe.

Bluegills do get that big. You catch a few dozen in a lifetime of stalking them that hit nine inches. A dozen might make it to ten inches. I've caught one that was an honest eleven inches. And make book on it, I've been a serious bluegill hunter long enough for this country to have fought three serious wars.

A seven-inch bluegill, on a fly rod is a trophy for anyone who knows the difference between twelve-year old Scotch and iced tea. An eight-incher is glorious. (So is iced tea.)

But this was a night loaded with seven- and eight-inchers. The kind of evening that, well, when you tell her about it, you know she is gonna think you've been into the Scotch.

So you cast, tighten the line and leader, lift the long rod at the strike, and watch, and yes feel, it throb against the side-wise slice of the fish. It went on. And on. Several dozen. Like it would never end.

Utter ecstacy!

So much so that you begin to feel it is time for moderation. The shadows are stretching. The rachet of the fly reel, the whir of the fly line, the splash of the bluegills — all become too repetitious as fish after fish comes to the waders. You start to think you shouldn't over- do a good thing. You haven't and won't kill a fish. But something inside tells you to sip, not guzzle, a fine thing.

One more cast, one more fish — you promise yourself. It is rapidly growing dark. You've reached the time in life where she worries about you stumbling around in waders after dark. I think it's time to quit.

That was a dozen fish ago. Still — one more cast. Then another.

Sitting on the tailgate, peeling off the waders, there is a flood of euphoria. The little boy, peering at the fishing tackle catalog with visions of wilderness magic stabbing his dreamy world, is here — with me. "We made it, together … still."

I reached out to touch him, thank him. He had gone. (Gosh, Mom must have told him to put out the lantern and get to sleep.) But, for that brief moment, we were one — again.

Settling behind the wheel of the big Suburban, which suddenly seemed lavish and extravagant, I was haunted by the hope that he understands I have done my best to live up to his pledge to look after the quiet places, the lonely places, where a boy could sneak away and escape with the books Mom brought home from the library, and with his dreams. I hoped he forgives me for the failures and that he knows I still see the wonder and magic in dragonflies, fireflies, tadpoles, and moonbeams rippling on pine needles.

As the car slid by old Phelps Station (it seemed to know its own way back to Mary Lou and Nails), it dawned on me that he must know this to have survived so long and make the journey back here to be with me, and our Martin Blue Chip.

You know, just maybe that's why I've always found it difficult to put out a campfire's last embers.

The Magic Of Spring
June 8, 1983

The afternoon was dreary, gloomy. Like so many have been this spring.

The mildest winter on record has been followed by a wet, cold, mean spring. You gotta pay your dues if you live in the northland. You accept it, even as you gnash your gums at it. That's the way it is.

Every trout fisherman I'd talked to complained that the rivers were over their banks and dirty. But not *the river*. Despite the rain and near freezing nights, it was clear, at normal levels, and the thermometer said fifty-three degrees.

Lampricide and road silt long ago did the bug hatches in. They come, now and then, but they are so irregular and sparse that the few trout that have survived the salmon no longer count on them. So it was a streamer day.

Rusty Gates had introduced us to a strange creature: a thin strand of rabbit fur tied along the top of the hook and extending well beyond the bend creates a slithering, shimmering, come hither lure for fish.

Seven regulation-size trout — seven to nine inches long, browns and rainbows — had struck. I wasn't here to gather a meal. They'd been returned.

It was no surprise when the phantoms appeared like mist from below the overhung bank; steelhead cling to its secrecy. They were smaller — maybe three to four pounds — than the fish that had taken an egg fly two weeks ago. But they were fresh, and bright.

A single trial cast and the new-fangled rabbit fur thing dug into the current. It snaked down through the dark water where the little steelies darted for protection. Cast after cast and not a strike.

An egg fly was fitted to the sturdy but still dainty Bob Summers cane rod. A dozen casts and nothing.

Maybe they were spooked. A twenty minute squat on the bank, a full pipe. Then more casts with the egg fly. Still, nothing.

The streamer fly book is filled with concoctions from a dozen or two books and as many, or more, magazine articles. But it always comes down to a Roxy. This time a red Roxy.

On the third cast one of the ghosts lurched at the yellow marabou feathers. The little rod snapped upstream, bending through the corks. Then downstream, as the fish dove for the dark water under the bank, his silvery side glistening in the dull light.

If he had charged upstream or down, the hook might have driven home. But it was over in seconds. The fly came back. (Roxies are hard to tie, so why complain?)

Enough. The walk back, along the ancient railroad grade, was as rewarding as the fishing.

With a few exceptions, the yellow blossoms of the marsh marigolds have wilted to a dingy brown. Where balsams haven't invaded, strawberry blossoms fleck the moss between the rotting railroad ties. On the hillside, trilliums are a fading glory. Smaller wildflowers and morels are hidden under the swelling head of ferns, grasses, and doomed maple sprouts.

Around the bend, where I always sit for a final pipe before leaving the river, two kingfishers wildly chase each other through the cedars and tamaracks. Back and forth they go, their chattering sounds like something you'd imagine coming from an asylum. Courting?

The evening before, at Lake 26, the thermometer said the water temperature was only about fifty-seven — at least ten degrees colder than it should be by early June. In the branches of an overhanging basswood, a pair of cherry birds (cedar waxwings) courted slow and deliberate like.

Both were on the same limb, as one would daintily hop three to six inches down the branch, then return. At that point they'd touch beaks. Then the other would sort of dance down the limb in the other direction, returning to touch beaks with a kind of embrace.

In a feral snowball bush, a lady hummingbird hung suspended, wings beating dizzily, while her gentleman friend performed a frantic horizontal-vertical helicopter-like performance for maybe thirty seconds. Suddenly, they mated and flew off together.

Is there something to be learned from the hectic courting of the kingfisher and hummingbird? Or is the lesson in the gentle pulsing of the cedar waxwings' love making? They must not hurry the nesting, waiting for the cherries to swell. So, do they savor its wonder, while the others rush desperately to it?

Why should an old man, without teeth or hair, ponder?

The first strike that evening produced a better than eight-inch bluegill. The Washington nymph (a terrific combination of peacock herl and ringneck pheasant feather, originally by Ann Schweigert in Roscommon) yielded several more, including a four-inch rockbass.

But the gloom gathered in the sky. If it must rain, let it be.

Dusk was filling the sky. The new leaves on the birches and popples hummed as the rain blew in from the southeast. The parsnips, radishes, carrots, brussels sprouts and other seeds would welcome it. The new asparagus roots haven't poked their green noses from the trench. (With hopes high we look forward to the first meal two years from now.)

Driving slowly down the trail through the cornfield, we approach two giant Canadas, strutting erect side by side, sometimes moving close enough to touch flanks. They are oblivious to the vehicle. The eggs are in the nest. Maybe the young ones have hatched. Are they here taking a break from their duties just to enjoy a few minutes with each other?

Where the narrow swamp bottom between the drumlins breaks out into the hayfield, a marsh hawk beats powerfully to rise above the road. It looks like a baby rabbit in its claws. Not more than four inches long.

Spring!

The cedar waxwings surely understand its magic better than you and I.

My Maybe-Crick
June 4, 1986

It isn't much of a crick. It doesn't even have a name — not even "no-name crick." Just isn't deserving of that distinction.

The folks who did the topo and the DNR county maps didn't find it worthy of a scratch mark. It is a sure bet they didn't find it.

You could convincingly argue that it doesn't even exist. But you'd be a darn fool to get into an argument over it. Why you can't even rank it as a real creek.

It is just this little trickle of water that comes and goes, now and then. But still, all and all a sorta important crick, as such things go — and if your values are twisted that way.

It seems to sorta start at a miniature spring seep on the side of a drumlin. You can hardly see the bubbles coming out of the ground. In the fall, leaves cover it. If you should step into it, you can shake the water off your boot and it would dry in seconds. You can get a lot wetter foot just tramping a few yards through wet ferns.

This little crick ambles on from the hillside — usually no wider than an open hand — as it drops from sight where the junipers and popples come together. It skips down there, somewhere, under the hardwoods, and then shows up again better than a football field away, at the edge of the cedars. Sometimes, where it runs the length of a tag alder swale, it is wider than most young men can jump. But there's no jumping room, anyway. It just sorta, but barely, flows in a lazy course, from one almost stagnant puddle to another, over and around roots and grasses. Not many folks would agree that it is a crick. Just a bunch of water.

It disappears, again, where the gully ends at an old hayfield. You really have to do a lot of easy, mindless rambling through drumlins and wet places to pick it up again at another cedar outpost where it is now trying desperately to be an honest, sure-thing crick. At this time of year, it is a good foot to eighteen inches wide and six to eight inches deep — in places. It has some deeper holes where it has gnawed a gentle path for itself around the roots. Sometimes, if you look close — like down on your belly — you see things swimming in it. Even little fish.

In the fall, I once saw some small brook trout — three, four inches long. Now they didn't come from nowhere; they had to have swum upstream from a legitimate creek.

I tried fishing, not to catch a fish, but because I figured my attention sorta gave it some dignity. And it is probably the only place I'll ever fish where no one else has fished.

The cedars, and my crick's discernable life, end at a perpetual bog, where everything is wet. This jungle of woody vegetation ends at the bottom of another drumlin. On the other side is a grown-up creek. If forms part of the headwaters of the Torch Lake system (or Elk River watershed) which empty into Lake Michigan at Elk Rapids.

Clearly, this tricky wisp of a tricklet becomes a part of something mighty big and fine, though with its comings and goings you've walked less than a mile — if you know the route.

Important things happen along its meanderings, too. Like showy and yellow ladyslippers. Chickadee nests. Morels. Thirsty fawns and king birds. Grouse and woodcock nests.

It also gives a perspective to bass fishing on Intermediate Lake and to watching sunsets on Torch Lake. If you don't understand where the roots of a thing are you can never appreciate the whole.

Somebody's gotta worship at the wonder of its insignificance. But I'm pleased that I'm the only one who does. This little crick somehow makes life a whole lot richer. Hope you've got a maybe-crick of your own — if not today, then someday.

Where Loons Continue To Play
June 19, 1985

As the decades fade into yesterday, time increasingly seems to become the enemy. You try to ignore it. Then you try to deny it. Then, dammit, you know you have to admit it — to yourself.

It starts with the rivers and lakes you love becoming polluted with people, with canoes, with speed boats, with sailboats that corrupt remote Great Lakes islands with litter and stereos, and with cottages and fertilized lawns. It spreads and infects rustic wilderness campgrounds with trailers and all-night orgies.

Doc Spencer calls it Condo Mania. It has contaminated and obliterated the sunsets in northwest Michigan like urban blight in once-proud Detroit neighborhoods.

For us, Lake Charlevoix tells the story best. We've been fishing in it, swimming in it, and raising kids in it for thirty some years. The kids are grown and we now recommend that the grandkids do not swim in it. It is foul. It is dirty!

We still fish in it, sometimes. But your cannonball disappears in a foot or so of water.

So we fish Torch Lake. Down there folks have been willing to put their money up when the condo polluters came to desecrate. The other day the thermometer said fish in fifteen to thirty feet. We did. And we counted well over a hundred lake trout in thirty feet of water.

That's great. Until you remember that it used to be that way in Lake Charlevoix, where now you can't see the end of your paddle and in Walloon Lake and Burt Lake and — where else?

It's not just the big lakes that have been mutilated. We had a going away party for Sue Zurawski today. Sue's twenty-one — I think she said. A beautiful young woman. She now has two years in the Peace Corps in Africa ahead of her.

Sue's family moved onto the lake across from us more than a decade ago. They were the first to break the barrier. Until then there were five places on the hundred-acre lake. Most of them were used two to four weeks a year. It was quiet. Mine.

The Zurawski's had a flock of kids, and a bigger flock of cousins and aunts and uncles. They built this big place on this little lake. And the cackle of the kingfisher was drowned out by the laughter of happy children doing what happy children should be doing — having fun outdoors.

Then, as always happens, more people built more places. At first, like the Zurawski's still are, they were content with little motors and little fishing boats. Now there are pontoon boats, with big growling motors, and sometimes even a ski boat.

It is still a wonderful place. The bass and bluegill fishing is about the best in these parts. And to nearly everyone it is akin to wilderness experience — if your memory doesn't reach back over a decade.

The places remain where the loon continues to play. The scheme is to celebrate them without being haunted by the reality that someday they, too, will be lost. It is not easy.

The Civilian Conservation Corps
March 30, 1983

The memories here reach back well beyond today's generation. Memories that many today could not comprehend because the country has changed so much.

The scenes include an aged lady casually climbing the steep hill from the spring to the oak ridge. They are also of tent camps, of a first trout hooked with Dad's help on the rod handle, of a giant brown that taunted me for years and finally came to the net — to be released. The flashes of mind-pictures include deer that flashed from the cover of a fallen pine and a wire-lashed pit latrine built thirty-five or more years ago, the evidence of which I (and maybe only I) can still find.

Memories are of the first otters, the first eagles and mink, a bobcat's wail, friendly chipmunks, and of the night when a tornado tore a swath through the pines and oaks only a few hundred yards away.

Recalling them from the memory bank could fill most of these pages; they have produced the spark that kept life going — several times.

I am continually fascinated — and puzzled — that so few of today's sportsmen and instant environmentalists have any grasp of our conservation heritage. Too few trout fishermen understand that the Au Sable of 1983 is a far finer, clearer, and more beautiful stream than it was when the first Civilian Conservation Corps recruits awoke to reveille near its banks fifty years ago.

A few years ago, Dave Borgeson was asked by an attorney just how precious or how small a small Michigan trout stream is. Dave answered that in all the world it has to be considered a rare and precious resource.

Dave, you see, had to hedge his statement. He could not honestly say that the Cedar River is rare and unique in Michigan. Why? Because we are blessed with so incredibly many rare, unique, and precious trout streams. We truly have a large store of the world's entire inventory.

Sure, as you youngsters and newcomers to the northland tell us, that's because God gave them to us. Yep. There's truth to that. But it is only part of the truth.

He created the groundwater, soils, and other conditions that add up to such incredible treasures. But we humans went on a crazed rampage in the late 1800s and destroyed them. We robbed the land of its roots and shade. We filled the streams with such ungodly loads of sediment that it still clogs the Au Sable, Jordan, Black, Manistee, and dozens of others.

Today's Au Sable, Manistee, Pine, and Pere Marquette are not the same creatures this guide inherited when he came squalling into the world. Back then nature had started her slow healing process of a land dominated by charred stumps. A trout was to be treasured. Grayling were still talked about as though they had been here only yesterday. But wise folks sadly knew they would never be again.

Standing on a ridge, back then, in what is now the Mason Tract along the Au Sable's South Branch, you could see for miles. Deer browsed in herds numbering a hundred or more — almost like cattle. Sharptail grouse could be ground-swatted like grasshoppers. Ruffed grouse were nearly as sparse as eagles.

Outdoorsmen met by "the pine who bends down from the High Banks," or "the pine" downstream from the meadow, or "the pine" below the Flats. These were the individual trees that had somehow been overlooked by the loggers. They stood out. They were the only survivors.

Today, tell one of Opening Day's trout fishermen to find a pine, any individual pine, and he will be lost until the last mayfly has hatched in November. The pines, the cedars, the oaks, the popples, the hemlocks (who ever knew of a surviving hemlock in 1933) are everywhere. And they are big. And many are so old they are dying.

The CCC "lads" made much of this happen. They marched across the scorching, barren, sodden, dreary, and, yes, ghostly, skeleton pine-lands like locusts. But this time locusts that gave. Sweating, and uncertain of tomorrow, they plunged tiny pine seedlings into poor sand, and they began to eliminate the erosion that was epidemic across millions of acres into our streams.

They built bridges, logjams, buildings, roads, telephone lines, and fish hatcheries. They lay in their bunks and dreamed of home, and feared for a country where a man-sized boy had to work for the government. (When Roosevelt couldn't cure the depression with his programs they marched off to war.)

A half century later, few of them will be seen on the stream when trout season opens in a month. But their legacy will be with us.

It is a legacy that those too young to remember the burned-out land should be reminded of. It is a legacy of tall pines, clear waters, gravel bottoms, mayfly hatches, and the spirits of young men who came to the land to heal and left to fight the ugliest demon ever loosed on mankind.

It is a legacy as big as the northland. A legacy so rich it will never be trifled with a eulogy. Unless we betray it, it will live forever in the northland the CCC boys rescued from our earlier madness.

Brook Trout, Dry Flies, And Wildflowers
May 17, 1989

The first sign that something was happening above the river was a pair of swallows slashing and darting between the cedars, hemlocks, and tamaracks. Leaning back against the ancient cedar stump, when the sun slanted just right, you could pick up the twirling outline of a few Hendrickson mayflies.

These are survivors — the last remnants of the flurry of big mayflies that fed magnificent wild brook trout before they started lacing the river with lamprey-killing chemicals in the 1960s.

The chemicals, sand, and salmon teamed up in the last two decades in a juggernaut that had humbled the river, the insects, and the trout.

A fella we met on the road a few days before, from Clarkston, put it this way: "It just isn't as good fishing as it used to be."

He came here knowing that. But he still came. So do I.

It is still a grand place. A few wild trout still live here, with a few glorious mayflies. The water remains cold and clear. Under the sand there is a trout's and mayfly's treasure chest of habitat, and a lot of people have been working to uncover that treasure.

In another five to ten, or even twenty years, when the sand is purged, the chemicals and salmon cut off, the wild trout and their mayflies will heal themselves. They will return.

Though those few mayflies and a few trout — the seed stock for the future — hold on, the hatches are not dense enough to bring many trout to the surface. When they do rise, it is more likely to be for terrestrial insects.

Some unknown bugs were being swept into the eddies this midafternoon. Though the sun was bright, the temperature was only in the mid 50s — about the same as the water. Old blood, that doesn't run as hot as it once did, sent me to the bank to bask in the sun.

Once the waders warmed, the innards started to yawn and the little cane rod began to nod. The swallows and murmur of the current were only a blur when the steady slash of the trout down and across the stream managed to seep through the fog.

The fish, not a big one for sure, was feeding on the inside, downstream edge of a stump that, until the sand piled up and widened the river, was several feet from the flow. It would be a trophy to hook, due to the difficulty of the cast, not the size of the fish.

It took more than ten minutes to work into casting position. Even with all that caution, the fish quit feeding. Were the insects gone? Had I put it down? Stand still, impatient feet, and wait.

Minutes later it started feeding again. I had knotted a size 16 black ant to the 5X leader. Just a guess. Certainly, there weren't enough Hendricksons to bring fish up. And those remnants that were here were still dancing far above the current. An Adams might have been a better bet. But fish an ant pattern just under the surface film when you aren't sure, and the odds are looking your way.

The first three or four casts were short or too sloppy. They were aborted before the fly could drift into the fish's feeding lane.

Finally, looping a slack leader at the end of the cast sent the little fly twirling in the eddy around the side of the stump.

I felt it — but didn't see it. The fish was on.

Nothing like the stuff they write about in the magazines and on the outdoor pages. But the four-weight rod throbbed respectfully as the fish fought it and the current. Seconds later the hook was twisted from the jaw of a nine- (ahh, maybe eight-) inch brook trout.

It felt good. Yes. Several smaller, and larger, browns had hit streamers when the adventure started. But here was the prize. A true trout, where true trout belong, fooled by a self-tied floating fly.

Forty feet downstream another trout fed. It, too, took the ant. This time a brown trout. Fair enough — but not the same: an intruder into true trout country.

Leaving the river I took the sloshy route to the car, which meant mucky waders to be hosed off at home. But I couldn't bear to tramp on the trilliums blooming in the upland trail.

You gotta have your priorities. Mine just happen to be brook trout, dry flies and wildflowers. I've said it before and I still suspect these are the places where God likes to spend His time.

Mayflies, Grayling, And Lady Slippers
May 20, 1987

The season's first yellow lady slippers forced these waders to take a detour on their way to the river.

Those who fish the Au Sable's Holy Water and other better known trout waters of the Michigan northland wouldn't consider this much of a river. It is short, narrow, and filled with obstacles that fly fishermen curse. It plunges wildly in places. Yet a state fisheries executive once told a court that it is a resource that would be considered rare in most of the world. Yes, rare, and precious.

The waters are so clear you can wade armpit deep, look down, and think it is only knee deep. They are so pure that even after days of mid-summer ninety-degree heat its warmest waters barely nudge a degree over fifty-five. Mayflies that defy identification bulge the stomachs of its brook and brown trout.

Some of the recently invading browns grow big. There are rumors of six- to eight-pounders being snatched from the deeply undercut banks. The true pilgrims who journey to it seek, instead, the dazzling little brook trout and the tranquility that my friend, Omar Jabara, knew here.

The sun glistened on the red and grizzly points and spines of the over-hackled, spent-winged Adams dry fly as a gust of wind sent it skittering across the riffle into a deep, quiet pool under overhanging cedars. Even wimpy old eyes could see the fly sparkling as it paused then snapped as the leader tightened. Just then, a fish bulged and sucked the number 14 hook into the depths.

The little seven-foot Bob Summers cane rod's tip nudged the leader taut. The barbless, sharper-than-needlepoint hook sank into the afternoon's sixth grayling. It darted into the current against the 5X leader tippet, then turned upstream. Its lavender side glowed in the high sun as its sail sparkled in a low, maybe two-foot-long, arch of a leap — the bushy fly in the edge of its jaw.

Seconds later, its gleaming, nearly ten-inch-long body plowed a wake up to the waders and, with a sharp shake of the leader, dropped back into the current, righted itself and darted for the depths of the hole.

Having caught hundreds of grayling in Alaska, I knew they would be taking refuge in the quiet water. I also suspected it was possible the ten-incher, the day's largest, would strike again. In

Alaska I'd taken as many as three on a cast — but only once — using three wet flies.

It was time to rest on the river bank. Listen to the current. Massage some circulation back into the numb left leg and ponder the magic of catching grayling in Michigan.

As a kid listening to elders talk of the incredibly inexhaustible grayling in the Rifle River, Klacking Creek, and other fabled waters, I developed a penchant for daydreams about finding the last Michigan grayling in some hidden, unknown crick. For a couple of decades, probably, I secretively pursued this unconfessed mission.

Of course, it was hopeless. Grayling were gone for good. Every effort to bring them back failed. A Michigan kid had to go to Alaska to catch his granddad's grayling.

Returning to the stream, the Adams sunk like a split shot on the first cast. Oh yeah! Grayling have a way of gooing up a fly.

A dunk in my last reservoir of Schweigert's dry fly dope cured that. But with it came reservations. I'd hauled Jack's distinctive-smelling fly dope all over the grayling waters of Alaska and the trout waters of Michigan. Some time next season it will be gone.

New high tech fly floatants, I'm told, are far more effective than Jack's smelly old deer tallow juice. Yet, fly fishing will never be the same without the odor that escapes the little bottle.

Anyway, the third cast brought up another grayling, which as usual, hooked itself — about seven inches. Re-dunking the fly and several casts later hooked the eighth of the day. About the same size.

Enough. These are hardy young fish. Hooking them and gently releasing them will not curtail their survival. But the dream — the karma, for now had been fulfilled.

Moose, pheasants from China, and battling summer steelhead make the big outdoor press headlines. I suspect the lady slippers cherish the return of the grayling far more. I sure do. Maybe because grayling live in places far more amendable to mayflies and gentle, quiet souls.

Maybe because having them back is sorta like paying a debt my great granddad owed Nature.

Rip Van Winkle
May 3, 1989

I was certain that Rip would be there. But turning the Suburban into Whippoorwill I wasn't sure I'd run into him.

Rip VanWinkle has been coming to this hallowed water on the Au Sable's Mainstream for a half century. Now in his late 80s, he doesn't battle the current or hatches like he once did. But he still comes to "the river" for the first couple weeks of the season.

He has a little cabin up off the river, on a rise. At noon he still has his beer and cheese.

I parked at the "new" cabin, where most of the old-timers stay, just off the river. It has benches where you can sit and watch the mayflies, river, and its currents. I spotted a hunkered figure down in the bush at streamside.

There was Rip, with one of those metal bucksaws. He'd been clearing "his" path to the river: a spot where the current is gentle enough for old legs.

The eyes sparkled. The nostrils may not flare as they did when we first met — probably twenty years ago. But he still snorts flame when he knows there's a chance to talk conservation, rivers, trout, and fly fishing. I knew I was in for a protracted stay.

I plopped on the upstream bench, my feet almost dangling in the river. Wrong bench. Rip declared the downstream bench the better of the two. I moved.

We talked about the guys who used to come but are gone now. Rip can do it without taking his eyes from yours. It is the way it is. This is more than a life-long commitment to friendship that we are talking about. It is a lifelong (and long life) commitment to tradition — started long before plastic or graphite fly rods. Tradition that has a gentleness inherent in its roots. It is a tradition that was strangely strengthened — and, yes, sweetened — by wars.

A few livery canoes went by. Some angry words were exchanged. Rip looked away. That tightness I've seen snap at his jaw and eyes over places like Filer Creek, the Cedar, and Bear was there again — just briefly. He knows it is too late to turn the clock back.

Then a canoe came down with a young fella in his twenties, and a tad of a son, with plastic bag-wrapped camping gear between them. Rip was up, vibrant, telling them what a wonderful adventure was ahead of them — coaxing them on.

He saw a rebirth of the cycle. I did, too. I thought of Dad, Mike, and I, and those forty and more years ago. The patched and recovered Old Town piled high with camp gear and canvas (no plastic back then) easing our way toward campsites on the Au Sable and other streams. It was a different world. By the 1950s the livery canoeists had run us off the rivers. The fun, the quiet was gone.

Rip remembers the country as it was: scrub, with a few sentinel pines that escaped the loggers, and whole sections of CCC-planted, knee-high pines stretching to the horizon.

Openers then were for hearty men — and boys. Breakfast was bannock, bacon, and eggs over campfires; few could afford a Coleman stove.

The Friday night before opener meant a visit to Schweigert's Rod and Fly Shop in Luzerne (later Roscommon), and then shivering to get the tent up and the fire roaring. It meant the same tent site at the real Canoe Harbor (gone these twenty years, due to canoes) and knowing who was in every other tent, because they, too, had been coming forever.

Opening meant the dare of a bare butt dive into the South Branch or Mainstream. We didn't know we weren't immortal. (Try that now and they'd march you to the slammer in Grayling for indecent exposure.)

Those were the times when George Mason and others still owned miles of the South Branch. When many cane fly rods were ten to twelve feet long, and, honest, some browns went to ten pounds.

For country boys trying to adjust from kerosene lanterns, outhouses, and wood ranges to electric light, indoor plumbing, and central heating from coal furnaces it was a time of awe. The Au Sable Country was big, magnificent.

Did we really want those changes? Could we keep up?

Would plunger starters on the floor, and then key ignitions, ever really replace automobile hand crank starters? If they did, would our world be as secure?

We tested the mud of North Downriver Road and Chase Bridge Road. As they were replaced by gravel, and then paved roads, we yearned for slower times, but loved the convenience. (Ahh, roads have murdered much of the best that was — but we gotta have them.)

Yet the trout, the mayflies, the clear, cold water, and a few of the sweepers remain. The tools have changed. The yuppies now wear strange uniforms. The rods are sleek counterfeits. The waders last forever. We no longer soak our leaders and scrape and coat our fly lines.

But we come back to "the river" every spring.

In all of those years I remember only two trout. One, a fifteen-incher I caught on a bee imitation fly on a scorching hot day in July to impress a buxom young thing who had the keys to a glorious cabin upstream, and a nine-pounder I returned to the river.

So, it isn't the trout that keep Rip and the rest of us coming back. Dave Borgeson sent along some quotes from Roderick Haig-Brown writings that sorta tell it: "The real truth is that sport is made by and exists in just three things; tradition, ethics and restraint. Reduce, remove or destroy these and nothing useful is left."

Rip would agree. He'd add that it is the places where trout live that keep the sport — and us — alive. And you know, I must believe that these places where wild trout live are much bigger and more important than we.

Spring Bass And Bluegills
May 21, 1986

Moving instinctively, about three feet to the north while wading east toward a favorite spring bluegill hole, brought a chuckle. Funny how a guy remembers where the boulders and snags are without even thinking about them for months.

Finally in position, several chunky shadows moved slowly over the sandy bottom. Seemed early, but bass were already holding down the fort. To heck with the nymph. Tie on a big streamer.

The wretched typewriter was a bully and the sun had been driving me nuts by 3:30 p.m. Mary Lou agreed that a mess of bluegills would make a nice supper. Maybe she'd have to dig into the freezer. Though bass were out of season, bluegills would have to wait for a few tries at the bass.

Pitch the streamer out, let it settle slowly while its long saddle hackle tail fluttered toward bottom. Then dart it in short jerks along the bottom.

The third cast connected. Whoopee! Winter's really over! The fish slammed against the rod and reel in a short, but muscular, burst. It then exploded through four feet of water, big mouth gaping and shaking, water frothing.

It threw the fly. Who cares?

A few casts later the fly hung onto a drowned branch that had been about five feet to the south for about five years. Storms and ice must have moved it. I straighten out the rod and break off.

Some good-sized bluegills take to nipping at the next streamer, which gives me thoughts of supper. Maybe I should go back to the nymph. Naw — keep trying for the bass.

Finally, another one takes — strong and mean-like. This time I'm fast enough at lowering the rod tip when he jumps, not once but three times. The brawny cane rod digs in as he dives for deep water and sulks. The bamboo beats him and soon the fly is slipped out of his jaw.

In the next half hour four more, twelve to fifteen inches long, take the fly and win their freedom.

A pair of mallards seems to be nesting up the lake a way. The drake comes down to check me out three times. The kingfisher is showing off. Swallows are everywhere. A rose-breasted grosbeak serenades a lover back in the birches.

This little lake — once remote, isolated, but now busy and developed — is amazing. There's a guy up the road who takes as many as 200 bass from it a year. Kills them all. And he's deadly. Never any thoughts to next year's fishing or what those grandkids he's gonna have in a decade or so will find.

There's another guy who rents boat launching rights on this all-private water. Even a few of the true-blue bass boats have discovered it.

In summer, the cottage kids, whose dads are down in the city paying taxes, haunt the bass and bluegills endlessly.

Yet the fishing survives. Every spring I fear the worst. But always the bass are there, and a few nice — not lunker — bluegills.

When you should have Her figured out, Nature throws you another curve. Not even the fellows with the big degrees and years of studying bass-bluegill dynamics have it doped out. In most lakes the usual theories work. Elsewhere they don't, and the researchers never seem to get closer to a pat answer.

Though you grope for the answers to many apparent mysteries, do you really want them? It is more fun to guess at them. If you had 'em down as prosaic facts, plain and simple, the "mysteries" would become common, and forgotten.

Like why are there so many orioles this year? Far more than we've ever had. Is it something to do with subtle habitat changes? Or has it taken them so long to find the hummingbird feeders? Maybe it is simply just a couple of good years in their migration routes and on their winter ranges.

A few mornings ago these tin ears thought they distinguished cries from four distinctly different owls. A first. It doesn't really matter that I'll never know.

Heady stuff for a guy who's just had to release five nice bass and must be content with fresh-from-the-garden asparagus.

Denali

June 15, 1988

Denali poked her aging bow out of the pierheads and swung hard to starboard, until the lubber's line on the binnacle locked on 345 degrees, only fifteen short of north. Easing the throttle forward, the Chris Craft conversion Chevy V/8 throbbed.

The mahogany laps of the hull lifted out of the water until the tach registered 2,400 r.p.m. She'll run faster — up to 3,600 or 3,700 r.p.m. But at 2,400 to 2,500 she's comfortable, making between seventeen and twenty m.p.h. Kick her up to her max and she's only doing three to five m.p.h. more, and she's straining. No sense in it.

This old gal has led a leisurely life. Launched in 1960, the hull and engine have spent only 215 hours underway. Why ask them to labor now?

Besides, there was no hurry. The day was warm and clear. The wind gentle. Mary Lou and I had decided in midweek that no one would be home to answer the phone on Saturday.

Once outside the Pine River piers, and on course for the can (buoy) that marks the east entrance to the strait between Garden and Beaver Island, there was nothing to do but check for any oncoming boats (none) and sit back and wait for the teapot to brew on the little alcohol stove, glancing now and then at the compass to be sure we were still on course.

Having piloted a boat to Garden, Hog, and High islands almost as many times as I have steered a car on I-75 south of Houghton Lake, it was rather routine.

Not a mile out of Charlevoix, the shoreline of Beaver Island snapped into view. You can sometimes see Beaver from the bluffs overlooking the piers in Charlevoix. It isn't common, but it isn't rare, either. To see the Fox islands is far more routine, occurring maybe one day out of ten.

To see clear to Beaver from the waterline, or a couple of feet above it behind the wheel of the boat, is very rare. Maybe I've experienced it a dozen times, mostly just at dawn.

But there it was. Some twenty miles to the northwest the sand dunes on Beaver's easternmost knob looked like slivers. It had to be a perfect day for this adventure.

As it turned out, it was to be an adventure in modern technology, as well.

Mary Lou is into computers, and stuff like that. Her pride is a Loran — an electronic navigating tool. It does amazing stuff. But this spring she's been finding it talking back to her.

If you totally trust in the Loran you forget the compass, watch, and chart. Dead reckoning, if you are that trusting, can be forgotten.

I'm not that confident of anything with a bunch of solder in it. A compass, watch, and map (or chart) have taken me to many faraway places and brought me back. I'll stick with them.

The Loran kept telling Mary Lou that the compass was off. That we were headed for some unknown, uncharted place in the middle of Lake Michigan. She kept grinding at my ear, telling me I'd better change course. Silently, I kept the lubber's line on 345 degrees and counted down on my watch.

Sliding up to the northeast corner of Beaver, with Hog off on the northeast and Garden dead off the bow, the Loran demanded that we turn northeast for a half hour. That would have taken us right over the top of Hog Island and its shoals.

The tension was mounting. A divorce lawyer, if he'd been aboard, would have been rubbing his hands in anticipation of a fat fee, when I told her to look for the can: "It is right off the bow there, somewhere." (Her eyes are better than mine.)

She didn't believe it. But she doesn't have any more fondness for attorneys than I do.

"There it is. Don't you see it?" (There was a note of, "Hey, old man, what good are you?")

The green can was directly ahead, not a half mile away, bobbing in the swell that land breezes so regularly create around these mid Lake Michigan islands.

Denali swung close to the can. Mary Lou punched in the location of her Loran. She had earlier pushed the wrong button, or something, as we left the pierheads at Charlevoix. Now the space-age wonder was doing its thing again. (But it isn't replacing the compass.)

Flipping on the depth sounder, Denali churned west-northwest. The blinking red light told us we were not over any of the treacherous boulders that haunt this narrow passage.

Just under five miles later, we turned east, for the long probe into Garden and Indian harbors. Here, misjudging your location by a few feet can rake the bottom out of any hull on rock piles as big as a house. But the old landmarks came into view and Denali held her pace, with plenty of water under the hull.

Minutes later the anchor dug into the sand in five feet of water. It was only a short row to shore in the small rubber raft. Another pot of tea simmered on the stove. Ham sandwiches came first.

A luxury sailing yacht was anchored a few feet away. Six people, in two small aluminum skiffs, waded and cast for smallmouth bass.

The thermometer said the water was barely fifty-five degrees. Three decades of fishing these waters has taught me that the small-mouth do not move in until the temperature is above sixty; sixty-five to seventy is perfect.

We half-heartedly poked hooks through minnows and threw out bobbers, mostly for the pleasure of watching them bob in the clear water, as we sipped the tea.

Having known this fishery for going on thirty years, we expect it to be fickle. There were the days, back in the early 1960s, when if you hit it right it was common to catch so many one- to four-pound smallmouth, cast after cast, that you became bored. It was also almost as common to catch nothing, as wind-swept currents churned into the bays that fringe Hog and Garden islands, lowering temperatures ten to fifteen degrees in minutes.

Mort Neff, *Outdoor Life*, and the Detroit newspaper outdoor pages ended the great days. Fishermen came, and they stayed. Once I counted about a hundred fishermen in one little five-acre bay. The fishery eventually caved in.

This is fragile habitat — extremely limited. The bass never recovered. They probably never will. More people have more boats with more time and more money.

That's sad. But we can't undo it.

The important thing is that here, in the middle of the wilderness that is Lake Michigan, the outer islands have not changed. There are no condos. There are no Tinsel Town gift shops and restaurants. The yuppies may come, but they leave even faster, with no shadow or stain to mark their passing.

Denali gets about three miles to the gallon. That's expensive — by car standards. But darn good for a twenty-seven-foot power boat. A more than reasonable price to pay for a ticket to escape the tarnish people have left on the Lower Peninsula's northwest coast.

The supper hour was gone. The breeze was turning cool. Time to haul anchor.

It was tempting to dig under the bunks in the cramped cuddly cabin for the bottle of single malt Scotch. The trip back would be slow and peaceful. But, as long experience has taught us, it could without warning turn into a challenge — if the big lake decided to have a sudden tantrum.

The Scotch would wait.

At about 8:00 p.m., Denali slid between the piers and headed toward the condo ghetto of Charlevoix.

Home From The Keys
April 19, 1989

It was almost breathtaking as the Piedmont 727 broke through the clouds over southwest Michigan and the fields and woodlots became distinct. This is a land I never considered loving, but at that moment it grabbed at me and I reached out for it.

Here was land — real land. Big hunks of it. In some places whole forty acres with nothing built on them — still in browns and black, from winter's edge. But, oh Lord, thanks, land!

A week in the lower Florida Keys does that to a guy who keeps his fly rods over his desk and his bird dog under his desk. The water there is beautiful. The flats or "back country," as they call it, is fetching. The weather is boring: seventy to eighty-two degrees every day under perfectly clear, sun-baking skies. Though oldtimers like Gary Schnicke won't return because they say the fishing has been ruined, it is beyond comparison for newcomers.

We caught tarpon (small — ten to twenty-five pounds), snook, snappers, grunts, barracuda, jack crevalle, and others unnamed — all on fly rods and light tackle spin rods. A ten-inch snapper will outfight a three-pound bass or five-pound coho. Really!

But when the fishing is over you gotta go back to the land.

What? There ain't no land. I mean it's gone. All there is is pavement and buildings. The land has been consumed. And that's the truth. After a few days in "paradise" you are doing mental exercises to keep from screaming at the s-o-b's for what they've done.

We land at Grand Rapids. and soon are in the fifteen-year-old Olds 88 on Highway 131, with the cruise control set at fifty-five. Traffic is almost nonexistent after we clear the last Grand Rapids exit. Past Cedar Springs we sit back and know the north woods is on the horizon. By Cadillac we have returned to a true paradise.

There has been more arc in our rods in the last ten days than we will probably experience all summer, but thoughts are only on those little cane fly rods, with 5X to 7X tippets and flies no bigger than the point on your pencil. Our thoughts now are on streams so clear we still drink from them. Of tiny brook trout we will swoon over as we gently twist the hook from their jaw.

We muse on a lifetime of campfires along the Jordan, Black, Au Sable, Manistee, Fox, and in the Dead Stream. And we remember deep dark woods that reach farther than a man's boots can in a day's travel.

We picture little lakes, with shimmering — yet quiet and gentle — sunrises and no drug patrol planes snarling over them. We remember bluegills (even though tame by Keys' standards) slurping in a bug as a kingfisher chortles at the feebleness of humanity.

Once home, you step purposely to avoid squashing the nubbin of green that will become a leek or trout lily. You are stunned at the coldness of the Cedar River, yet you plunge your whole face into it just to taste its sweetness.

Yeah, this north country is for you — where you can heal. This is where you will fight to keep it from becoming another Florida. Where you listen to the frogs and squeeze her hand — giving thanks for being here and with her.

The grouse are drumming. The bird dog is moaning at her confinement.

We are rejoicing at just being here. Being home.

Have you ever seen anything more majestic than a Hendrickson mayfly? Maybe a blue-winged olive? A trillium necklace around a sweetwater spring gurgling from moss and pine needles?

The Right Stuff
May 23, 1984

His arm and the graphite fly rod worked like a piston-driven lever in an assembly line. Every move, every cast was perfect.

The line and leader responded as though they, too, were part of the machine, dropping the number ten Washington nymph exactly where it belonged. At the other end of the boat I was fascinated, almost hypnotized, by the precision of it all. His dad never cast half as well. Nor do I. These young guys, with their computer-designed rods of miracle fibers, their fly fishing school technique and dedication to excellence are, indeed, in a world we never entered.

I'd known him since he was in high school. His dad and I fished together, lied together, drank together. After the fishing we'd often put a bottle of Scotch on the table and settle down to an evening of lying competition. We'd talk about this fly or that, this fish and that one, and war stories.

Though he was under age, we'd make sure he had a beer to sip on. And he'd sip on it. Not chugalug it like we knew he did when he was out with the guys.

Sometimes we'd pick on him. And he'd love it. When he thought we were fighting, not understanding Army-Navy rivalry, we'd see him look worried, get fidgety; and we'd stop.

He liked it best when we'd agree. When we'd both be cursing the politicians.

He was a sensitive, bright lad. It was the Vietnam era. He couldn't accept our war stories. The ones we told and retold, like neither of us had ever heard them before: "Did I ever tell you the time the ensign ..." or "Bet I never told you about the corporal who fell in the sergeant's fox hole and ..."

It bothered him that they were always funny. That no one ever died in them. Twice, as I remember it, he puckered up the gall to challenge us. "Damn it (he was proud of himself when he cussed, like us) war isn't funny. How come you always make it out like it is?" Something like that.

Both times we looked at him — and then at each other — amazed that he didn't understand that the fun is all that sane people want to remember. Both times it sorta soured the Scotch.

Early on, he decided he'd be an attorney. He could then do important things — help people, and the world. And have some influence in conservation.

He loved and respected his Dad, but considered his trade —
accounting — to be money grubbing. When he died, Jack (that's
what we'll call him, after a favorite uncle) almost died as well.

In the last few years he has learned that passion, brains, guts, and
do-gooder ambition don't change the world. He and two other
young guys have a law business in a southern Michigan town. He
makes a comfortable living. But he hates grubbing with divorce
cases, defending petty crooks, and the other ninety percent of any job
that is just labor.

He called and said he wanted to go fishing again. This time he
wanted to talk about going into politics. If he did that, he explained,
in the boat casting to panfish, he could make it happen. Right?

His plan is to run for the state House, then Senate, then Congress.
By damn, he'll see justice that way!

Could be he'll get elected, if he can come up with the money.
He's handsome, articulate, and an all-American young man. He
understands what's wrong. He's gutsy enough to stand up to the
special interests, bureaucrats, and political prostitutes.

I am pleased, and proud as blazes, that he wanted my endorse-
ment. That he somehow figures talking to me is like talking to his
Dad.

But I couldn't give it. I had to tell him that it is the takers, not
givers, who make it in politics. The system rejects the good guys. The
only way to beat them is on the "outside," constantly pounding on
them. That they will chew you up and spit you out if you try to do it
without being one of them.

He expected that answer, but didn't like it. I told him that he
must have patience. There are no miracle reforms. It won't happen.
But if you keep clawing at them, snarling, never purring, you will
keep them marginally honest. Recognize them for what they are —
and never take the pressure off, though it is frustrating and exasperating, and you'll make the system work; far more than you will pat-
ting butts from the inside.

It's the case of the one rotten apple in reverse. If a good guy gets
elected, they squash him. He has no influence, no clout, until he
becomes one of the bushel of rotten apples, or when he leaves.

As I was giving my sermon, he missed a strike. The sunfish were
hitting. Nice plump seven- and eight-inchers. The bluegills hadn't
moved into shallow water.

"You're a damned cynic. (He was mad.) You don't believe in anything. If you're right, the country would have collapsed years ago ... How come you keep trying, if you don't believe in it?"

"I do believe in it — the system, the concept. It works and survives because of those of us on the outside — the people — who keep their claws sharpened. ... I've worked in both Washington and Lansing. The politicians and bureaucrats are not the government. We are. Trouble is, too few of us are willing to take the responsibility for being the government."

There was a long, half-hour long, pause. We fished. Him expertly. Me awkwardly, as always. Then: "Hey, I brought a bottle of Pinch. Want to come to the motel and drink some of it with me? We could invite Mary Lou and go to Duffy's for dinner."

"Nope. We'll do that some other time."

Several fish later: "What do you think Dad would have said?"

I knew it had to come sometime and was ready.

"I don't know what he would have told you — but he'd have told me: the kid's taking on the world and making his own decisions. No matter what he does it will come out right ... he's good stuff."

The sky was orange over the drumlin to the west. The light dim. But I could see his mouth hang open, a bubble caught in his throat. He coughed it out. A tear, maybe several, hung in the eye the setting sun reflected into through his glasses.

I took my glasses off and used my shirttail to wipe them clean. He pulled out a hanky; I did the same. I caught his smile; sorta brave, like he'd been honest enough to do it.

I kicked the little electric motor into gear and headed for the landing. He said, "Hey, I remember catching you and Dad crying once — had you just had too much booze?"

I almost told him we had been talking about a ship he'd been on that went down; and, sure, we'd been drinking too much. But, instead, pretended I didn't hear him.

So I got two tin cups out of the Suburban and splashed some of his Scotch into them. We sat on the shore and sipped it, warm and pungent.

He'd have preferred a Strohs. A blackfly drowned in my cup. I poked at it with a finger, then drank it down.

He's a man now. His Old Man can be proud.

But we'd both prefer he — and we — never had to grow up.

River Lunch
May 9, 1984

The big, old four-door Chevy was a surprise as I passed the turnout along the river. It's been a regular fixture here for six or seven years, but never until early July when the "summer people" migrate to this part of the state.

The car, in darn nice shape, is probably a late 1960s model. It belongs to an old gent whose family has owned one of the many mansion-like summer homes here for three or more generations. It is common for them to keep an older car stored at the "cottage" as a second car during summer. (They bring a limo with them.)

Before the Chevy it was a big, old four-door Buick that took him to the river.

We'd crossed paths on the river a dozen or so times in the last twenty years. Just a "how's fishing," "nice hatch," "lots of mosquitoes" sort of crossings. I should remember his name but never do.

Unless someone else was using the car, he was "up" two months early.

I forgot the puzzle after the first couple of casts. Small caddis were hatching and small fish were rising. The river was clear and laced with spiritual tonic; within minutes the overpowering calm that trout streams, bird coverts and the end of a battle produce had taken over. Everything is clear and right. There are no sorrows, no joys, no questions, no goals, no failures, no pressures.

Coming around the bend I was disturbed to see someone sitting on the bone-colored sweeper. My sweeper! Where would I take a break to light the pipe and dream with the current?

To hell. The sweeper is big enough for two.

It was the old guy with the Chevy. Tall, sorta angular, white haired, wearing no hat. The waders and vest were old.

"Join me?"

"Sure, if you don't mind sharing my sitting place."

He chuckled. "Pretty good fishing, aye? I've heard about this early season fishing ... didn't think it was this good."

"It isn't, always. This is sorta unusual, but it happens more times than we remember. The river isn't like most others; it doesn't dirty up as fast and is pretty stable."

"Yeah, but not as stable as it used to be before all this sand. Most of the places I've been fishing for more than forty years are just sand flat runs now. Too bad ... it used to be really good.

"Mind you, I'm not complaining for me. It's too late for that. And I never see anyone else, except you, here in the summer. Used to be a lot more fishermen in here ... when we still had brook trout and hatches."

"Maybe we'll get something done about that."

"I know you're trying, but you don't seem to get anywhere.

"Oh, I read the *Call*, been a subscriber for about twelve years. I know who you are."

Oops. Caught me off balance. It could turn into shop talk. Don't need that on the stream.

But he changed the subject: "Have a good winter?"

"They're getting too long. Not as much fun as they used to be when all the parts were working right. How about you, good winter?"

A long pause. Eyes downcast, looking at the waders.

"No, lost ... ."

I didn't get the name, but obviously, his wife.

"That's why I'm up so early. Without her, or my work or the kids there's not much there for me ... but I couldn't take one of your winters.

"Couple of the grandkids — eleven and thirteen — like to fish and stuff. They're gonna spend the summer with me, when they get out of school. Trying to talk the housekeeper into starting early, too.

"Even up here it is kinda lonely. The evenings can be hell. Don't think I'll ever get used to it ... hope I don't. Damn it!

"But the kids will take the sting out of it. Hope I don't spoil them too much. The housekeeper is good, she helped us raise our kids. She'll find chores for them."

There wasn't anything to say.

The cane rod was old, a Leonard, I guessed from the wrappings and handle. Looked like eight and a half feet, and in excellent condition, judging from the windings and guides. Only the handle really looked used. The reel was a Hardy. The vest was lean, not bulging.

"What's that rod of yours?" he asked.

"Oh, a Bob Summers', made by a friend of mine; seven-foot. Nice rod ... here," I handed it to him.

"Ummm," flexing it and checking the cane for nodes and finish. "I've seen his ad in your paper. Thought you liked his seven-and-a-half footer for four-weight line."

"Yeah, it's my favorite. But this one's a little faster and stouter, for five-weight. Good in the early season ... with these big flies." (I was using a 14.)

"I keep thinking about getting a new rod. Just might this year. But it's sorta late for that. She got me this one right after the war. Maybe I'll go down there (Traverse City) and buy the kids rods from Summers."

"Now that would really be spoiling them. Never appreciate them if they get them that easy."

"Ha, ha ... you've got as many opinions in person as you do in writing. I like that. And you're right. I bought them a couple of Fenwick glass rods. Might send them to that T.U. fishing school you mentioned in your paper. I wrote to 'em. Looks good."

"It is. I've never talked to anyone who's been there who didn't rave about it. Some guys can't get enough; keep going back, year after year. I know some of the instructors; they're great guys.

"You gonna fish some more?" I asked.

"Nope, had enough for today. I'm hungry and it's a long drive back to town. You gonna?"

"No. (I fibbed, I had planned to.) Come on. I've got a stove and food in the truck. We'll brew something up."

"Hey, that sounds great." His face lit up and he stepped off the sweeper in a strong stride.

After shucking the waders, I drove down to his turnout, fired up the Coleman and opened a can of stew and one of peaches. The stew simmered on one burner and a pot of water for coffee or tea on the other. Then I spread out crackers, peanut butter and jam and popped open two small cans of sweet juice.

"Whoa ... almost forgot." Digging in the Suburban's grub box turned up a can of smoked oysters.

"Hey! Hey! This is great!" He was joyful — delighted. Crackers and peanut butter were disappearing into a smile I was sure hadn't been there for several months.

He sipped the juice, then: "Oh, geezus. Forgot. I got something to contribute." He almost trotted to the Chevy and came back with a little cooler containing two bottles of cold beer. He popped them open with a Swiss Army knife that came out of a vest pocket. I couldn't pronounce the beer's brand name.

Piling the stew on the little tin plates, he pushed it on his crackers with the spoon and kept dipping dripping fingers into the oysters, between swallows of beer.

"Best damn meal I've had in months … no make that years. By damn, I really do believe that stuff you write. Guess I didn't think anyone could live this good."

"It ain't bad, is it? Cheap, but who can be richer? Tea or coffee?"

The food was about gone.

"How ya gonna make it?"

"Instant coffee or loose tea."

"I'll take tea, if it won't screw you up."

"Nope, just carry the coffee for company." The tea came out black, strong, and blistering hot.

"Hey, you mind if I take a picture of this?" he said heading for the car.

"Heck no."

He came back with a Leica 35mm reflex, which had a self-timer.

"I have a tripod in the car. Let's use the self-timer and we can both be in the picture."

"Good idea."

He arranged things so the stove and cans of stew and peaches were in the picture, and reset the shutter until he had four or five shots.

When I took the camera off the tripod I couldn't avoid fondling it. It was worth more than the six or seven cameras in the truck. My heart plopped when I saw his eyes look from me to the camera and back and start to light up.

"Tell you what …"

(Damn, no. I don't want your camera.) He caught himself. He sensed that it wasn't right and stopped.

"Tell you what," he started again, as I was packing stuff. "Next time I see you here I'll have a can of stew and peaches. You bring the stove and tea."

"Ya gotta deal."

We shook on it. The shake was strong. The shoulders were back and kinda bouncy.

He fired up the Chevy and leaning out the window, almost giggled and asked, "Hey, Shep, you wanna race back to town?" Then chuckled like mad.

"That one beer was too many for you," I told him. But I knew it wasn't the beer. It was just plain damn feeling good, and whole and worthwhile, and part of something real again.

SUMMER

Puppies And Tamaracks
August 26, 1987

Nails, the bird dog pup, didn't know what to make of the river. She's come to know lakes and cricks in our ramblings. This was her first excursion to the river.

It is wider, noisier, faster, and more tangled and jumbled with logs and sweepers. Up here it twists and darts around overhanging loops and undercut banks.

Nails stabs her nose and then her paws into it. Then springs back. Only to pounce again to confront this new creature. Is it friend or foe?

There are high-powered bird dog folks who say you have to keep the pups on the fast track. Don't let 'em mess around with butterflies, sparrows, and stuff like that. They sigh and blubber if they see the pup pointing and chasing a grasshopper.

Yeah. Their dogs, somehow, remind you of the kid out of a high-powered private military school who went to hell the first time he faced somebody coming up the hill delivering live rounds.

So Nails gets all the time it takes to be a puppy. All the time it takes to learn that this business about romping and prowling is supposed to be fun.

I was thinking about that and smirking sorta, when she landed in my lap.

She's a little thing; only about thirty-five pounds. But a bundle of her up tight to your belly with your waders dangling in the river can be a jolt.

Yet she didn't want anything special. Just to say hi — like do you want to come and play?

Nope. It was play time, for her. But not me. The trudge to the river was as much as I could muster. Nearly a month with a tormented back had made getting the last issue of the *Call* out a blur of sentences that seldom meshed into paragraphs or whole stories.

Things like that ultimately wear on your mind and nerves. Even if you hobble, the options are a retreat to the river for therapy or succumb and become pain's vegetable. Mary Lou has more vegetables than we can handle in the garden. Nails and I went to the river.

As eyes grow older fly fishing becomes far less cluttered. When you can no longer accurately gauge which of the myriad of may, caddis or stone flies are hatching, you simply determine if they are up or down wing and guess at their general color; dark or light.

So you fish a swept wing, spent wing, or upright wing imitation in olive or tawny colors. And geez, you wouldn't believe how well it works. Just try to get the size pretty close. If it is over size 14 it really isn't much fun anyway.

Of importance are the tug of the current on the waders, the kingfisher chortling down the river, the leader spinning out in the current, and the bird dog pup up on shore wondering what it is all about. That you can no longer see the fly at the end of the leader becomes a matter of small concern.

Though I no longer use more than seventy percent of it, the bulges of stuff in the fly fishing vest remain treasured. Gosh, there's a little doodad that is supposed to take all the puzzle out of tying leader and hook knots. The instructions are still wrapped around it. I have never used it, and can't read the instructions. But I wouldn't be without it.

You just gotta have all that stuff to enjoy fly fishing. You really do.

And there's the little packet of streamside fly tying gear. About the size of two clenched fists. I could — when my eyes were prime — tie just about any pattern with the materials and tools in it. I used it once, in a practice session at the fly tying bench behind Mary Lou's TV. But I wouldn't think of leaving it at home.

A trout rose for the third time across and just downstream from a hole I've fished for more than twenty years. Before brown trout, steelhead, and salmon drove brook trout from this water you could sometimes take up to an eleven-inch brook trout there. Now it is three feet shallower and holds only brown trout.

Some folks, who haven't been fishing long and who have a questionable heritage, regard brown trout as the ultimate game fish. Those of us who have been around a while and who have deep roots in the trout fishing business, regard brook trout as the only honorable char.

Regardless, it seemed appropriate to flick the little Bob Summer's rod and drop a spent wing Adams into the current that bounced over the hole.

On the third cast the fish took — an eight-inch brown. It skittered over the water and shook off when I grasped and jiggled the hook.

Nails took it all in, her forelegs submerged in muck along the bank. Returning I tried to reassure her that she was where she belonged, that Toots was here somewhere with us.

A mahogany-colored maple leaf floated by, bouncing and coursing around and under a sweeper that has probably dangled over the river for a century.

A kingfisher darted and laughed over the river. A frond of gold-leafed tamarack needles swirled in a miniature undertow.

In a month or so it will be time to take Nails to the grouse and woodcock woods. The cane rods and the creations of hackle and fur they cast will be set aside for another winter.

Spring's pup will learn the wonder of a nose full of grouse and woodcock scent. She will learn slow and easy. The kill will be rare. The taste of feathers will not be part of the learning.

That's the magic of hunting with bird dog or hound. Like fly fishing, you can take the pleasure from the point or the chase. You don't need to kill to claim your trophy.

Autumn is closing in fast. People who don't understand that confuse an old guy sitting on a river bank.

And geez, I wanted to ask that last cluster of gold-leafed tamarack needles just where it was going and what it had seen since May.

If you haven't, take the time to become mesmerized by a tamarack. Become spellbound by the things it has seen that you never will. If you really get into it you'll find that your bank account really isn't all that big a thing.

Precocious Warblers
September 18, 1991

Hey! We all know the guy (pity sakes, could it have been a gal?), who put this big glob of a world together, was at his finest when he deposited us human folks here. For sure, we are evolution's finest creation.

You believe that? No way.

Take a minute and consider that with sixteen to twenty years of schooling we still don't know how to help make our place in the world better than we found it. For a fact, we don't know how to find our way at all. For a double fact, the chances are we will trash what we found.

But consider a fragile little critter, not weighing as much as my thumb, with a brain maybe not weighing as much as my little toe-nail: the Kirtland's warbler.

Now if our mass of brain matter, or whatever it is, were even an infinite fraction as highly evolved as that of a Kirtland's warbler we might have something going for us.

This comes to us via Jerry Weinrich, a wildlife biologist out of Houghton Lake.

These little birds have a lot of caretakers. Jerry just happens to be one of the best of them. He's what a wildlife biologist is supposed to be: as concerned about dinky birds as he is about elk, as interested in snakes and turtles as he is in orchids.

Jerry Weinrich is — just maybe — what you perhaps secretly have always wished you could be. What you would have been if you'd known those many years ago that you could put the Wheaties on the table with a job nurturing wildlife.

Like all good folks in his trade — and there are a bundle of them — Jerry never has enough knowledge. But he knows enough to know there's a bundle he doesn't know, and that there's even more he would like to know.

(But do you suppose, that knowing all of it might take the magic out of it?)

Enough of the gibberish? Hang in there, Shep.

Jerry and I were talking about the Kirtland's. He's elated. This is the best year the endangered little fellas have had in at least thirty years. Nearly 350 males showed up in the jack pines to nest this spring. At least that many youngsters left the nest and are already wintering in the Bahamas — or are on their way there.

Scientists have been studying Kirtland's for the past three or four years — studying them "hands-on." That was taboo until a few years ago. The scientific community was deeply divided on whether "hands on" studies (capturing and banding them) would endanger them even further and possibly contribute to their extinction. But the hard decision was made and the studies were very cautiously launched.

Baby birds are taken from nests and banded. They then are recaptured when they leave the nest to begin exploring the pinelands.

Scientists expect to learn how many survive, what kind of nesting habitat produces the most young, how many make it to their wintering grounds in the Bahamas, how many come back and where those that do nest, what their nesting success rate is, et cetera.

What they've discovered will blow your mind — and your ego if you are stuck on the proposition that two legged critters are superior.

We all know — well, don't we — that baby birds pick up and follow their parents thousands of miles to and from their winter homes, and those who follow them back play house where their folks did. Naw! Not true.

The researchers have learned that when a Kirtland's is a few days out of the nest it begins exploring for next year's nesting habitat. Almost invariably they are found in better nesting habitat than their parents used. That's primarily because new, and improved, habitat evolves annually.

Immature birds will be found in the finest nesting habitat in July and August. Next year those same birds will return there and set up housekeeping. Virtually at the very spot they picked a year earlier.

Pretty savvy, right?

But that's not the best of it.

Those kids, those month-old to six-week-old kids, don't wait to follow momma and poppa to the Bahamas. They begin arriving in the Caribbean islands in mid-August, as much as two months before the adults arrive.

I mean, they just pop up into the air, buzz over Cleveland, Atlanta, Miami, and across the ocean to the tropical islands their ancestors have wintered in forever, without anyone showing them the way.

How do they that? Ha! And you thought you were blessed with the answers. Think again.

All this doesn't leave you feeling real important, right? Unless, that is, you really are wise enough to know you don't have the answers, and that our kind better get smart enough to understand that deficiency, and treat with greater respect the other creatures we share this planet with.

Treat them as equals? Not really. Not until you can march to that distant homeland your ancestors came from ten thousand years ago without a map, or compass, or even landscape bearings.

(But, egads! After what we've done to the land, not even your ancestors would want to go back, let alone recognize the landscape.)

A few years ago a Grayling Chamber of Commerce official suggested Crawford County would be a better place if they'd pack all those pesky Kirtland's warblers into a National Guard helmet, gas 'em, and eliminate their interference with the good weekend warriors. Huh! It is those weekend tank commanders who can't find their way from one forty to another.

Don't you love it?

Nails

August 8, 1990

Rans Hill said she was gonna be one heckuva bird dog. "Bidable, a tiger on raw beaver meat, and a feather-snortin' bird dog." That's sorta how he put it when she was a wobbly-legged pup about the size of a shell vest pocket.

Well now, Rans didn't tell the whole story. This little creature who came to live with us after our Toots left us, is a lot more than gentle, loving, and bird snorting.

For openers, she has never had raw beaver meat since she left Hill's quarters on Higgins Lake. She's had to survive on a bland diet of what veterinarian Dave Norton calls Science Diet pellets. It is kinda expensive, but Dave says it might have prevented the cancer that took my Toots at ten years old.

That was five years ago. I'm still nursing a hollow ache up under that hand that mends fly line as the current brings it back to me.

I remember when Dave was a gangly kid — about the tallest in high school. Not really an athlete or a savage competitor, but if he could reach over the heads of the kids from Boyne City, East Jordan, and Gaylord to grab the ball off the backboard he'd do his part.

His Dad, John, ran the Standard station. That was back in the 1960s, when the "town" Standard station doctored your car, like Dave now does our Nails.

I wander, but it has always seemed right that Dave saw fit to come back. He left for a decade or so, to study pet doctoring down in East Lansing, and then practice it until he felt he had the hang of it.

Not many of the kids who leave to study big time stuff manage to come back. We needed Dave. We're fortunate that he needed us.

Just the other day, Dave gave Nails her annual allergy shot. There's something out there that gets her to scratching and nipping at herself every August.

Do you suppose it is anxiety over the pending bird season?

Captain Hill (as he answers the phone) didn't tell me this pocketful of feathers would be so fragile when he told me to come and pick her out of the kennel. He didn't know. But what do you expect from a guy with white hair who is still sporting tracks?

(Tracks are something us kids saw on our shoulder and collar when we were young enough to smile all the way to the end of a five-mile run with a fifty-pound pack on our back — before we'd taken time to go potty that morning.)

This business about making Department of Natural Resources regional law chiefs captains will never make sense to old infantry-men. Colonel's eagles would look more appropriate on Captain Hill, who stepped down as the state top fish cop to return to the field as a lowly "captain."

That is class.

Ever know a general who didn't talk more about the company and regiment he commanded than he did about the division? But ever hear of one with the guts to cash in his stars to get his eagles back?

That's what Captain Hill did.

Right now, as these scrambled thoughts come to mind, the bird dog he entrusted me with when she was still intimidated by grasshoppers was showing anything but class.

We were checking out the grouse covert her predecessors and I had hunted since about the time Captain Hill was checking out of the Marine Corps and dreaming about a berth in the Michigan game warden corps.

She was going stiff-legged on me. That could mean anything — robin, snake, grasshopper, chipmunk. You guess.

We were at the edge of a popple stand, where it breaks into a swale. She was about to catapult into the thick grasses and muck of the swale when I called her short: "Stop! Stay!"

Her springs were so taut when she came to attention that she nearly fell. But she held. (Colonel Hill would be proud.) Stomping in ahead of her, I kicked out a cottontail rabbit.

She streaked past me like something fired from a rocket launcher. My "Stop! Nails; stop!" got lost in the laugh.

Hey, General Hill, where did you come up with this breed of bunny hound with the long hair and a knack for pointing birds when they can't find something else more fun to distract them?

Drumlin Bassin'
July 1, 1987

Dragonflies can really mess up, or juice up, a guy's bass fishing.

Now, bass fishing is supposed to be serious business. Right? Well ...

The Sunday before, I'd watched three different boats, with two guys in each, bass fishing in Antrim County's magnificent upper chain of lakes. There was all kinds of good stuff to do. Miles of undeveloped shoreline to gawk at. Swallows, kingfishers, at least one mink, muskrats, even dragonflies. And the fish weren't biting worth a dang. (Not even Killer Bing McClellan was catching them.)

But these guys were swishing away as though their arms were windmills. Mean, serious! Man, were they serious.

It turned out to be a low key bass tournament.

At a retirement supper, former DNR director Howard Tanner once said he was going to take the time to "smell the fish." Those guys weren't even doing that.

Well, everybody to their own. As long as they're not messing up mine.

Bass fishing has come a long way in the last twenty or so years. But you'll be hard pressed to convince me it is any more fun than it was forty, or fifty, or even sixty years ago.

Sure, it is in some ways, easier. The magnetic cast control plug reel and graphite stick I was plunking with work far better than the old metal club and Pflueger Summit reel I was so proud of as a kid. (Still have that Summit and the Supreme I was even prouder of a few years later.) Electric motors have oars and paddles beat hollow for quietly positioning a boat against the lily pads.

But, geez, have you ever looked at all the bass fishing baits in a Bass Pro catalog? There are dozens and dozens of pages of them. Complex? Whew! Used to be a guy knew he had the right stuff if he had a couple Hula Poppers, two or three Jitterbugs, and some of those Heddon plugs that ran deep, along with a Silver Minnow.

And back then you didn't get run over by water skiers and guys on snowmobiles that run on the water.

Ah, well. Dragonflies haven't changed and there is still enough boy left in the man to be fascinated by them.

There wasn't another boat on the little, private lake. Just Nails (the bird dog pup) and a babbling old editor. It was after supper, but the temperature was still in the seventies, with a slight breeze. In other words: perfect.

And the dragonflies seemed to know it. They were everywhere, in lots of dazzling colors shimmering in the still-high sun. Some as small as an inch and a half. Others, probably, over three inches.

All of this was so intriguing that I'd put the rod down to take it in. Then I saw the wake that made the lily pads churn. Muskrat, was the first thought. But it was no muskrat. It just had to be a damn big bass taking something near the surface.

Wished I'd had a top water plug on, but snapping up the rod, decided to go with the spinner bait.

It was about a thirty-foot shot. The big bait hit the water rattling. Hung a second on a pad and started sinking. About two seconds later I started churning it through the salad — as they say.

It stopped. Caught on a weed — or a bass. I leaned into the rod. It gave, like a weed breaking loose, and then lurched toward the rod. A tail came half out of the water as the fish turned. Then half the fish surged out of the pads, twisting and diving.

Grinding at the reel and horsing the rod, I threw him off balance for a second. But he made it to the weeds and dug in. It was tug-of-war for a few seconds, but he came loose and the hefty rod and ten-pound-test line half skidded him out of the pads and into open water, where he made one leap and dove again.

That's when I remembered the pup. Hell, she coulda been drowned in the weeds by now. Nope, she was there, on the middle seat, head over the gunwale, back straight, tail doing little circles.

The fish came up. A good eighteen inches — maybe three pounds. Biggest bass of the season. A pair of pliers eased the hook out. The fish never fully left the water before diving again for the deep sanctuary in the weeds.

Nails forgot about the dragonflies until one landed on top of the tackle box in front of her nose. She put the point on it while she sat wagging her tail.

Three much smaller bass later it turned chilly. Switching to a small jig produced a half dozen, or so, nice — six to eight inches — bluegills on the ultra light spin pole.

The sun was dropping behind the drumlin when we got the boat and tackle loaded.

And Dad said his oldest would never amount to anything.

The End Of Summer
September 12, 1984

The old blackberry patch is slowly fading. Young popples are invading like squash vines as they spread out from a nearby beaver cutting. But the patch remains generous. A capful was picked in a few minutes.

There's a special knack to eating wild berries of any kind. Properly trained folks don't daintily eat them one at a time as they pick them. Some dour brutes wait 'till they have a handful and then jam them in their maws. That's bad, but better than one at a time.

The approved tactic is to wait until you have a capful then mash one fistful after another into your maw. If you're really good, your tongue will keep up with lapping the juice as it drips from your purple lips. That's talent!

Thoughts of the bear cubs seen here some years back were interrupted by the biggest darn mayfly or caddisfly the river has ever produced. It swept in on huge wings and landed on a weed. The weed, a big thistle a few feet out in the clearing, bent through ninety degrees then swayed back and forth.

Big dang bug — sorta olive drab gray. Way too big for the four-weight cane rod. Gotta figure out a way to capture and identify it.

Then momma or poppa buzzed in. Damn. It was a baby goldfinch. The juice from the berries must have squirted in my eyes — or maybe they were fermented.

The unofficial end of summer does that to folks who live in these boonies. When the caravans of fudgies head down the highway, heads become giddy and a youthful stride returns and shoulders straighten. The condo dwellers and folks up for a quick fix are a terrible burden.

But all that's behind us until next June.

Though there were blue-winged olives on the river, the trout weren't interested. It was too fine an afternoon to fish nymphs or streamers — besides, a lousy salmon might take one, which could shatter Bob Summer's artistry.

An imitate-nothing downwing Leon Martuch Hillbilly looked good in the fly box. With its red wool butt it is fun to watch in the current's swirl.

A little brook trout — maybe six inches — clumsily grabbed it as it bobbed through slack water above a sweeper. Ha, fun on the little stick. Several casts later, a brown, maybe eight inches, sucked it down as it skimmed in the current along a sweeper that sways with the river.

A fish started rising, across and downstream, over a slight indentation in the tons of sand that choke the river. The size 16 fly swept across and dimpled the surface. Four feet downstream, the brown took. A brute: just about a half inch under ten inches.

Then as the released fish darted toward a stump slumping into the river, a big fish slashed at him. Wow! Not big enough for a salmon, but couple pounds at least.

A three-inch marabou streamer rapidly replaced the dry fly. It cast awkwardly on the little rod and plopped into the river upstream, bringing it to the surface, then let it sway with the current by lowering the rod tip.

Wham!

He missed it. Wham! Blasted back and took it on the second slap. Geez.

The rod hummed deep into the corks. The miniature reel, hardly bigger than two silver dollars, screeched as the 5X leader followed the first dash downstream.

Not giving much of a diddle dee if I landed him, I kept the corks straining, hoping for a jump. Instead, he turned into a sluggish fighter and maybe two or three minutes later slid to the surface.

Silvery, heavy pale dots, probably twenty inches and about three pounds. A lake run brown. He wallowed off into the current, with none of the zing of much smaller resident trout when released.

A kingfisher flapped by, cackling at all the commotion. The berry juice was feeling sticky. A half dozen mouthfuls of river water washed most of them off or down.

Several bushels of grapes are ripening beyond the garden where there are enough tomatoes, squash, broccoli, peppers, beets, carrots, swiss chard, parsnips, and other goodies for two households full of kids. The second round of apples and peaches, plus pears, is due in a coupla weeks.

The arthritis is gnawing at Toots' hips, but she keeps a beady eye on the gun cabinet, yearning for bird season.

The baby goldfinches are now coming to the feeders at the house. Bucks are rubbing moss off antlers. Young bucks will be making scrapes soon. The first geese and tawny popple leaves are due.

There's a cricket chirping in the woodpile behind the stove that's been fired up several cool mornings.

There's a somber, ominous tint to the Big Lake. A warning that her gentle time is over. *Beware: I'll become a brute with no notice in the days ahead; no lover will ever tame me.*

Ah, ain't it all grand?

The Tric Hatch
August 1, 1984

The thermometer registered an uncertain forty-seven degrees in the pre-dawn mist. A chilling shock compared to the warmth of the blanket and the low 70s the night before at bedtime.

Closing doors and windows to ward off the dampness, even if it was too late to shut out the cold, I was tempted to unplug the coffee pot and retreat to bed.

But more sleep and warmth would not heal the wounds of too many people, too much talk, and too much typewriter bondage. A down vest over the flannel shirt and T-shirt, with a spill-proof mug of coffee steaming onto the fog-shrouded windshield, were a better antidote.

Shortly before 8:00 a.m. after the curtain of fog lifted, the first miniature mayflies appeared. Nearly forty-five minutes later there were hundreds, then thousands, up and down this short run of smooth slackwater. I was already far too warm for the vest; it was left to decorate tag alders.

I'd meant to tie the 6X, then 7X tippet, to the standing 5X the night before. By the time company left it was time for bed. Now it was a trial and error torture test. (I blamed it on John Tanton instead of age.) But, in time, the size 24 Tric was secured.

A few fish started feeding about 9:30 a.m. Two small brook trout, probably six and seven inches, sucked the little fly in. Upstream there was more action: four chinook salmon smolts slashingly took the fly in a matter of seconds.

It was time for more waiting. The white-winged blacks would start to spin in an hour or so. The flannel shirt became another bank decoration.

The raspberries were ripe and swollen. Some nearly as big as a trigger finger's nail. Back from the river, blueberries were so thick you walked gingerly to avoid squashing them.

By 10:15 a.m. the T-shirt was too hot under the fishing vest; it went into the big back pocket. The thermometer must have been well into the 70s.

Isn't a northern summer wondrous?

The little flies were now like a cloud of rising and falling miniature snowflakes. It has been years since we've had them like this — since before the last lamprey treatment.

Several dozen fish started feeding, their body forms like liquid shadows just under the surface. Brook trout came easily. They were released; too few have survived the ravages of road silt, lamprey chemical and salmon. But before 11:00 a.m. there were four 8- to 8 1/2-inch brown trout in the vest pocket, next to the streamer fly book.

At the upstream end of the run a good fish kept rising — maybe twelve inches. The undercut sod bank, and a sweeper downstream, create an eddy just above the slot. It has bedeviled me many times before.

Shoot a slack leader upstream and it floats neatly through the eddy. But the second it bobs into the slick just below the spinning water it is sucked under. This rarely seems to spook the feeding fish, but the fish never sees or touches the fly. The trick is to cast across and slightly upstream, into the maybe four-inch slot between the eddy and the rising fish, with enough slack to keep the fly from being sucked under, yet tight enough for the tiny hook to grab some flesh when the fish takes.

Beavers are a scourge here. They have devastated the stream with dams and flooded cricks. About a mile of former bird hunting lands are awash.

They leave, however, bushels of tiny aspen limbs that burst into instant fire. In less than five minutes the four-inch-wide fire was crackling hot, charring the gutted trout as they perched on the stick, sliding back and forth just over the flames. Minutes more and the smoke-blackened flesh started to crumble off the skin. Peeling carefully, the fresh trout fell onto eager fingers that were dipped into the hat full of berries and plunged down an eager throat.

Some folks who are pretty savvy about water chemistry and stuff, tell me that drinking this river water will someday kill me. Someday wasn't that day.

The brunch break took less than a half hour, maybe twenty minutes, while the trout still sipped in Trics between the eddy and the sweeper.

On my second cast the fish took, and the flimsy little hook grabbed. Now there are folks who spend all night throwing grenade-size blobs of hair and feathers at thigh-size brown trout. There are guys who stand in snow-bitter water chucking lead-laden gaudy hunks of fur and plastic at steelhead and salmon as long as and thicker than an arm.

That's all fun, mind you — until you discover real fly fishing. It is called "Tric fishing." The highlight of the trout season is letting that ten-inch brown go, after you're stuffed with half-raw trout and fresh berries and you've washed 'em down with crick water. (Even makes you wonder if twelve-year-old Scotch really tastes good.)

Grasshoppers And Grouse
August 10, 1988

Nails' head snapped around, like some kind of whiplash victim, until her nose and rump were six to eight inches apart. She locked on the quarry like a robot on command.

Cautiously, an inch or so at a time, she unwound, her rear end slowly twisting until it was behind, not beside her nose. Then again, inch by inch, she crept forward in a full stalk mode: tail nearly on plane with her backbone, front paws, one at a time, reaching out at creep speed.

Carefully stepping in front of her, it took several seconds of close scanning to pick out the mottled dark grey and brown form. The little gun came up. A puff of yellow, green, and cream was blown some two feet through the air and landed in a clump.

Ha! My second kill. And only sixteen rounds fired. Darn good for a guy who never qualified with his Service 45. (The range guys always qualified us. The colonel, though a pistol sharpshooter, insisted everyone in the outfit carry M1 Garands. "Can't hit (blip) with a damned pistol when they're shooting back at you," he'd explain.)

This pistol is a Colt Ace .22 rimfire auto loader. Built on the same frame as a Service 45 — one heckuva little plinking piece.

The thermometer on the office window read ninety-five. Everyone I'd talked to on the phone had snapped. Air conditioners in DNR offices around the north country were out of commission. So were tempers. The drought and the heat of summer 1988 were wearing on nerves.

After forty years of banging at typewriter keys you do it almost instinctively. The fingers snap and the words slap down on paper. But when sweat drips off your nose onto your belly it is time for a break.

At least Nails thought so. She came from under the desk, clawing at my knee; she wanted out — time for a hunt.

The little bird dog is going on seventeen months — a classy little critter. Bidable — but wired with 220 this summer. With day after day of ninety degrees, she hasn't been getting into the action she savored in the spring when woodcock were nesting.

So she's taken to pointing everything. From the chipmunk that cleans up the leftovers under the bird feeder to the Coast Guard helicopter that flies over several times a week. Her current favorite is grasshoppers.

They are an old favorite of mine. Great sport with a little hand-gun. But extra special now when there is a dog to point them. One day two weeks ago I hit nine hoppers. Didn't count how many rounds it took, but my loading hand was getting raw from feeding .22 shells into clips.

There are a lot of folks out there who would ban all private own-ership of handguns. I can understand where they are coming from. If I believed for a second that it would end the killing of kids and other innocents I would eagerly give up the handguns I own and immensely enjoy.

There are some factors, however, the anti-gun lobby hasn't con-sidered.

Next time they go to Congress with their plea they should be asked how we would control the grasshopper blight on the drumlins in southwestern Charlevoix County if that old newspaperman didn't have his .22 pistols.

When you're in the grouse woods this fall and the grasshoppers are gone so your dog doesn't have anything to point, consider that one.

Which, after a long hike, gets us to bird hunting. It has been fes-tering at me that wildlife biologists just don't know what the blazes is happening to our grouse. For decades they told us the population fluctuated on a seven- or ten-year cycle. And for decades this seemed to be so.

Folks who remember the great bird hunting in the 1930s, 40s and 50s will tell you they could set their watch by the cycle. And it worked.

It sure as blazes hasn't since the 1970s. That cycle got smashed flat on the low end. Why?

The theory that grouse only inhabit stands of young aspen is about as valid as the theory that every handgun owner is a nut and murderer. I've had good hunting all of my life in hardwoods, in tag alders, in cedars and birch. Sure, it is often better in cutover aspen. But it was always good in other habitats, too. However, only if there wasn't much hunting pressure.

Though we are still losing far too much aspen, we are also regen-erating more of it than we ever have. The "grouse cycle," however, is running on a flat tire.

I'd like to brag that Nails and I are making a big dent in the grasshopper population. You be the judge of that one. I do believe that the September 15 to January 1 grouse season is making a tragic dent in the grouse population. Let's cut it down to October 1 to November 5.

The next guy who tells you that this reduction is absurd ask him to explain what happened to the "cycle" us old bird hunters could rely on.

Hey, things ain't what they once was — and they ain't ever gonna be. Too many guys are out there reading Gordon Guillion and buying Bean bird boots, Browning doubles, and a snazzy little setter like Nails.

Grouse killing has become almost computerized. Nature didn't create this king of game birds for computerized hunting.

Nails and I have located several broods of birds. We'll hunt them this fall. I won't shoot at one out of five; she'll be disappointed. (Love to eat 'em but just have to figure the hunting has deteriorated to where the dog's point is the pay off.)

So we'll do our part.

And some slob will come in after deer season, when a legitimate hunter (one with a pointing dog) can't hunt in the snow, and blow them out of the trees like shooting squirrel nests.

Geez, man, I've been doing this too long to believe that is bird hunting.

A Mid-August Hike
August 15, 1984

After nearly a week of mind-sizzling heat and humidity so soggy that paper stuck in the typewriter, the morning was uncommonly kind: fifty degrees with a light breeze just after dawn.

The old bird dog was intent on sleeping in. She hadn't moved when the kibbles rattled in her bowl and the heart worm pills clinked in the jar. But she came up like a pup chasing a butterfly when I jingled the bell from the pocket of my hunting vest. It took some persuasion to get her away from the door and into her food.

With berries ripe in the upland away from the river, it seemed like a good morning to look for the brood of grouse I'd seen once some weeks ago. Despite old joints that are getting creaky, Toots flew into the back of the Suburban, feathers streaming. She knew exactly what pocket I'd put the bell in and wasn't going to let it out of sight.

Some guys wouldn't be as happy with a new Cadillac as she was when I clipped the bell to her collar. Instantly, she was lost in the ferns, leaping high every few feet to make sure I wasn't lost.

Not seventy-five yards from the truck she was on point.

Too easy. She was in a stand of over mature popple with light ground cover.

Moving in behind her, I was even with her nose when the young woodcock fluttered up not three feet from us. Ten feet farther we had another point and another doodle. It went like that four more times, within a twenty-five-foot area.

These young woodcock are dandy little birds. They are small, noticeably slower flying than they will be in mid-September, and with brighter tawny markings.

But that was it — no hen bird.

A quarter mile or so from the truck she dove into the berry bramble and the bell went still.

Moving in slowly, one of the young pats flushed before I saw Toots about five feet from me. Carefully now, watching her head turn and following it, four more birds flushed. She moved, maybe twelve to fifteen feet, crouching low, and then locked on again. Stumbling a couple of times, I flushed the hen bird well ahead of her. Then getting in close, two more youngsters, light colored and sorta wobbly fliers — but strong — left the berry bushes.

That was enough for me. But she deserved more, so I headed her away from the river bottom, toward easier walking, expecting no more action. Who could have asked for a more rewarding morning?

After less than a half mile, she was on point in thick ferns under a stand of birch mixed with some beech and maple. It didn't seem to be right, but summer birds are unpredictable. The hen flushed first, probably thirty-five to forty feet away, swiftly streaking between me and a beech tree. Then, not seven feet from Toots' nose, three young birds went out. Before it was over, nine little ones left the cover.

Whoopee! Ding-a-dee doo! Old Lady, we're gonna have us one helluva hunting season.

But her day wasn't over.

The sun was rapidly warming both dog and man so we headed for the little pond. Just a nothing-place, where there are frogs, turtles and cattails. People who come here are looking for trout. Probably not more than one out of a thousand visit this small twenty-by-twelve-foot pond.

Toots roared into it like a young Chessie chasing live ducks. She landed in the middle, the water deep enough that she had to hold her snout up to keep it dry. Several frogs leaped from shore, plunking into spreading riffles. A small turtle on the clay bank watched, then slowly slipped into the water.

It took Toots about five minutes, just standing there with water up to her back, and drinking about a gallon, to cool off.

Knowing what to expect, I ordered her to the opposite bank when she came out. She sat there, her feathery hair soaked and dripping. She looked up anxiously, then down and away, when I took the bell from her collar. She knew it was over, but didn't know why. Though it was more than a half mile back to the car, there was no bird cover on the way, so no sense in her wearing the bell.

On the stroll back, she tagged along, just ahead or behind me. About half-way through a stand of large, old, long ago, heavily over-browsed cedar I lost track of her. Searching, I found her on point about a hundred feet away, near the trunk of a blowdown cedar at the edge of the stand.

Moving in I spotted the bird, a big cock bird, under the stem of the tree. Toots knew she had a veteran at bay, holding a good twenty feet away until I moved in, then she inched forward as I took short, slow steps ahead of her.

His tail fanned out. The pat stood frozen until I was less than twelve feet from him, then erupted like a volcano.

I clipped the bell back on Toots and let her wear it all the way home and into the house. She had earned it.

Blackbirds are ganging up in these precincts. The last fawn I saw had nearly lost its spots. Most of the swallows and bluebirds are gone — somewhere. Farmers are hustling to get crops in. Cherries have been picked. Trees hang heavy with apples. The freezer is rapidly filling and a few more tomatoes ripen every day.

Mayflies are still hatching — and will be for two months. Guys who go for such things are catching salmon as mechanically as Ford workers assemble a car.

And Toots and I can't keep our noses out of the gun cabinet, and I can't keep my hands off the little double.

National Priorities
August 24, 1988

It wasn't something I'd normally do. Nails and I were in the garage turning on the little black and white television. And it was bedtime.

But nothing had been normal for several days. A malarial-like viper that's been trying to take control of my internal thermostat and blood cells for more than thirty years had made another visit. The thermometer had skipped between 105 and the low nineties. By late evening, the fever, chills, and delirium were stabilizing. But the chair and bed didn't fit. I'd sorta worn them out.

So Nails and I trudged to the garage and snapped on the TV, without even thinking.

I read the papers. I knew the Republican National Convention was in process. That George Bush was due to accept the nomination this night. But it didn't mean anything; didn't really register. Couldn't care less.

Then here's this guy, standing at the podium hands fluttering as he tries to start his acceptance speech. A human tidal wave of crazies are screeching and shrieking. The air is full of balloons and junk.

These are the people who control our political process. They seem to be totally barren of rational behavior. The guy hasn't said anything yet and they are behaving like 1950s' bobby-soxers at an Elvis Presley show in an intellectually barren land.

I should not be so alarmed. For more than twenty years, I've been convinced that it is rationally impossible to be a Republican or Democrat.

But the clincher was Nails. She stood between me and the little ten-inch TV screen and moaned. (Hey, this little bird dog can make some weird noises.) Never before in her year and a half on this earth has she done that.

When that didn't convince me to shut the thing off, she went behind me, got up on her hind legs, put a paw on each side of my neck and nibbled on my ears. Never did that before, either.

Folks with fancy degrees would say we'd be wrong to jump to conclusions about her behavior. But the only conclusion I came to was that she must be wiser than those folks in New Orleans who were acting like idiots. She might be nuts. She might be retarded. But she isn't an idiot.

Despite the protest, I was too weary to get up and shut it off. So I halfheartedly listened.

George Bush said some good things. I really picked up on his — and I didn't catch it all — promise to tackle acid rain. That sure is a break from the present administration. But it is only a political promise.

As determined as a guy is to do his civic duty and listen to such drivel, he has to terminate it when his bird dog starts nipping at the hair around his ankles like she was after fleas on her belly.

She was content, however, to snuggle up on the swing on the west side of the drumlin. It was perfect weather — just under fifty degrees a few minutes after 11:00 p.m. It also was later than we are used to being up. The old winter-weight robe and pile-lined slippers were designed for this.

The moon was just breaking half full. Stars glistened among the strange new man-things that have been flickering in the sky since the mid 1950s. Ears numbed by vapors from a skull that had been an oven for days had trouble picking up the night sounds.

Something yapped in the swale below the drumlin. Maybe along the east shore of the lake. Then again — and again. Sorta shrill.

Nails' chin came off my lap and she unwound from her berth on the oak slats of the swing. Stiff legged, she looked over my shoulder — uncertain.

A series of yapping sounds began from along the west shore of the lake to the north. A fox vixen and her pups? Learning to hunt together?

It was fun to think so. Though all wild creatures are magnificent, none are more so than the fox. At least not in this old fox hunter's opinion.

The make believe of the political charade that has afflicted this land for so many months started to fade in the real world of a family of wild canines. Creatures, who have learned to survive and prosper despite the curse of mankind, make a presidential election pale to insignificance — trivial and worthless.

Between now and early November the political cheerleaders and spin doctors will try to convince you the future of the world hinges on the outcome of November 8. Maybe so for the future of their cramped, personal power. But not the future of the real world that you, the fox, bird dogs, chickadees, and brook trout live in.

A fish biologist friend said, very sincerely, the other day that probably the best thing we could do is forget about having a president for the next four years. The only problem with that, far as I can see, is that newsmen wouldn't know what to write about. Maybe they'd have to discover the magic of sunrises, fireflies, fox kits, and the first fall snowstorm over Brockway Mountain.

Wouldn't it just be a better world if those were our national priorities?

Sporting Hoppers And Big Bluegills
September 6, 1989

During the waning days of summer, the stress of trying to fulfill an agenda that was drafted during leisurely (uh, make that boring) winter nights overcomes some normally rational, and at least marginally bright, people.

Pete Petro and Bruce Richards have become pathetic examples, both verging on demented behavior as they race to beat the inevitable changing of the seasons.

Let's start with Pete. He's the guy who owns that nifty wildlife art gallery — Chandler's — in Petoskey. Picture this: Pete's sorta stumbling through a just-mowed field, bent forward, nostrils flaring, sweat pouring from squinting eyes, the end of his tongue turning pasty gray where it protrudes from clenched teeth, neck muscles drawn so tight his head seems to be rolling on his shoulders.

"Hey, Pete! Take it easy. This is supposed to be fun. You're taking it too serious."

"Fun, hell! Sheppard, you're out to kill me, you want blood — all mine. You know where you can go. I'll beat you yet. You've been doing this for years. I haven't. You think I'm a patsy," he blurts back, the stub of his tongue wagging loosely.

The knuckles of his right hand are wrapped so tightly around the heavy frame of the .22 rimfire-bored Colt .45 service pistol they are the color of parchment.

"There's one! There he is! He's mine!" he screams, his voice starting to rattle as his squinting eyes turn to bulging marbles. The pistol comes up. Blam! Blam! His body shakes and rattles. Blam!

"Haa — haaaa," he babbles. "I got him, blew him away." He lowers the pistol, snaps out the clip and unloads its chamber.

It is the showdown at the first annual Chandler's/*North Woods Call* Sporting Hoppers Invitational. The rules are simple: .22 rimfire pistols, solid point rounds (hollow points and bird shot are ruled out), only one pistol loaded at a time, don't shoot yourself or anyone else, only shoot at stationary targets, when you locate a target you shoot until it is dead or has fled out of safe range, if it flies out of range you can pick another target until you kill one of the vicious devils, but mainly don't shoot yourself or anyone else.

Oh yeah, I forgot, the only legitimate targets are grasshoppers. No dragonflies, butterflies, etc. And only on-the-ground grasshoppers. You can get as close to them as they will let you before they fly and, I repeat, don't shoot anyone!

Pete already knows who the winner is. I told him when he started taking the pistol from his Blazer. The only guy who can possibly win is the guy who has the newspaper to report the results.

He bellowed about some things his customers wouldn't want to read when that sunk in.

Now, he'd killed his target. I picked one. He's watching the muzzle of the old Colt Woodsman wobble in an about eighteen-inch arc as I try to pull the trigger when it passes over the grasshopper. He's starting to smile now, figures he has me beat.

After I empty one ten-round clip and reach for another he's getting obnoxiously elated. "Haa, I thought you were good at this," he babbles as he's sorta hopping up and down like his son Jud on Christmas morning.

"Hey," I straightened him out, "you don't seem to understand the point of this shoot-out. It is to shoot. You hit 'em right off and you gotta clear your piece and stand around while the other guy is having fun shooting."

That does it. His eyes are spinning and there's a fiendish, sorta insane chortle coming from somewhere in his chest.

For the next hour and a half we slaughtered maybe two dozen grasshoppers with several hundred .22 rounds.

Over a late afternoon beer Pete concedes it is a lot more fun than shooting Sporting Clays and — always the entrepreneur — is figuring out ways to market it.

Now to Bruce Richards, the guy at Scientific Anglers down in Midland. This day he's squatting in the center of a sleek low-slung Tupperware canoe on Wakeley Lake. The day is perfect. Showing his usual lack of humility and grace, Bruce is effortlessly casting perfect loops with a five-weight fly rod and dropping poppers and nymphs sixty and seventy feet from the canoe.

That stuff is OK if you're at some sports show and want to impress people. Or if you are teaching people to fly cast. But there's no place for it a few yards from a guy who's been flailing the air with a fly rod some thirty years longer than you have and still ducks on every third, or so, cast to keep the popper out of his neck and ears.

Bruce is almost as frantic as Pete was. He needs to prove that he can catch a bigger bluegill than I have. He claims he caught a twelve-incher from Wakeley Lake several years ago. He knows we all know he's an utter, absolute, prideless liar.

The biggest bluegill that ever lived in Wakeley Lake was eleven and one-quarter inches. I caught it. Many people saw it. If there was a bigger one in the lake I would have caught it. Simple as that. Everyone but Bruce will accept that as gospel. Right?

All that egotistical artistry he does with a fly rod cannot undo that truth. But he's determined.

Fishing is good. Panfish suck at the poppers consistently. Most are small, too small to inhale the bass-size bugs. But the action is steady. We could be fishing bass. But big, and I mean big, bluegills are the target of choice.

Mary Lou's joints start to ache so we paddle to shore and I strike out alone in the long, bloated old tin canoe. Maybe sixty feet from the landing a ruddy bass gulps the chartreuse popper and dives into the weeds. No way the 3X leader is going to horse him out of there.

I give a couple yards of slack line and wait. Either he'll swim out with the popper still connected or I'll end up breaking him off. He frees himself of the weeds, but not the hook and leader. I lift the eight-foot seven-weight cane rod high and turn him. He thrashes, but can't beat the rod.

Geezus! There are wide flashes of yellow and red. It is a sunfish. A bi-i-i-i-g sunfish.

"Mary Lou! Mary Lou! Get down here. Hurry!"

I gotta have a witness before I let this wallhanger go. Like proof — you know? (Wakeley Lake is no-kill, artificial lures only.)

No Mary Lou. She's wandered off to unknot the crick in her hip. The other canoe is across the lake.

Fumbling in my vest I find a tiny tape measure, lay the fish — ohh, he's big — on my knee and stretch out the tape. I'm shaking. Never heard of a red-ear sunfish this big. He measures an honest ten and one-half inches. Get that: ten point five.

Sure, Bruce doesn't believe it later around the campfire. But Mary Lou, Bud Jones, and Bruce Lanphar do (I think).

So now you know how big bluegills and sunfish get in Wakeley Lake. If they got any bigger, I would then have caught them. Got that Bruce? Take your fancy casting and show off somewhere else.

It takes years of intense participation to master the lazy days of summer without becoming its victim. Maybe the haze will clear from Pete's and Bruce's minds by mid-winter.

Small Pond Bassin'
June 22, 1983

Toots crouched, rigidly on point, her nose maybe a foot from the marshy lake edge. If I couldn't see the in-between-size bullfrog I'd have guessed she'd trapped a woodcock probing worms from the muddy soil.

It was a good minute. Then the bullfrog vaulted maybe three feet and a foot high. Toots pounced, like a fox hunting grasshoppers. Her muzzle slammed into the water, and came up empty.

She'd been in the house when I left. Mary Lou, tired of her whining, had let her out to follow me down to the lake. When I prodded the bow of the 35-year-old plywood boat ashore, she jumped in to take her sentry's perch on the front seat.

As I rowed down the east shore, her nose followed every swooping swallow. She also tracked the kingfishers as they cackled across the north shore. A lone Canada swooped into the weed-filled channel to the south. It's my guess there are goslings down there on one of the hummocks. Mallards have nested on the east and north shores of this isolated, completely private lake.

The third cast brought a strike to the little bug. The bluegill engulfed it before I could twitch the rod to set the hook. It was about six inches. Now there was a strike on virtually every cast.

When a fish struck, and every time it splashed fighting the rod, Toots would tighten, her head following the action. In her young years I had to restrain her from diving after them. No longer. Uncle Arthur Itis has been visiting her joints this spring.

Switching to a bigger bug, a sloppy deer hair gob, I cast it to within two inches of shore. The wake that sped toward it was no surprise. A heavy bass bent the long, five-weight graphite to the corks. Line sped from the reel. Toots braced for the counter attack.

The bass got into the weeds, twisted and held stubbornly, but finally the six-pound-test leader and the muscle of the rod brought him out. Spent, he slid to the side of the boat and was released — about fourteen inches.

No more than a half dozen casts later, maybe ten feet up the shore, another largemouth nailed the bug. The sun was over the drumlin, turning the edge of incoming Lake Michigan clouds an orange glow. The strike was unseen and explosive. The kind that even oldtimers thrill at.

He bore for the lilies and the rod couldn't turn him. Then, right at their edge he smashed into the air, thrashing and throwing water, and the bug. The line was too tight. I should have been ready to lower the rod.

Down the lake a loon cried. Or maybe it was on the next lake.

The third cast right into the lilies brought another jarring strike. Sliding the rod horizontally, I skidded him out of the pads while the hook was setting. As he turned back to his safe haven, he felt the rod and dashed into the rapidly developing darkness. This time I was ready. The hook held. A few seconds later the second fourteen-incher was released.

John has a rule for the few people he lets fish the lake; release all bass fourteen inches and above and all bluegills over seven inches. It's been working well as shown by my fishing experience. It would do wonders for hundreds of public lakes. But people are greedy — and that leads to mediocre fishing.

She wallowed as I strained at the oars. No threat of her going down, but enough water to be uncomfortable and cranky. I've put off deep-sixing her for at least a year. Guess I'll try some more caulk. She's quite a lady. She's seen the majesty of Lake Michigan and now keeps a lonely watch on the wonders of the little lake.

The scales from hundreds, maybe thousands, of panfish and perch, from dozens of pike, bass, and lake trout have washed in her bilge. Kids have shrieked from her gunnels as they dove into the water. She's even shared a few romantic moments.

Darkness came fast. The flashlight in the tackle box came in handy as we approached the landing. She was so heavy with water her bow crunched to a halt more than a foot from land. Wading through the lake, its water seemed warmer, somehow, than the water in the bilge.

For a few seconds I doubted I had the strength left to beach her. The bailing bucket helped and she slid onto the grass. Turning her over was another groaner.

With the tackle packed, I dropped ice cubes from the cooler into the Scotch I'd brought in a container in the car and returned to sit on her overturned bottom. Halfway through the double shot, the thought of cold well water tasted better. Slowly, respectfully, the Johnny Walker black label was poured onto her scarred bottom.

Feeling not in the least like a fool, I saluted and lead Toots to the car.

A Hot Day In July
July 20, 1983

The parched grass at the pond's edge is brittle. Squatting in the shadow of the cattails I found the ground warm, the ferns already amber and brittle.

The waves of heat that roll off the tepid water seem more than my imagination — they could be felt. Not even the dragonflies are buzzing. At ninety-five in the shade, the grasshoppers in the hayfield are also lethargic.

Too hot to fish. Too hot to walk — to put on waders. It has been this way for days. This searing heat makes no sense, here on the brim of the Big Lake.

A red-winged blackbird sort of fluttered in, landing on a cattail. The long stalk teetered under the weight. A breeze, ever so slight, came down the hill. It felt good on the bare chest and heavy eyelids.

On the nesting box just to the east, the male bluebird suddenly broke into song. They have already fledged two — or maybe more — young. Are more coming?

It has been a good year for bluebirds, swallows, orioles, rose-breasted grosbeaks, purple finches, canaries, and — we think — hummingbirds. Though we're not sure if we're seeing their young, we saw the hummingbirds mating again this weekend.

The kingfishers were also acting pretty silly the other evening. Do they raise more than one brood?

The wind, like the water in the pond, evaporated. The heat returned like a weight. Only a few feet away the blueberries are swollen but still a gray-blue — not yet ripe. Without rain the sugar will never reach them. They harden and drop off, lost to us and the birds.

I remember an afternoon on a lower slope of Denali. The weather had been in the sixties. The canteen had been filled at a freshwater (not glacier-melt) stream. The sun was warm. The blueberries ripe. For three hours we lay there, filling ourselves with blueberries and dozing. The four of us gorged on berries without ever getting up, just twisting around to find more, and napping. (Then we spent the night beating a path from the tent to latrine.)

A few days before, high on a glacier, the temperature had been around zero. How good that sounded now.

The northland will survive this parched, sweltering torture. The drained lakes and streams will come back. The insects, plants, and fish being lost will recoup. Most creatures have adapted comfortably. The fawns come to the pond unaware that their first months have been a period of uncommon stress.

But the hen mallard that started with eight balls of fluff is down to four near-replicas of herself. That's not unusual, probably, but I wonder if low water in the lake made the youngsters more vulnerable to predators.

Grouse broods should be thriving, but I haven't seen them since mid-June. They probably have retreated to the coolness of the lake edges.

During the week a pack of assorted demonstrators, without the sense to wear all their underwear or boots, had ranted and whimpered about that ELF thing in the UP.

Why can't such energy and passion be directed at a real cause? Like let's fight the schemes to enslave our rivers behind dams, the politics that allow a super class of citizens to butcher our fishery resources, inane proposals to sell public lands or develop them, and underhanded moves to politicize conservation decisions?

Why must so many people be so afraid of dying, they fear living?

Even in this clawing heat, the bluebirds make more sense than they do.

The Hard Life
July 25, 1990

The sun must have been giving the DeTour passage her first blush as the old Merc sputtered and snapped to life. The sky here, just below Dollar Island, was the color of the inside of an empty Korean War C-ration can.

Like opening that can, you had to want to believe in its promise. But here, some thirty miles west of the entry to the St. Mary's River and just north of the Les Cheneaux Islands' Middle Entrance, you knew it was gonna be better than that.

With the lines pulled aboard, the sixteen-foot Dunphy slid through the channel at a whisper. The four cylinders of the 1960 outboard thumped the little plywood hull along at about seven miles per hour.

Around Conner's Point and across the mouth of Sheppard Bay, Cedarville was still slumbering as we turned downbound along big LaSalle Island, through Government Bay, around Island No. 8 and the north nose of Coryell Island into Moscoe Channel.

Conservation officer John Caroffino had said there was an outside chance — really way outside — we'd find enough keeper-size perch here for breakfast. Knowing the odds, I wasn't counting on it. But if they were here I had more than three hours to find them.

Mary Lou was back in the cabin and wouldn't be awake until 9:00 a.m. or later. Besides, I was here courting the sunrise — not perch.

The anchor snubbed in about twelve feet of water. I set the bobber about ten feet above the minnow and poured a cup of coffee from the thermos.

The sun was now threading wisps of pink, purple, and amber through the fleecy clouds. It was gonna be just right.

Slowly, subtly, like fireworks in slow motion, it brightened, until somewhere over Port Dolomite an explosion seared the sky with dazzling orange.

By 7:30, two fishing boats had invaded the retreat. A half dozen or more, or fewer, rock bass and three-finger-long perch, had been released. The thermos was empty (and I needed to find a place to empty what had been in it).

A guy back at the resort had commented the day before that these northern Lake Huron islands and channels are one of his favorite places in Michigan.

He is wrong. The Snows remain one of the world's great treasures. The developers haven't, yet, got the formula for stealing their sunrises and sunsets with condos and gaudy half-million-dollar summer "cottages."

We had launched this journey into summer with a rendezvous of Wakeley Lake veterans at the walk-in, no-kill bluegill-bass-pike lake west of Luzerne. Again, experience proved superior to athletic prowess.

Bud Richards and your guide, the senior fly flingers in the crowd, scored on braggin' bluegills. Bud landed eleven bluegills between nine and ten-and-a-half inches. I landed six the same size. The others, including Bud's impetuous son and master fly caster Bruce, had to settle for seven- and eight-inchers.

There had also been an afternoon and morning dropping flies on the "home fields" of the Au Sable South Branch's Mason Tract. Younger folks say the Mason Tract hasn't changed. That it is like it always was. They are wrong. Much has changed.

Old landmarks have disappeared under a matured forest. Stream cover — holes, riffles and runs — bear little resemblance to what they were fifty years ago. An oldtimer has to set his clock to today. If he tries to fish a bend the way he did back then he is in the trees or on the bank.

Three fishermen, two in their forties and one in his twenties, resting on the bank, commented that this is still the same wilderness it was when they discovered it twenty years ago; maybe the only place they know where nothing has changed.

Newcomers like them are wrong. It has improved, due to vehicle access closures and limiting canoe landings.

As the euphoria of the Les Cheneaux Islands was starting to wear off, Jerry Rakoczy prescribed a day of big water trolling far off shore for open water steelhead. I had my fill of serious Great Lakes trolling many years ago. But far out in the open water it is still a wilderness experience, despite the mechanics involved.

Rakoczy fishes out of Frankfort a week every summer, with his Dad, Jack. We boated four steelhead on the surface. One cleared the water more than a dozen times. And we never saw a hint of another human being.

That, thank you, is a quality experience.

With deadlines approaching, Bill Rustem called from Lansing. He had to be in Traverse City. Could I meet him the next morning at Skegemog Lake (with a boat and tackle) for some muskie fishing?

Skegemog is another of the northland's jewels. Conservationists have saved its wetlands, preserving a "far north" wilderness environment. And it has muskies (as well as great smallmouth).

The only trouble is I have never landed one of those muskies. After several hundred hours trying I should know I'm not destined to. Still, it could happen. And a chance to fish with Rustem beats the pants off spending the day with this computer.

Yep! We had a great time going around and around and around, then around again, in a circle, dragging plugs, spoons and spinners almost as long as your lower arm. The sun glared. The wind purred — and snorted, a little. We lied and recalled conservation battles.

Winching the old fourteen-foot Starcraft onto the trailer a deep sorrow wrenched my sensitive soul. I planned to flip some bugs at bluegills that evening. I mean, could I take any more of this hard living?

And lucky Bill. He got to return to his high salaried job in Lansing. He didn't seem to appreciate how fortunate he is to be pulling down those big bucks. I almost had to hit him to get him into his car and on the road to the "good life." And him all the time babbling about wishing he could move "up north."

He just doesn't know the sacrifices it take to survive here. (Oh, and pass the aspirin. My casting arm has developed a knot. Maybe I'll rest it — around October 1, when bird hunting becomes respectable.)

Late Summer Storm
September 11, 1985

Thunder rumbled over Lake Michigan. Lightning ripped and slashed. Perched on the top of this drumlin it was easy to imagine you were a casual, uninvolved observer as the big guns softened up the beach at Inchon.

Chickadees and nuthatches passed each other coming and going to the bird feeder a few feet away. There was a constant flow between the feeder and basswood tree; sorta like traffic on a freeway.

Visibility was down to about a quarter mile as the storm churned over the big lake. Like the smog hanging over a battlefield, but here, though, the odor was sweet.

The news the next morning would report tornadoes made a couple of landings just south of us in Antrim County. John Kantola reported silver dollar-size hail in town, eight miles north. The rain gauge said two and one-half inches fell on our drumlin.

But at the moment it was an unfelt drama. Nature showing off her majesty and might while Thumper slumbered under the picnic table and a ham about the size of two fists simmered over charcoal and apple twigs.

(Great way to prepare a small chunk of ham, incidentally. First soak it for several hours in a mixture of pineapple juice, brown sugar, and cloves. Then cook and smoke it gently on a covered grill. Don't fail to have a knife handy to "test" it as it browns.)

Along the roads, some of the maples are starting to display small clumps of red leaves. Whitetail bucks, since they started sprouting antlers, are seen more often. Spots have disappeared on most of the fawns.

Crows are flying in flocks of up to 200. The hummingbirds seem to have left. Muskrats and beaver must be exhausted from rearing what seems like a record number of young.

You have to hustle to get in an hour's bluegill popping after supper. If it is overcast, it's dark by 8:00 p.m. In town you can find a place to park and chances are you won't get run over if you absent-mindedly cross Bridge Street in the middle of the block.

In backyards you see guys honing up on their archery when they aren't off chasing salmon in Lake Michigan or Lake Charlevoix. The chinook are already surging up the Jordan, Boyne and other rivers and cricks.

Thanks to Jerry Manz, Rollie Harmes, Steve Swan and John MacGregor, the DNR is hustling to get a salmon-blocking weir in the river. Several thousand have probably already gone above the weir site, but it may — at best may — stop the bulk of the run.

Conservation officers are, for real, risking life and limb when they enter the Jordan Valley. A few salmon poachers have no more respect for a DNR lawman's life than they do for natural resources. They consider the salmon a personal possession and are out to kill every one of them in any way they can.

It is one of fall's tragedies that such magnificent fish have to bring such disgrace to our streams and to mankind. Only civilized humans can be so gruesome.

But such matters seemed puny sitting on the drumlin listening to and watching the clash several miles out over the lake. Better to savor the magic than to ponder the tragic.

The Discovery Of Denali
August 31, 1984

The vagrant perpetrator of this nonsensical charade, and his partner in publishing and other endeavors, have acquired one of
those holes in the water you plug with money. (Money we're not
sure we have.)

It was advertised for a coupla weeks, or so. Every evening I'd
check the want ads to see if it was still there — always secretly hoping it would go away. For days Mary Lou kept gently pushing me to
call the next day.

It was too good to be real. A 1960 Chris Craft Sea Skiff with but
109 hours use in twenty-four years. For those who are into plastic
boats and motors that stick out of the transom (rather than sit under
a proper box near the middle of the deck or hang on the transom), a
Sea Skiff is a lapstrake wood boat with an inboard engine. It is one of
the finest sea boats ever made for these waters. The engine is an
incredibly reliable Chevy 283.

Our kind of boat!

Before giving up a regular paycheck to ramble across these
pages, we'd had several good-sized boats — not yachts. The finest
was a 24-foot Lyman, built in the 1950s.

Since giving them up we've had to be satisfied with a beamy
fourteen-foot tin boat with a thirty-year-old Johnson.

But when the big lakes are in your blood there's an empty niche
in your soul if you have to give up those camping trips to High and
Garden Islands, and the runs to the Snows and Manitous. And once
you've felt and listened to a wood hull there's a hardness, an
unkindness, to a plastic hull that takes the music out of the lake.

And after owning three inboard-outboards there's the conviction
that they don't handle like a boat should, compared to a straight-
drive inboard.

So we kept kidding ourselves over the years that someday we'd
find an unwanted wood-hulled inboard we could afford. Something
we could enjoy working on together in the fall and spring and cruising to the lake's still wild places.

Finally I called. The boat was at Walstrom Marine in Harbor
Springs. The salesman was Dave Lyle. We'd met his folks at a *North
Woods Call* Subscribers' Copper Harbor Gathering. Lyle, who has
sailed the world, turned out to be as candid as most Keweenaw

natives.

He was selling the boat for a fella in his 90s. It had been purchased at Walstrom's in 1960 and kept there at a covered dock and in
indoor storage all these years.

Not only hadn't the boat been sold. No one had been interested
enough to look at it — and the family wanted to get rid of it. Lyle
agreed to have it pulled from the water so I could give it a thorough
poking. As sound as new! The engine purrs and throbs like it did in
1960.

Friend Dave Irish, who owns the marina next door, advised that
we couldn't find a more seaworthy, dependable stink boat.

We made a deal even we can afford — we hope.

In a philosophical mood one day, two decades ago, hardware
vendor Clare Staley, gazing out the window of his store, observed, "I
don't know how anyone can live away from these big lakes."

Water is a marvelous tonic, whether its a spring frog pond, a
crick, or a full-blown trout stream. But nothing quite compares to the
freedom and freshness of being out of sight of anything but the wildness of the big lakes. An evening campfire on the dunes of High
Island is as near to heaven as newspapermen are allowed.

While there are an estimated quarter-million people in Michigan
with boats capable of open water cruising on the Great Lakes, most
beat a direct path from one port to another along the shore, fish for
salmon, or never get more than fifteen miles from their home port.

They ignore the remaining wilderness islands. The quiet bays
where you can wade to shore carrying tent and sleeping bags and
truly sense and be a part of Michigan as it was 300 years ago.

Most islands have been lost to those who seek true isolation. You
might encounter a camper or hiker anytime on Isle Royale or South
Manitou. Beaver Island and Mackinac Island are afloat in plastic.
Drummond and Bois Blanc are still rustic, but heavily populated.

But there are the others — and they beckon. Only big mountains
can compare. Truly big mountains, the kind that this old body with
its mangled drive train can no longer traverse. Denali II will carry us
back to the true wilds of Michigan's big lakes.

A Hot Summer Day
August 31, 1983

The chilly fifty-eight degree water flowing around the too thin stocking-foot waders topped by the bald noggin sweating in ninety-degree heat gave me an idea what a Sanders hot fudge sundae must feel like.

While not as plentiful as on the Au Sable, the little white-winged black mayflies had been plentiful enough to bring fish to the surface. The spinner fall came about 9:20 a.m. and lasted nearly an hour. More than twenty six- to nine-inch trout, mostly browns, had been released.

Toots, however, had been bored, or possibly frightened.

A few days before I nearly lost her under a sweeper. The big bird dog likes to frolic in the river like a pup. She puts down more trout swimming behind and ahead of me than I do with my clumsy casting.

About a week ago she'd been sucked under a sweeper. I saw her going and pitched the little cane rod on the bank and headed her way. Before I got there she went completely under. Twisting frantically to rid myself of the tackle-filled vest, I was sure I couldn't dive under there — who knows how deep and stub-filled it was — and grab her in time.

I figured the vest would catch on the log jam just below and pitched it. About the instant it hit the water she came out the lower side, paddling desperately.

Today in the heat, she just sat there, belly-deep, at the edge of the river.

Coming out of the stream about 200 feet upstream of her, I cautiously checked the blackberry patch. Several years ago two cub bears tried to stare me down from this patch. I've been mighty careful about it since. No bears today. Collecting a cup of berries took less than two minutes.

Downstream, where Toots waited, the little alcohol stove came out of the backpack, along with the tin cup and tea. A scoop in the river and tea was on its way, while I shed the waders, dunked my sweat-soaked shirt in the water and wrung it out.

The contrast between the tartness of the strong, black tea and the sweetness of the berries, with my bare feet soaking in cold water, almost compared to a tall Scotch and ice after a day bird hunting.

Not to be left out, Toots gobbled the two packs of stale soda crackers I fed her in pieces.

I was going to be drenched with sweat before we got to the car anyway, so why not see what is left of the brood of birds I'd flushed twice in late spring. Then there were around ten tiny chicks, not yet flying. This was Toots' first trip here. I hadn't wanted her disturbing them until they could fly.

We turned upstream, just at the edge of the little knoll that rims the cedars and popples along the river. About seventy-five yards and she started spinning and jerking.

Birds!

Maybe fifty feet farther and she slumped into her classic (not stylish) sitting point; her tail cocked up about forty-five degrees, her shoulders hunched, neck craning, fanny on the leaves. Her nose siphoning air — and bird smell.

Sweat soaked the bifocals and I headed into the tangle where she pointed. At about ten yards into the brush there were still no birds. I called her. She came up, swung around once, and dropped into another point — same direction. The humidity must have carried the scent well.

About twenty feet farther in, from the middle of a small blackberry bramble, six birds exploded. Only five youngsters had made it, but they are flying strong.

A rare find this late summer.

Our pre-season explorations have located only four broods, where we've never found fewer than seven in other years. In good years there have been as many as a dozen.

Good sense says forget the grouse opener, leave the birds alone until early October, when the leaves are down and the hunting cooler. But we're selfish, too. With so few birds, these and the others we've found will be well shot over during the first two weeks of the season.

So what? Like the fella says about brook trout, the pleasure isn't in the killing, it's in being where such superb creatures live. The old gal and I finally got that straightened out.

Back in the car, we stopped at the little feeder crick. She lay belly-down in its gravel. I shed the shirt, used the cap to pour water down my back and belly, toweled off and sat watching her watch a school of minnows — maybe tiny trout. Neat the way this system keeps on doing its thing with no help from us.

September Trout
September 7, 1988

Summer is ending in the northland. Near the river, your waders brush against blackberry bushes that are turning brown, while underfoot, blueberry stems crunch like October leaves. Though the sun will hang over Lake Michigan for another four and a half hours, now at 4:00 there is a chill in the breeze.

A welcome chill, after weeks of hot days that kept you out of waders and fly vest. Daily temperatures that edged up to and above ninety, keeping even the bird dog pup huddled on the basement floor in front of the fan.

The lakes, including Lake Michigan and — even — frigid Torch Lake, remain warm, with surface temperatures around seventy. The salmon continue to baffle the folks who never forsake the downriggers and cannonballs.

Ah, but here on the upper Jordan, there's a tingle to the water, which rarely hits sixty degrees. As it swirls around your thighs you scrunch your shoulders together to shake off the shivers. You love it. You dip your hand and then bathe your arm up to the elbow, rejoicing in its wildness, its purity.

They can torment and torture Michigan's best trout streams with sand, canoes, roads, salmon, steelhead, and lampricide, but the rivers respond with oxygen-rich, cold, untainted water, just waiting to welcome back the brook trout and mayflies that are their heritage.

On this day, wispy clouds scud the sky. The wind gambols through the hemlocks, cedars, and popples, driving more warm water onto shore from the southwest. Twenty miles to the west, salmon trollers curse their misfortune, and blame the DNR, somehow for failing to deliver five beast-size fish to every customer on the charter boats.

Though no hatch is evident, an occasional trout slashes at the surface. Black ants!

An easy fly to tie. Take a number 14 or 16 hook. Wind a clump of black thread, yarn, or fur less than halfway down from the eye. Twist on a few turns of red hackle, then another clump of black. I like to top it off with a dun hen hackle tied flat on the back. But that isn't necessary.

Then dunk it in your Jack's Rod and Fly Shop, dry fly dressing. Ha! Don't have any left, do you? I'll run out next spring. Found a big bottle last year that I didn't know I had. Maybe I'll set what is left aside, just to open the lid now and then and sniff the deer tallow. It is an odor that has been a part of my fly vest for forty-some years.

Things change. Darn few for the better when you put on a few years and cling to cherished memories of slower, less anxious, less crowded times. You yearn for the times when yuppies, canoes, and complex formulas did not intrude on your fly fishing. Times when an Adams, blue dun, black gnat, and quill Gordon were about all the dry flies you really needed — or wanted.

Back then you could have still seen 7X tippets but they didn't make them and you didn't need them. A few guys fished with size 18 and 16 flies. But they were show offs. They kept enough gut leaders soaking in their boxes to sink a small canoe. And, hey, darn it, we didn't always believe it, but they caught fish.

The little 7 1/2-foot, four-weight Summers rod flicks the ant out just above the sweeper, dropping it and the 5X tippet at the edge of the swirl. Three or four casts later the trout struck.

I was too fast. Took the fly away from him.

Maybe five minutes later with the second cast he struck again. This time I let him take it. Hook up.

Not much of a fish, by most standards. Maybe eight inches. Probably closer to seven. But it arched the rod, and the varnished cane glistened in the sunlight emerging through willowy clouds.

It felt good. Better, much better than the chinook Mary Lou and I landed in the big boat a few weeks before.

Downstream, where the river splits around an island with a nearly century-old cedar stump that is almost half as big around as the fly rod is long, a fish fed steadily. Apparently a stream of half-drowned ants flowed with the current.

It was tricky casting, trying to keep the leader from dragging the ant. A loose coil of leader was required. No telling if the fish struck the fly or a natural — just let it float through. Pick up at the end of the eddy, and trust the fish to hook himself.

This went on for more than a dozen casts. Then the leader tightened as the rod arched.

Hey! This guy wasn't any yearling.

The rod came up. The bamboo bent. Maybe not deep into the corks, but well into the butt section. Six to seven feet of line came off the little reel before I tightened down on it.

The fish headed for the roots of the stump that keep the island of sod anchored in the current. The rod stopped him short. We hassled each other for a few seconds. He then darted off for a sweeper that bobs in the river fifteen feet to the east and dived under it. We jousted there, until I decided if I played the game much longer I'd wear him down to the point where he might be too exhausted to release.

Now, bucking the current and the fish, the little rod did strain into the corks as I lifted the trout from the hole and forced him upstream to me. Best catch of the year. Might be stretching it some, but he looked like twelve inches as I twisted the hook out of his jaw. As he swam off, I noted his spots were already turning spawning color.

A trophy! At least by my standards.

A wild trout in a wild river. Things don't get better than that.

Yeah, and it was Sunday. Some folks figure they can find God in a building with a steeple and cross on the roof.

Everybody to his own.

Grasshopper Sparrows
September 19, 1990

G rasshopper sparrow? Huh?

I've been eyeballing birds and bird books for decades, but "grasshopper sparrow" was a new one on me when biologist Jerry Weinrich popped it the other day during a discussion of the controversy over clearcutting state forests.

There's a whirlwind of rebellion brewing out there over clearcutting. People are getting up short about the miles of clearcut forest land they are seeing along our roadsides.

Clearcutting is a double-edged dagger.

They should be upset about much of it. There is no excuse for wasting thousands of acres of public forest land just so the governor and legislature can stroke the timber industry. The nine million folks who own these forests would bolt at their being used as commercial tree farms to benefit about one percent of the owners. But the practice continues because so few of those nine million know what is going on.

Most sinister is the clearcutting of popple, beech, maple, oak, hemlock, and upland cedar to make way for the red pine plantations favored by industry. There is absolutely no way the "owners" would tolerate this if they had any notion of what is going on.

But then you get to grasshopper sparrows — and vesper and clay-colored sparrows, upland sandpipers, bluebirds, sparrow hawks (kestrels), snowshoe hares, and Kirtland's warblers. Held in special esteem are the endangered and hallowed Kirtland's warblers.

Much of the disgust with clearcutting focuses on the seeming devastation of jackpine plains in the Au Sable Country. DNR and U.S. Forest Service personnel are under increasing assault from people who consider the pinelands wasted. Over the last year, the *Call's* editor has had well over a dozen people call demanding that he denounce this rapacious disrespect for our timberlands.

Whoa! These horizon-hugging clearcuts are not a plot to enrich the timbermen. They are designed to enrich the world by ensuring the survival of Kirtland's warblers.

Though this department's guide finds a dynamic beauty in many clearcuts, if erosion is prevented and logging roads are closed to vehicles, he can understand that those with a more casual, postcard perspective find them ugly.

This year's experience with Kirtland's warblers — one of Earth's most threatened species — dramatically demonstrates that it takes huge tracts of immature jackpine to assure their survival.

People who find the clearcuts, and subsequent planting of jackpine seedlings, eyesores, sometimes find it hard to balance the value of a tiny warbler with this temporary "blight."

That's where grasshopper sparrows come in. Jerry Weinrich says, yeah, he can understand where some folks regard the clearcuts as ugly. But geez, they should get out of their car and tromp through the "wasteland."

If they did, they'd be certain to meet the grasshopper sparrow — "the most nondescript, little brown bird." Just over four inches long, grasshopper sparrows have no distinguishing markings or characteristics, except they chirp like a cricket. And they love jackpine clearcuts.

And they keep damn fine company — like Kirtland's warblers, bluebirds, upland plovers, vesper sparrows, snowshoe hares, and whitetail deer.

That's good enough for me. I'm gonna look me up a grasshopper sparrow next spring. While I'm at it, I'm gonna pray that your great, great, great granddaughter hears a Kirtland's warbler court a mate on a June morning in the jackpines. And that while she's at it she is savvy enough to know it happened because you and I cared enough to cherish grasshopper sparrows.

Damn! I love the little beggars and I've never met one.

Thumper

July 31, 1985

"It is the things you know for sure that aren't so that'll get you in deep trouble."

Dad, or someone else less important, used to plant that absurd bit of wisdom on this boy who knew everything for sure and wasn't gonna let go of it. He repeated it so many times it kept ringing in my ears whenever I'd tangle with somebody I knew for sure I could kick the pants off but found out I couldn't.

The ringing has pretty much disappeared in the last few years. That's probably because I've decided my fanny-stomping days are long over.

However, it came back about three months ago. A guy who is a lot smarter than I could ever be offered to give me a dog. He was sorta apologetic about offering. Said he'd take him back anytime I didn't want him.

Both of us know for sure that free dogs are worth about as much as a free 1947 Nash. And we both know for sure that kind people don't offer to give their friends free dogs.

"What's wrong with the dog?"

"Hey. He's about the best looking bird dog (English setter) you'll ever see. Big, too. Strong. Healthy. Spent fifteen hundred dollars having him trained (He's got more money than I do, too). Should make you a fine dog."

"So what's wrong with him?"

"I don't have time for him ... already have four or five other setters. Oh, he's young, in his prime, only four years old."

"So, damn it, John, what's wrong with him?"

"Uh, why don't you come down and look at him. If you don't want him that's OK. If you take him you can always return him."

"Come on! How come you don't want him," I snapped.

"Well," sorta sheepishly and under his breath, "The trainer says he seems to be a little gun shy. I don't know if he is."

So, somewhat reluctantly, Mary Lou drove down to Traverse City with me. We'd been looking for the right puppy to replace my wonderful Toots who died in April. Mary Lou was still hanging tough for a puppy. And she didn't want a male dog. (We had always got female puppies and had them fixed before they came into season.)

The dog emerged from the kennel. Wow! Handsomest bird-killing machine I'd ever seen. Just a knockout. Tall and long. Mostly white, with some blue ticking and a tad or two of orange.

A friendly brute, too. But, clearly a little hesitant. He went through the sit, stay, and come paces well.

"Does he like birds?"

"Don't know."

"What did the trainer say?"

"That he's gun shy, but why not see what you can do with him?"

He had a deal. But when I went to load "Sonny" in the Suburban John says he'll loan me a metal dog cage to take him home in. I protested that I didn't need it. He assured me I did. And I did.

Friendly? Did I say that? Geez. The big guy had never had him a one-on-one buddy before. Thought he'd take over the driving.

By supper time we had something of a deal: I wouldn't squeeze his paws if he wouldn't land them on my ears. He didn't stick to his side of it long and my hands became so sore from squeezing paws the size of my palms I had to give up.

The problem became evident while I was cooking on the grill that evening. Every time I'd wave the tongs I was using he'd cower and crawl under the picnic table, trembling.

Someone had beaten the hell out of him — busted his spirit. Someone had pounded his soul as well as body.

Damn! You might be able to make a case for beating on people. They can understand it and can get even.

He's gun shy, I learned, because obviously the beatings came when there were guns around and he didn't do whatever it was he was supposed to do to satisfy the trainer.

He was trained on one of those hunting preserves by a field trial specialist. He points grandly. He knows and loves bird scent. He also works extremely close — far too close for most hunters and all field trialers. He will only hunt favorably for the person whom he has developed confidence and trust in.

He's sorta klutzy. You should have seen him trying to figure out how to navigate stairs.

He's been renamed Thumper, because of his big paws and mostly, because Mary Lou didn't like Sonny. He picked up on his new name in less than a day. He learned his house manners in less than two days until one of the girls brought a just-about-in-heat yellow Lab up with her.

We'll see. He might just be staying. He sure plans to.

Little Things
July 29, 1987

It is a bigger threat when you are young. But even as senility becomes something you very privately begin to ponder, you must work hard to keep little things from becoming big things.

The hi-tech watch read something like 3:?? (can't read it without glasses) in the morning. The eyeglasses were several feet away — up by the compass. The head room clearance in Denali was minus zero, less than in your half of a GI shelter-half.

We'd sat up late — just past midnight — sipping Scotch, then tea, and night watching at Hessel Bay. The little bunks on the old 27-foot Sea Skiff had felt like the kindest refuge in the hemisphere when we finally cuddled in.

But now, at somewhere between three and four, the latrine was calling. Activating the potty under the bunks meant disturbing Mary Lou, who was in a deep slumber that would end with a mad scramble for the head about eight.

Lumbering to the latrine in the Hessell Marina seemed the more gentlemanly thing to do. It meant squirming into a pair of britches and trudging, half blind, some sixty or so feet. Finding the latrine key on the dash of the old wooden boat was the major challenge.

All of that accomplished, plus the primary mission, I darn near did it again when the telephone bleated in the harbormaster's office, some fifteen feet from the latrine door.

Suddenly you're home again. The office phone is ringing. Gotta answer; shucks, somebody might wanna know when bird season opens. Then, you think any s-o-b who calls in the middle of the night can go to Hades.

They — hey! We're on a holiday. We're a hundred miles from the office and the telephone. That ring isn't for us. Get your buns back to that bunk and curl up with your partner and forget it, Shep. Ha! We're free.

It takes a while for it to really sink in that you are disconnected from the mainstream. You can't do it in motels. And not even in campgrounds. (Your car registration will always lead them to you, whereas they're not likely to trace a boat registration.)

I slept in. Mary Lou nudged me several times, with a sleepy question, "the coffee ready yet?" before I realized it was after eight o'clock.

Denali's alcohol stove makes coffee almost as good and as aromatic as the stuff we made on campfires along the Jordan and Au Sable forty years ago. It permeates the canvas-shrouded deck as the morning sun dries the dew.

The coffee is ready after a quick shower in the modern harbor building and the one block trip to the Hessel Grocery for the *Free Press* and *News*. (They sell just about everything you need, including first class newspapers, like the *North Woods Call.*)

Strip down the canvas, sit back with the coffee and newspaper (I'm addicted to them) and the world turns into a Disney Land. No cares. No worries. Just lotsa friendly folks. The kids from the other boats stop by to ask if they can play with the pup (Nails).

The Les Cheneaux Islands are like that. Stop in other harbors around the lakes and folks are in a hurry. Or they are showing off their boats.

At Hessel, Earl Godby and Bill Geer are up from Tawas with their boats, wives, and pups. They launched the boats at the marina and lined them over to the dock. They've been there several days. They're not even sure the boats run. The agenda peaks with a big bobber and minnow. If a coupla twenty-inch pike are landed, the day is perfect. If no pike are landed, it is also perfect.

Oh, sure, if the weather is bad or if Mackinac Island's zoo doesn't have room for more boats, some of those in the fast lane nudge their way into Hessell. But they're gone in the morning, looking for more action, and the gift and clothing shops of the Gold Coast.

If you are beginning to get the notion that we are sorta infected with the freedom of exploring the upper lakes with an antique wooden boat, you have caught on. It took several years to get the 27-year-old boat ready. It was more than worth it.

Isle aux Galets lighthouse (Skillagilee, or just plain Skille) is one of the most dramatic statements of wilderness in the big lakes. There it is, more than five miles off Cross Village, a jumble of rocks, gnarled vegetation, and a massive man-made structure. Out in nowhere. Only terns and gulls come here.

We hadn't been there in more than fifteen years. We couldn't resist; we circled and circled, despite the haze that obscured the mainland to the east.

The DNR's new marina at DeTour has brought new life to the old shipping and fishing community. There are restaurants and gift shops. The folks who run the marina are doing a first-rate job. The

DNR — and we as Michigan citizens — should be proud of them.

We chanced into DeTour harbor on the evening of the Fourth of July. The local folks were staging their fireworks just off the main breakwall, right across from old Denali. Nails stood on the boarding ladder cheering.

We tied up on Lime Island, up the St. Mary's River just a few minutes from DeTour.

Lime Island makes coming back to work sweet. It is 900 acres of mostly wilderness — very accessible wilderness. Just a few minutes off the Raber Launching ramp.

Once on Lime the rest of the world is forgotten.

The DNR had planned to turn the island over to the developers. The *Call* helped DNR director Gordon Guyer change that. It will remain largely wild, with an improved harbor, some hiking trails, and rustic campgrounds.

Though it was sultry hot, we opened a soda and saluted our part in that decision. (Too early in the day for a slug of that sipping Scotch we'd toted along.)

Later, after cruising the west shore of Drummond Island and its gem-like outer islands, we anchored and popped the tops on the Scotch and Mary Lou's suds. We raised our glasses to salute. A salute to a boat built in Algonac more than a quarter century ago and still as sound and seaworthy as a new yacht.

But mostly to Michigan; as old as the eons, as abused as the bloody hills of Korea, but still magnificent.

If you doubt it, go visit Skille next week. Shut the motor or sails down. Just ponder how it all happened and how it all is.

Big things will seem mighty small in a mighty big hurry.

Summer Backyard Birds
August 12, 1987

Feeding songbirds, shaving, and taking showers have a lot in common.

I guess you didn't know that.

It dawned on me the other day. It was the first time in several years that I've gone to the former grain elevator to buy sunflower seed for the bird feeder without Mary Lou. The last time I had to pay the bill I was in shock for days. Since then Mary Lou has written the check while I toted the fifty-pound bag to the car. I never asked how much it cost.

You can get away without shaving or showering. If I knew what either cost I might.

Some time ago I was buying razor blades. There was a bulk pack of fifteen, which I figured must be a real steal. So I checked the price on packs of five- and ten- and the fifteen- blader. Geez! Even at a reduced rate per blade, the fifteen-blader cost about a third what I recall making a month as a grunt private.

If you get your electricity from REA (Top O'Michigan here) and heat your water with it, the cost is enough to make you want to wash in the crick or pond — about a third more than Consumers Power, according to my estimates.

But, you gotta shave and you gotta shower. And in our case, we gotta feed the birds. So you just don't look at the cost of any of it. (See, what'd I tell you?)

The point of this tortuous struggle is that summer bird feeding has never been as wondrous as it is this year in these precincts. Since birds started nesting in late April, we've gone through seven fifty-pound bags of striped sunflower seed. And you can add quart after quart of sweet water for the hummingbirds and orioles.

Ah, let's start with the orioles. For more than a decade after the Dutch elm disease devastated this country, it looked like orioles — which depended on the elms for nesting habitat — were gone. Then slowly they started to come back. At first a few nested in the big silver poplars around the old farmsteads on these drumlins. Now they are nesting in the maples and popples.

Before they have young, while sitting on eggs, and after the little ones hatch until they are fledged, the orioles are addicted to the sugar water in the hummingbird feeders. At times we'd have as many as eight or ten on the feeders or waiting their turn. Mary Lou was mixing two quarts of sweet water a day.

Like hummingbirds, they'd come within two or three feet of us as we sat by the feeders on the porch. The music wasn't good; it was heavenly.

Oh, yeah, let's talk about the sunflower seed.

There has been an eruption of rose-breasted grosbeaks this summer. It has been common to have more than a dozen at a time at the three feeders. Early on, there were the scraggly little ones perching precariously on the side of the feeders squawking for their folks to stuff seeds down their craw.

They still come, but now they are self reliant. The juvenile males continue to stand out; kinda raggedly and blotchy black and white, with just a touch of the gorgeous rose on their breast that will so distinguish them next spring.

A decade ago we cautiously snuck outdoors to get a better look and listen when a rose-breasted showed up. We still stand and gape in awe. But now they are common; we see them more than we do robins.

Why?

We'd like to know. But we've learned from years of asking such questions that if we had a PhD in ornithology we wouldn't know the answer. If our staggering investment in sunflower seed is the reason, all the better. But I suspect there is a far more magical explanation.

It has also been a banner year for nuthatches, chickadees, and blue jays.

The other day I carried my daily three three-pound coffee cans of sunflower seed to the feeders and the bush next to it burst into a blur of the little folks. There must have been thirty to fifty chickadees. They landed in the tree about thirty feet away. To my eye it seemed that a heavy rain — which we hadn't had in weeks — had tattered their feathers. They were just babies.

Chickadees are common pals here. But usually you see little of them in the summer, when they are more independent. Obviously there has been a massive hatch.

Have you ever seen baby nuthatches exploring the bird feeder? They look like something the ink blotter got mixed up with. If you didn't know better, you'd like to snatch them and make them pets.

And then there are blue jays. The bird dog pup was helping fill the feeders the other day when a blob of juvenile and adult jays burst from the bushes. There were at least twenty of them. Mary Lou says they are homely and noisy. Sure, but heck, she says the same thing about me. And Nails loves putting the point on them.

You can make a strong argument against feeding birds. I wouldn't consider feeding deer, grouse, ducks, or geese. They're supposed to be wild, and I hunt them.

Does that mean I respect game birds and animals more than song birds? Geez, I don't know. But I don't think so. Yet I think it is true I enjoy the chickadees, nuthatches, grosbeaks, and woodpeckers I see while dozing in the deer woods more than I do those at the bird feeders.

Life, though, would hardly be tolerable without the year around visitors to the bird feeders.

Right now we're waiting for the goldfinches to nest and bring their babies to the thistle seed feeders. That's gonna happen any day now, a couple weeks ahead of schedule, because the hot dry summer has already produced weed seeds and they nested earlier than usual.

Matt, Poopa, And Feeshing
August 22, 1990

There are times when this editor should feel thoroughly culpable — when the guilt should be a suffocating, unbearable burden.

Like the other afternoon.

The desk was smothered with heaps of notes and reports that should be turned into stories for folks who pay the bills by reading the *Call*.

The day was pleasantly warm, with just enough cloud cover to keep fish active and just enough wind to keep the bugs down. A lousy day for sitting in front of this wretched monitor and keyboard. But that's the job; deadlines are an old nemesis.

Then Sass called. She announced that two-and-a-half year old Matt wanted "Poopa" to take him "feeshing." (He calls his father Dadda and his grandpa Poopa. Don't 'spose he's smarter than we suspect and already recognizes a b-s artist, do you?)

Now this Matt is some kind of guy. He started life sleeping eight hours at a shift, with no complaints. He only bawls when he really hurts — and then reluctantly. When he gets a notion that won't fly, he scowls briefly in response to a contrary order; he then smiles and goes to something else.

He loves the dogs, cats, and everyone he meets.

And this summer he's learned to love catching "beeg feesh" with Poopa.

Those big fish are really four to six inch bluegills, from a small lake just a few drumlins east of this drumlin. His biggest has been a nine-inch rock bass. We had to hold onto him to keep it from taking him off the dock. Most days the bobber makes a dive on every cast of the worm-baited hook.

That's the way to get a kid hooked on fishing. Nothing serious — just lots of action. Keep it simple. Take along a bucket to let the fish swim in for a few minutes. Then explain to him that they want to go back into the lake. They'll buy that.

And (this is critical) when they become bored, pack it in. Don't force anything. No pressure — just lotsa fun. Which may include wading in the lake after the rod is hung up. Or trying to catch a frog or dragonfly. Point out the birds, clouds — or anything that can enrich the experience.

So you got it, I deserted my post. I let you down. Mary Lou and I packed the rod, life jacket, and worms and made a dash for Matt, then the lake.

And I still don't feel one twit of guilt.

Matt hauled in a coupla dozen fish, from three o'clock to nearly four.

When we got back home I had honorable intentions of battling the computer. Matt had other ideas. Grabbing me by the paw he towed me downstairs to the gun cabinet.

Shortly after he was born, I saw this replica of the Red Ryder BB gun I had craved as a kid. It found a slot beside the "real" guns. Matt has learned to "shoooot" this summer.

He can't hit anything — can't even pull the trigger. But working together we get the job done. We blaze away at a target on the bales of hay. (I pre-punched some holes in it.) By the time the Red Ryder was retired, this old Poopa was exhausted.

Go ahead and fire me, if you figure I got my priorities out of whack. No way will I apologize for warping a twerp's values by taking him fishing and shooting. And I could never write anything more treasured than building a foundation for a lifelong courtship of bluegills and the reflection of birch trees in a northern Michigan lake.

It is true, some off-road vehicle advocates say mauling God's earth with those monsters is the only alternative kids have to drugs. Matt gets a bigger high on catching "beeg feesh" with his "Granna" and "Poopa" than they ever can with those mechanical demons.

Lord, ain't we blessed? Thanks!

Trout, Nails, And Bear
August 23, 1989

If you had a direct pipeline to God, you could not have ordered more perfect weather.

It had dipped to forty-five the night before. We had beech and maple snapping and glowing in the fireplace. Morning called for fleece-lined slippers and sweatshirts. By late afternoon it was lightly overcast with the temperature hanging between seventy and seventy-five.

Nails decided we should unplug the typewriter and see if the river had dried up in the last few days.

The fishing business isn't that serious with me anymore. So I selected a half dozen flies for a little box (two Adams and several downwing patterns), hitched into the waders, and snatched the five-weight Summers cane rod out of the Suburban.

From where we parked it is less than 100 yards to the river. In this stretch it is wide and shallow, where it used to be much narrower and deeper before sand choked and impounded it.

Now over two years old, Nails has settled down. I can now count on her to stick close, and patiently wait for me as I prowl the river.

As expected, nothing was happening at streamside. Just a ribbon of nondescript, cold, clear, drinkably-pure water. I didn't expect to catch fish; I just wanted to fish.

The fly assortment included some grasshopper imitations and a coupla things we call hillbillies. These are sorta generic downwing patterns that the late Leon Martuch — the inventor of modern fly lines and the founder of Scientific Anglers in Midland — originated as trout-fooling miracles. Former SA boss Bob Philip (now with Orvis) says he's tried them worldwide and confirms they work anywhere.

After squinting at the eye in the size 14 hook and 6X leader long enough to lash a crude knot, I discovered the English setter had deserted me. Nails was nowhere to be seen in the lush ferns and grass.

Poking the reel of the fly rod over a limb about eight feet up in a birch, I went looking. It made sense that she might be on point; the popples, birches, tamarack and dogwood along the river are prime bird habitat.

It took a while, but I found her, stretched taut, tail at about half mast, snout reaching, starboard-paw raised.

"Easy lady ... stay! Whoa ..."

Stepping in front of her about five feet a young ruffed grouse flushed.

"Whoa! Stay!"

Another grouse exploded. She wheeled. "Stay. Stay!"

Then another. Nails spun off to the west. Bolting.

"STOP! ... Good girl ..."

She came up, slowed and went into a crawl.

"Easy, lady ... good girl."

She was with it now. There were more birds, somewhere close by. The genes were in control.

This wasn't a spring chick she was dealing with now. As it moved, she moved, canted to the east, then toward the river — slow, careful, head high to get the scent, with her tail high over her back.

Ah, damn, man, it was beautiful. I had died and gone to bird dog lover's heaven.

There's a big blowdown cedar near the river bank. I've sat on its trunk watching the river, the mayflies, the swallows. That is where she froze — solid, with only her nose twitching.

With memories of my Toots blurring my eyes I felt kinda guilty. Here she was proving her stuff and I could only think of the gal I knew she'd never replace.

The waders crackled as I moved through the brush. The bird, I'm sure a veteran of these games, burst from her cover and bolted across the river.

Nails is a gentle, timid, sorta wimp of a dog. All she wanted now was petting and cooing to. She got plenty of both.

Back downstream, I retrieved the rod and studied the river. She sat on the bank, with tail switching every few seconds; head and handsome snout high.

At first I didn't believe it. The polaroid sunglasses indicated a form — a large one by my standard — close to the bank on the far side. I would have to move downstream and sneak across to make a cast; that took time and concentration.

A good ten minutes later I made my first cast with the Hillbilly, not knowing what to expect. As planned, the fly dropped into the current not three inches from the grassy bank. Then it aimlessly swirled and darted.

As I raised the little rod to pick the fly off the water before it could spook any other smaller fish just hanging around, this thing gulped it. The line came tight, then limp — then all bedlam and eruption. The little reel — about half the size of the palm of my hand — sorta wailed. I bowed the rod to half-mast, afraid to strain it too hard.

The fish started upstream, as I lifted the rod. This wild spotted creature turned downstream; I lifted higher and started cranking on the reel. There was a boil on the surface. The rod went limp.

I hadn't set the hook. The fight was over. By guess, the twenty-or so-inch summer-run brown had won. Enough. A guy only deserves so much gold in one afternoon.

And there was Nails, into the river up to her neck. Something was wrong. Unsure of something, she was spooked. Strangers and unknown noises sometimes do that to her.

Walking her to the bank I rubbed out her tangles and talked to her. She nuzzled and clung to me. Fearing she had been hurt while I was concentrating on the fish, I felt for wounds — nothing.

Heading back to the car she wanted to go upstream of the most direct path. I coaxed her downstream. When we came to a berry patch bramble she froze, and would not follow. She whined when I headed into it. On the other side I found bear scat — unusual here. She's never met a bear. Obviously, she doesn't intend to.

That's alright with me. If she's into birds and trout she's into the north's finest treasures. The bears are a treasure also, but better left alone.

Denali Ramblings
July 27, 1988

The boat ride from Hessel through the channels around the Les Cheneaux Islands is worth repeating. Not just once a year, but several times.

Though the islands and mainland are somewhat heavily developed, they do not insult you with the gaudiness that now prevails in Michigan's other traditional resort communities. The cottages remain simple, if large. There is as likely to be a wooden runabout at the dock as there is to be a plastic ski boat or yacht.

It remains what I call the "real world." People still come here to enjoy the scenery and to live a leisurely, uncrowded way of life that their great (or great-great) grandparents pioneered.

We savored the morning ride from the Hessel marina around Marquette Island, down the Les Cheneaux channel, past Larry and Liz's cabins, past Sheppard's Bay, Cedarville and LaSalle Island at almost trolling speed, under clear sky. The marine radio weather forecast warned us of what was ahead.

As Denali poked her wooden nose outside Government Island, clearing the green can and swinging almost due east, the sea and mist struck. Ahead lay twenty miles across northern Lake Huron in seas quartering off the starboard bow. The twenty-eight year old twenty-seven-footer would take it in stride, her lapstrake hull cushioning every blow while spray slashed across the windshield and the canvas top Mary Lou designed and sewed.

Though they had left Hessel with us and turned into Lake Huron behind us, Jerry Flint and Joyce Hagen were soon far ahead of us in their twenty-four-foot plastic boat. Even farther ahead were Paul and Mrs. Lyon of Onaway, in his brand new twenty-five-foot tupperware boat. Pat and John Kilgore would clear the Government Island (East Entrance) can nearly an hour after we did and almost beat us to DeTour.

Those tupperware boats are built for speed. They sorta skim over the water, sometimes pounding enough to make a former infantryman's hemorrhoids howl in agony.

In contrast, old Denali was built for the sea: slow, soft and sure — gently slicing through the heavy waves. Even through the spray and mist we could pick up the towering St. Martin Reef lighthouse some seven miles southeast of the Government Island buoy and four miles from the nearest shore when we left the islands and turned for DeTour. In the gloom it looked like the bow of a freighter headed our way until we got nearer.

While we seemed to be under heavy cloud cover, some two miles to the north over the southern crest of the eastern Upper Peninsula, the sun glittered on the shoals, boulders, and tiny islands that make up this rarely seen but splendid jewel from Michigan's rich treasure chest of wildness.

Probably about half-way there we picked up the massive DeTour passage light. It rises over the mouth of the St. Mary's River like some kind of god.

The St. Mary's River is a jungle of buoys and turns. Its water a tobacco brown, in sharp contrast with the emerald blue and inky black of open Lake Huron. Not that the river is foul. But it is "dirty" with the silt its current and the wheels of the mighty ships keep in motion.

Sliding into the DNR's DeTour marina after a windy, wet crossing is almost like becoming pampered royalty. The DNR crew helps you into the gas dock like old salts.

Old Denali has a rudder about the size of a supper plate. That just isn't enough to maneuver her hull in tight quarters. Experienced skippers can turn sixty-foot yachts with twin engines sharper than Denali will swing.

The dock crew at DeTour not only knows how to help, they are eager to help. Of all the marinas we get into on the upper lakes, only the crew at the Clark Township marina at Hessel is as helpful and as genuinely concerned that you enjoy their facility and boating.

(One guy who needed no help at the dock was Paul Lyon. He steers his 25-footer like the pro he is. When he's working, he skippers a 790-foot lakes freighter. He's been on the boats for thirty-nine years. When he isn't working, the Onaway resident is boating for fun.)

The new DNR marina at DeTour has done several things for the community. It has, of course, provided jobs. But new businesses have also sprung up to serve boaters, including a dandy little restaurant. Though we haven't seen their bank deposits, it appears that the cash registers in other businesses we stopped in were clanging a lot more than they did a few years ago.

Boaters appreciate the facility and exceptional treatment they get from its attendants. Not once during our stay at DeTour (two nights) did we hear anyone complain about the DNR — not once. And that is virtually unheard of anywhere in northern Michigan.

Compare that to the evening we docked at Lime Island. Several boats came in, docked briefly and their occupants walked up to the old town, passing us at the dock. More than half found something to complain about. One lady was really ticked at the "damned DNR" because there is poison ivy on the island.

(But if that's bad, DNR waterways chief Orie Scherschlight says a boater was giving him hell the other day because it let the water at his dock get so low this summer. "Now there's a guy who really thinks we have power," Orie says.)

The St. Mary's is as overpowering historically as it is naturally. Much of the early drama of European exploration and conflict took place along and through it.

And the next morning it turned rough, if not tempestuous.

The going was fair until we cleared the north end of 900-acre Lime Island. Turning for Munuscong Lake, Denali was slamming her bow into five- and six-foot seas. She'd take it, but it was no fun. We aborted plans to cruise the upper St. Mary's to the Soo and swung into the former ore carrier dock on the west side of Lime Island. A secure, snug berth.

It remains incredible to me, and many others including former DNR director Gordon Guyer, that some bureaucrats wanted to give the island to developers. It was, you see, a "nuisance" to administer. Though a true gem in public ownership, they didn't want to be bothered with it.

Until the 1970s, a company operated a freighter refueling station on the island. The old townsite complete with homes, a school, and playground equipment remains. Archaeologists are still exploring an ancient limestone quarry and lime kilns. There is some suspicion they could pre-date Europeans. Historical documents do not explain their presence.

By dusk we had the island to ourselves. The minnows I'd been soaking since midday were still unscathed and lively. Rather than unhook them, I left the rod in the holder when we wiggled into the smaller-than-pup-tent cabin bed. The next morning I unhooked and released a three-inch sculpin.

That was about it for our fishing success. One four-inch perch in the Snows. One sculpin. The herring were overdue. We were counting on them for at least a couple of meals. No one was catching them.

The mayfly hatch hadn't started.

The next morning Rollie and Lois Harmes arrived in a small boat about the time the coffee pot was empty. Rollie is the DNR lands division (now real estate division) chief who balked at giving away Lime Island. He's also getting the federal government to give the state some 500 small Great Lakes and inland islands.

Our kind of bureaucrat!

So we spent most of the day slowly cruising the dozens of small islands in Potagannissing Bay. Many of these will soon be owned by the state, thanks to Rollie. Neat little islands; like Propeller Island, Wreck Island and Love Island (ah, what a novelist could do with that one).

The only glitch in the day was lunch. While Mary Lou was whipping us up some sandwiches from ham I'd grilled over the charcoal earlier, Lois unwrapped some stuff (oh, she's gonna kill me for this) that looked like dehydrated pablum. Natural food. They want to live forever. Mary Lou made me try some. Sure, I confessed, I could get used to it (but I also once got used to cold C-rations).

It was Lois's first island-exploring adventure. Rollie says she's putting some heat on him to buy a boat big enough to make it an annual experience. With the family grown, he might be tempted into it. After all, at least one of those islands should be named Harmes Island. (Wonder what cedar boughs ground up with nuts, soy beans and dry cereal would taste like?)

After another night in DeTour and in Hessel, we decided it was time for a real bed and easy chair. The about eighty-mile run from Hessel to Charlevoix was picture perfect, including a family of loons off Dahlia shoal, in northern Lake Michigan.

Churning into the piers at Charlevoix was like taking a 75 mm howitzer smack in the gut. Tinsel town condos glaring their ugliness out over the lake. Boat traffic so thick it was stop and go, stop and go. Frightening, after a week in the "real world" with a few real people.

What makes it tolerable is knowing that within a half hour of the piers we are, again, free of this rat's nest that is the yuppies' condo ghetto.

A few days later we anchored in the protected harbor at the southeast corner of South Manitou Island. We shared the several miles of beach with only about a half dozen other boats, all widely scattered. Jeannie and Jerry Rakoczy anchored their Fish Buster fifty yards away. After swimming to shore and exploring we broke out the charcoal grill, swung it over the side and sorta warmed the blood in the steaks while I warmed the blood in me with Scotch. (The next night we grilled the steelhead fillets we'd taken off Leland.)

And when the next break in the weather and work came we were off to the Fox Islands, hunting steelhead and wildness. That's where it is — in the open water of the big lakes. ATVs, rental canoes, ski boats, condos, and tinsel will never prevail here.

Au Sable Country
August 28, 1985

It was cold enough in the little cabin at 6:00 a.m. You tried to hold the coffee cup with both hands to gather in the heat. I guessed it was in the low forties outside.

By 6:30 the shoulder-high fog over the lake looked about as thick as whipped cream. It was so dense I briefly wondered if it could be shoveled.

Anyway, it would have been foolhardy to race to the South Branch for an early start. Ninety minutes later, I was peeling off the wool undershirt before stepping into the river. I dropped it beside an oak with three stems that form a nap-inducing, late-afternoon backrest.

The river fooled me for a second as my mind switched back forty years and Dad was sitting there, in waders and fishing jacket, the old long Kresge cane rod across his knees. He looked young: not a line in his face. Startled me to realize how old his oldest son has gotten.

There wasn't a chance for a Tricorythodes mayfly spinner fall before the canoes arrived. But upstream, just into the no-kill water, a few small trout were sipping something near shore — probably terrestrials. So I tied on a small down-wing pattern that can imitate almost anything except mayflies.

The four-weight Summers rod sent the leader under the overhanging tags. On the third cast an eight-inch brookie took solidly. Within the next two hours I'd taken and released more brooks and browns than I've caught all year on the Jordan; the largest maybe eleven inches.

Hearing the first clang of a canoe upstream, I scramble for shore, not wanting to even see the intruder.

The hike back to the car was a journey in a time machine. Though looking at the land today, what I saw was yesterday. The land was bleak — stumps, stumps and more stumps. Only the few "surviving pines" — those that were too small to interest the loggers in the 1880s and 90s — and some young and some old oaks. Bending over I saw the beginnings of today's stands of pine.

At the car, I searched for the campfire ring I'd sat around in awe of the old people (whom I would now consider kids) as they talked auto engineering, debated the merits of engines and transmissions and what fly was best, or whether worms could outfish flies. (Flies were always the winner in my mind, I recalled.)

No campfire ring, of course.

Today it would take an hour's work just to clear a place for Dad's old silk tent. Then you could plop it anywhere that was level by just kicking away a few stones.

There was a flashback. Brother Mike, then a gangling kid, was again standing under some tags (now he's taller than they were) at the edge of the stream, water up to his knees, with his rod over his shoulder and the fly dangling two or three inches over the river. We were heading back to camp for lunch and I was bragging about catching the most fish. A little brook trout jumped out of the water, grabbed the fly and hooked itself.

We talked about it for years. I hadn't thought about it for maybe twenty-five years.

The river too has changed. Nature is responsible for most of the change, and also canoes. There are many times fewer fishermen now, except for the heavy night hatches. Back then we fished all day, every day we could. The canoe liveries ended that.

Even the fenceline that marked the boundary between George Mason's land and the Forest Service land is gone. Probably not ten percent of the people still coming to the river ever saw or went through it.

There aren't as many hog fish today. Fish in the four- to eight-pound range were never common, but a few were taken each year; many by guys fishing from the bank with fist-size gobs of crawlers in the man-swallowing holes that are now largely gone.

Overall, the fishing remains absolutely and totally incredible. And so does the river and the land.

On the trail back to the cabin, the miles of jack pine plantation added the last stunning reminder of how long I've been coming to this land. Back then the now-dying pines were just planted by the Civilian Conservation Corps. You could see huge herds of deer across the plains into the next forty. Now you couldn't see a bull moose twenty paces into them.

Where you now walk half a day to flush a couple of grouse, you could have picked off a limit (whatever the limit was) under oak or fruit-bearing trees with a .22 rifle.

I decided not to look in the mirror when I washed my face before lunch — didn't want to be reminded how the years have changed it, too.

Au Sable Guardian
September 5, 1990

If the Boss up there on that Perfect Trout Stream in the Sky tolerates swollen heads, Mr. Calvin (Cal) Gates, Sr. must be packing an awesome burden on his shoulders.

Mr. Calvin (Rusty) Gates, Jr. has done Cal mighty proud — damned awful proud.

Rusty picked up the charge when Cal saluted the Taps bugler for the final retreat a few years ago. He's turned it into a withering barrage for the Au Sable River that Cal Sr. lyrically worshipped.

A relatively young fella, Rusty has become the guru — the godfather of Au Sable conservation. He is a no-compromise conservationist who bleeds before our Au Sable feels the prick.

Those who have always been the defenders of this greatest of Michigan's treasures — the fly fishers — now worship at the little fly shop at Stephan Bridge that Cal gambled on and where Rusty carries on.

Sure it is a dandy place. All kinds of nifty, classy, and, yeah, expensive stuff. Like Orvis rods and clothes. Trout flies so perfect a guy who has been winding stuff on hooks forever swoons over them. The latest and best poop on hatches. Some of the savviest guides who have ever jammed a punt into the gravel of this Holy Water.

The beds and view are supreme. The soup is first rate. But, anyone could put that together.

What makes it special, what makes it important, is this tingling knot of a guy who picked up the baton when his dad passed it on.

You've known people who are what they call wired. Rusty is one of them. There are times when you expect him to explode into a zillion splinters. His intensity can drive your blood pressure up thirty notches. But that is only when he identifies (or in fairness, perceives) a threat to our Au Sable.

At other times he can create true artistry in the jaws of a fly tying vise, while grinning and joking. Or coax a riverboat through the river's most complex currents as casually as you and I brush our teeth or scratch our ear.

Rusty is one who is sensitive and articulate enough to be silent when the moon ripples on the current, to squeeze a big dog's jowls tenderly, and fall in love with the depth they measure the Grand Canyon by.

Rusty, some newsmen caution, is prone to fire at phantom targets. And you bet, I've known him to launch his missiles at imagined foes, or at targets not yet in range.

But, hey! I remember a valiant, brilliant, compassionate West Pointer desperate for supporting leadership telling a young, most undeserving rifleman: "When you don't know if you should hold ground, give ground or attack, always assault the b——ds!" (Or something like that.)

Rusty has made book on that. He ain't gonna give ground. It is far too late for his, Cal's, and our Au Sable to do that. Holding ground is also, a losing action.

So he's locked into butt-kicking mode. Stop by and thank him soon. He's doing your job for you.

And if you can read poetry you didn't know these kids could write, hire on for an Au Sable float with him.

This department's guide was an old Au Sable veteran when Rusty held his first fly rod, with Cal Sr.'s hand wrapped around his.

Rusty, old cobber Bing McClellan, and I floated most of the Holy Water the other day. I signed off throwing a salute to Cal, knowing that when I answer the final Taps I'll be looking Cal up to thank him for the guardianship he left us for the Holy Water.

Grouse Opener
September 20, 1989

Nails was literally slobbering in my ear as she leaned over the seat, like she was trying to push the car down the trail faster. She'd been down this trail just a few days before. It had been a bird dog's jackpot: two ruffed grouse broods, three single birds, and five woodcock flushed. All in a distance of less than two miles.

Nails, (and before her) Toots, and Thorne have been hunting this cover along the river for years. I've been coming to it for about twenty-five years. It isn't what it used to be. Beaver have flooded some of the finest woodcock plains. The popple is way past prime. Some of the berry brambles have grown old and stale. But there are still birds. If there were none, I guess I'd keep returning.

Where we turned off the main trail onto the two-track, I noticed that the sand pit at the base of the hill was torn by tires, but I charged it off to sightseers. This was opening day — a Friday, not Saturday. The cover was still jungle-thick. Other bird hunters would wait until tomorrow.

Turning the bend into the little parking cutoff, I learned I was wrong. Three cars were parked side by side; one of those customized Suburbans, a spiffy Wagoneer, and a Volvo. That's all the cars there is room for. That's more cars than I'd seen parked here during an entire season in years past. I shouldn't have waited.

Rejecting the urge to just forget it, we backed down the trail, around the bend, where there is room to pull off. Nails sprang from the car. As always, her initial burst of enthusiasm took her in a few fast circles. She knew the direction and stopped out about thirty yards, waiting. When I didn't follow she sprinted back. When she saw the shell vest and then the shotgun coming out of the case, she plunked her fanny on the ground, muzzle pointing at me, tail swishing, tongue lolling out the side of her gaping mouth.

This was different — not like the other day. She fell in behind and beside me as we walked down the two-track, past the parking jam. Less than a hundred yards up the trail, I stopped, talked to her, swung my arm into the stand of old spruce and told her what she was waiting for; "Hunt 'em up, Lady!"

Spruce? Sure. Odds were good some of the single birds had fled into them to avoid the mob of hunters.

Nails spun in about three fast half-circles, deeper and deeper,

into the spruce. I loaded the barrels with lowbase 7-1/2s and followed slowly. She started back, slower, casting. Then darted to the
north, turning east, then north again. She was onto something. Then
she had it. Body and tail stretching, almost tiptoeing, she moved
toward an ancient stump, nearly as big around as the little gun is
long.

Then she stopped. On point — hard and steady.

Promising myself I'd kill this first bird for her, I checked the safety and slipped my thumb over it. The bird held tight. This would be
easy.

No more than twenty-five feet away, with lots of air under the
high spruce boughs, he flushed. A big old dark phase bird. The barrels covered him.

Damn you, Sheppard. I couldn't do it. I pet her and apologized.
She didn't seem to mind. So I reminded myself that the business
about killing birds for the dog is malarkey. They, like sportsmen, live
to hunt; not to kill.

Maybe a quarter mile into the over-age popples, two men and a
dog came into focus, heading back to their car. As we got closer, they
appeared to be in uniform — wearing the same LL Bean (I guessed)
clothes and carrying smart-looking little autoloaders of an unfamiliar
brand. (Autoloaders! That's blasphemy in the bird woods. For ducks
and geese sure — but not for real birds.)

Their pointer had its tail between its legs and ears down. It sure
as blazes wasn't happy. It didn't want to play with Nails. Seemed
almost afraid of her.

"Any luck?"

"We flushed a big bunch of birds (young brood, no doubt) down
there a ways. They were wild as hell. Got off a few shots. Didn't get
any.

(Wild, my gazoo. Those birds were tame the other day.)

Stopping to listen a while later, there was a great commotion the
other side of the feeder crick. Yelling, cussing, and whistle blowing.
Some first rate cussing. Ha ha! Nails pulled in tight, walking at heel
without orders. Intimidated by the meanness she was hearing.

We ducked upstream to the log across the crick. A ways beyond,
a game-pocket-size setter, one of those radio things on her collar,
exploded from the tangle, tongue dragging, covered with burrs,
almost falling she was running so hard, eyes ablaze with panic.
Seeing us, she nearly fell over herself trying to stop.

Nails held back. I walked up to the dog, talking as soothingly as I know how, got her by the collar and rubbed her soaked ears and forehead.

"Hey! I've got your dog! Follow the crick upstream!" It took a couple of throat-rasping tries, but they finally heard me and started bolting through the tangle along the stream.

Three of them emerged — sweating, somewhat jaded. Disgusted. All wearing dandy new, but now disheveled, gear and packing little over-unders. The smallest of the lot charged, snarling and screeching at the dog and swung back a boot.

The bastard was gonna kick her! And she wasn't much bigger than his boot. Still holding her collar, I lifted her slightly and swung her away from him and let go of her.

He looked in his early thirties, and as overweight as I am. And I was betting, not near as many scars to have ground the meanness in when it is needed. Flash anger isn't my thing, but no one kicks a bird dog in front of me in my woods.

He didn't want to test it. Looked away and mumbled something. One of the other guys tried to be pleasant and condescending. They'd flushed the other young brood. The dog had gone wild. Sure thing, it never had a chance to learn its business or to trust these damned yuppies.

"You guys know the way back to your car!" It was an order. Not a question. They understood. "It is just about due west of that big pine you see there," I pointed.

They looked in the direction. At first, it didn't seem they knew what a pine was. But this one stands out, on a rise of ground. They finally caught on, leashed the dog and stumbled toward it.

My day was ruined. There was a bitter, sour taste deep in my throat. The good old days were the good days — at least in the grouse woods.

But, heck, Nails was still with me. So were the memories of those better times, before grouse hunting was a fad, with Toots and Thorne. We can confine our hunting to private land, where cowboys aren't welcome.

And geez, the best part was I hadn't killed that bird. Obviously a cock and a survivor of last season — and maybe more. Odds — according to the bio-statisticians — are that he won't make it through to next spring. Could even be I could kill him. But I'll hold fire in those parts for the rest of the season.

It would please me much if he entertains us during next spring's Hendrickson mayfly hatch from his drumming log.

And by the way, some of us old duffers have to hang around long enough to see these fashion plates get tired of trashing our grouse woods.

FALL

Woodcock Hunter's Heaven
October 31, 1990

From the top of the drumlin, you could see snow clouds brooding over the Fox Islands. Snow has been promised since last night. The wind that was to be its partner had arrived; it screamed through the maples and beeches. Lousy working conditions for a bird dog. But better than sitting home.

It was only a fifteen-minute drive; it took us nearly a half hour. But why hurry? We were in no race. Even this late in the season, it was certain that no one had seriously hunted this out-of-the-way pocket of private upland hardwoods, croplands, and swales.

Maybe a few guys, mostly kids, had walked through it, hoping to shoot a rabbit, squirrel, or bird. But I was sure that bird dogs had not explored its edges or probed its innards.

Each year we reserve this area for a try when things get tough in late October. Nails knows it well. The owner trusts us to respect his fences, to respect his privacy in deer season, and to never bring anyone with us.

Nails sat patiently by the tailgate of the Suburban as I shucked the wool coat, replaced it with a sweat shirt, and covered it with the orange-trimmed shell vest. Uncasing the old side-by-side caused Nails to shiver and shake, but she didn't bolt when I dropped a couple of low-base 7-1/2s into the barrels and snapped them shut.

"Hunt em up!" sent her streaking across the edge of the cornfield for the swale at the bottom of the drumlin. A couple of stern "Whoa! Easy ... easy, lady" commands slowed her down. She was in a hurry to get on with business.

As she threaded into the tangle, I came within a few inches of stepping on a woodcock in the mowed edge of the field. It fluttered into the air, not five feet away, and dove for the thicket.

I smiled at the thought of brother Dave in nearly the same situation — about a week ago. An easy shot. But I'd flushed the bird, and I had to order him to "shoot!" He knew of my dislike about shooting at a bird not pointed by the dog.

Today, the doodle made it into the bottom.

I realized Nails' bell was silent and tried to recall where she'd been when the bird flushed. Even with only the leaves on wild grape still holding out, I couldn't see her. Then the bell tinkled to the south. Only a couple of times. Then a few more.

She was seventy-five feet away, pacing slowly; right, then left, forward, and circling but a few feet. Confused? Too much wind, even down here?

By the time I got to her, she seemed on point one second, then, slowly — still with head held high and reaching, tail feathers swimming in the breeze — searching.

As I moved in, a woodcock flushed between us. Not a pointed bird; not a fair shot. When I was about five feet away Nails seemed to lock on. I lifted the gun, ready for the flush. She faded to my right, still tight on point. A doodle flushed. I dropped it.

Nails held. I moved to within a foot of her nose. Two more flushed. I dropped one. "Fetch!" (I knew she wouldn't.)

I broke the action and reached for two shells as I walked over to retrieve the birds.

Nails then bolted into some tag alders, came swinging out to the edge of standing water, covered with mud, and went back on point, not a hundred feet away. Closing on her, I wild-flushed another bird without shooting. As I approached, the bird I assumed she was pointing twittered into the air, and fell when the gun snorted. She still held.

Geez! We were in a woodcock hunter's heaven.

A bird wobbled into the air maybe twenty feet off to her right as I approached and fed another shell into the empty chamber. The bird she was pointing flushed when I was three feet away. I swung, but decided three were enough.

In the next forty-five minutes, she pointed more than a dozen woodcock and we flushed at least two dozen, without burning any more powder.

Climbing into the upland and heading back to the car, she managed to point two grouse. I was tempted to take the one that was a sure thing. But hell, it would stick around for the next time. Maybe even give us a brood next spring to keep the game alive — if some slob December hunter doesn't shoot it out of a budding tree.

Three woodcock, one at a time, wrapped in tinfoil and toasted on the gas grill, is enough "ordurves" to enrich autumn memories.

As we stood on the beach an hour later, the islands appeared as huge marble slabs. A blazing crimson sun was creeping behind them under a sky washed with ink that flowed into Lake Michigan. The snowstorm had died out there over the islands, perhaps with the last woodcock of 1990 disappearing with it.

We gave thanks for being able to celebrate another northern Michigan October.

Conversation
September 28, 1983

We knew the birds were there. We'd seen them several times since mid-June; a big brood.

The temperature was in the high sixties; too hot for real bird hunting. Crawling and climbing through the tangle along the river had been a sweaty affair. So I swung Toots back from the river, after a mile or more into the uplands.

Heading up a knoll into a blackberry patch at the edge of a stand of young popple, she went on point.

Moving in slowly, clucking "easy gal, whoa old lady," the hen blasted out of the pucker brush maybe thirty or forty feet ahead of Toots and sixty feet ahead of me.

I swung the old side-by-side I'd picked up last winter (but never shot), and missed. Clean. Knew I shouldn't have fired, but it was the first shot of the season.

As I cracked the piece open to pop in another shell, the bird Toots was pointing flushed.

Hey, you're slow and old!

Toots moved ten feet and was on point again. The bird flushed, and this time, I hit it. As I moved to pick it up she went on point again. I mentally pinpointed the dead bird and moved up behind her. The bird exploded from the briars and dropped ten feet away as the little 12-gauge erupted.

Geezus! Whatta gun.

I picked up the second bird and headed for the first when she was on point again.

Looking over my shoulder to be sure I had the first dead bird located, I walked up on Toots. The bird burst out of a tangle of dead elm and waist-high berry bushes.

It dropped not more than three feet over the berries.

I cussed at myself. What in hell did I need with three dead birds in under two minutes? Dumb. Mary Lou and I can only eat one at a sitting. Darn few people get in here, so they'll be here through October if I don't kill them.

Toots went wild. As I picked up the last two dead birds she flushed at least four more.

Good. Make 'em wiser. More fun hunting (harder killing) the rest of the season. Their tails were just stubs; juveniles. Let 'em grow up.

After breaking the gun, and as I was field-cleaning the birds, I caught a flash of orange to my left. A guy, standing under an elm skeleton had apparently been watching us. I waved. He waved back, but didn't move.

I finished gutting the birds and decided he wanted to talk. As I headed his way, the big English setter, much to my surprise pranced ahead of me. (She's like me — not much on people.)

She walked right up to him and squatted. He knelt down to pet her. (Hmm, obviously knows dogs like to be talked to on their level.)

I'd guess he was in his late sixties, but could be older; hard to tell. He was taller than I by a good four inches. A handsome, strong face; square shoulders, erect.

"Couple of damn good shots," he said, looking me straight in the eye. (He'd only been there for the last two birds.)

I wanted to brag on the old-new gun.

"Surprised me too. Missed the first one clean."

"Oh yeah, then you got the second one?" (He'd heard the shots.)

"Yeah, got three."

"There were more!"

"Three's plenty for opening day."

His hair was white under an old Jones cap. The hunting vest was well-worn, but well-bought. The double-fronted canvas britches were the only thing that didn't look years old. The Russell-type bird boots looked expensive.

His eyes locked on mine with every word; not challenging, but sincere and inquisitive.

But his shotgun — an old, cheap Iver Johnson single shot — didn't fit.

"You live here," he said as matter of fact.

"Yeah, how'd you know?"

"The tan, you're not in a hurry, and you didn't need to kill any more birds. People who come up gotta kill everything they can."

(Be damned!)

"Where you from?"

"We have a cottage over by Bellaire on the lake."

"Been coming up long?"

"Oh, guess it is going on forty years ... when did The War end?"

"You fish here, too?" he asked.

The Jordan was only about 150 yards away.

"Yeah, some. Do you?"

"Used to a lot. Still do, but not as much ... did a little better, though, this summer. It's changed.   The brook trout aren't here; flies aren't either, you know."

"Yeah."

"River's full of sand and silt; didn't used to be that way. And those damn salmon; can't prove it but I believe they've hurt the trout."

Since we were obviously going to talk, I rolled the birds out of the game bag in the back of the vest to start cleaning them.

He noticed me eyeballing the gun; the awkward single shot.

He reached over, touched it.

"All I've got left. Gave my bird guns to the boys. This is the one I started each of them with."

"How many boys?"

"Three. They don't seem to have time to come up hunting ... too busy making money. I didn't raise them that way. We always had enough money, I thought. (I was starting to feel like I was intruding too deep into his life.)

"I always made time to come up trout fishing and bird hunting. Bill (I think he said) would take my patients for a couple of weeks for trout fishing and two more for bird hunting. He likes to go to Florida in the winter and I'd handle his then."

He reached over and lifted the little single shot from the tree it was leaning against and put it across his lap, careful to break it so I'd know it was unloaded.

"Can't hit a thing with it. Too light. Not enough iron ... I don't know, just not right."

(Meaning the shotguns he'd given the sons were double barrels.)

He watched me skin the first bird, pulling out the breast and legs in a few seconds.

"Could I help you?"

"No."

Then, damn, it came to me. "You eat grouse?"

"Oh, Sarah loves them ... she's one of the best cooks ... but I haven't killed one in, geez, I don't know how long ... can't hit anything with this gun ... and it isn't any fun without the boys and Sam." (I guessed a bird dog he remembered.)

I flipped the uncleaned bird to him.

"Clean this one and keep it ... it's a young bird. Eat it tonight, if she'll cook it."

"Can't do that."

"Don't gimme that crap. It'll make me feel a lot better about killing it. Mary Lou and I can only eat one bird for the two of us at a meal; we don't need three, and I'd just as soon eat squash or tomatoes."

He whipped out a pocket knife and cleaned the bird as fast as I could.

"Can I look at your gun?"

I handed it to him. (It was broke and empty.)

It is an old piece. Probably more than fifty years old. But a masterpiece. Trouble is, the stock is only about 12 1/2 inches long, though made with beautiful wood.

He threw it up to his shoulder (we were sitting on the ground) checked the barrels, the action and the markings.

"Beautiful gun, but the stock's awful short."

"Yeah, I didn't know if I could shoot it. Seems to work OK though."

"Yeah, that was great shooting."

"Surprised me, too."

"How old is she?" pointing to Toots.

"Eight or nine. Sorta lost track. Best I've ever had. Better than I ever expected."

"Where you parked?"

I jerked my thumb to the west. "You?"

He nodded to the south, meaning he'd walked a half mile or more.

"You've got a long walk back," he said. (It wasn't more than a mile and a half.)

"Don't have anything else to do."

"Take good care of her (Toots). Wish I could have another one ..."

His voice trailed off wistfully, as he glanced away. He knew it and got up; no kinks in his tailbone.

Toots sat beside me as I watched him gracefully wade through the ferns, berries, and popples. I hoped it wasn't too late for the boys to learn that the most cherished thing the Old Man had taught them was to love bird dogs, fine guns, and the places where ruffed grouse, mayflies, and trout live.

Moving To Turkey Run
November 16, 1988

"If I ever move again it will be because I'm back in a wheel chair and you're too fast for me to catch. I'm gonna move to the old soldiers home and chase nurses up and down the halls."

Her eyes narrow. Her jaw tightens and her shoulders stiffen when I make that threat. (She should know I don't mean it — she's easy to catch. But, geez, she believes those stories I tell about running down nurses in GI hospitals. If they were true, everyone would be trying for a Purple Heart.)

We've had it with moving. Back in September, fish biologist Jerry Rakoczy and wife Jean came over. He walked in, stumbled over a couple of boxes and declared, "I thought that hurricane was down in the Gulf."

It is better now. But still a disaster.

It started about three years ago.

We were happy over at Matchett Lake. When we moved there, about eight years ago, we thought the owner would sell to us. The old farmhouse at Phelps Station had become too big with all the kids gone. And too many people had moved in around Lake 26.

The Matchett Lake place seemed perfect. The only home on a two-mile-long road. Lots of wild and quiet. A big basswood tree to talk to at sunset. Old buddy, Irv Drost had built it just right for him and then us. But the winters drove him out.

The owner wouldn't sell. And then some sneaky, mean stuff I'd picked up decades ago got to tearing me up. I'd managed to carry it pretty well when younger, but it really became ornery as the years piled up.

Sometimes we'd be snowed in up to six days. Mary Lou didn't want to live that way if I wasn't going to be around.

So we started looking. For a couple of years we looked in the Cedarville-Hessel area. Found one place that looked right — if a little cramped — on would you believe, Sheppard Bay. That fell through.

Then Sass, the youngest, and husband Don, after nearly a decade of marriage, announced that we were gonna be grandfolks again.

That did it. Mary Lou's roots were down. We'd stay in the shadow of the condo ghetto that is Charlevoix. No discussion. She wasn't budging. We started shopping here. I was happy in our rented place. So I kinda hung tight for a place on Lake Charlevoix, with a big boat dock and all, knowing we couldn't afford it.

Then wham! She comes up with this place about three miles from Matchett Lake. So deep in the woods that trees were wearing a notch in the roof from the wind (they're down now). Quiet. Secluded, but close to a paved, school bus route county road. Built by old pal John Pearl to last (before he got the lust to build a log cabin for bride Doris).

A contractor, John's first love is wood. He loves to build stuff with it. He loves to look at it, feel it, smell it. The house reflects that.

It is a fine place. But what sold me was the big pole barn. Room for the boats, the old Olds 88 and for the work shop. While largely non-functional, the two big fireplaces aren't bad either. (Fortunately, the two air-tight wood stoves are more practical.)

Without even looking to see if anyone is around, you can save wear and tear on the plumbing by walking out any door.

Northern Michigan is a big place. In our work we can live just about any place. At one time we even considered a magnificent place at the mouth of the Silver River, just downstream from the Silver River falls and in the shadow of Brockway Mountain. (We couldn't afford it.)

Despite the condos, the stolen sunsets, and the tinsel people, northwest Lower Michigan is still about as good as it gets. The U.P. doesn't have the mayfly hatches. No where else are the islands as close. The drumlins and the swales between them are still magic (the yuppies haven't found them).

So we're settling in. Next stop is the old soldiers home.

Our goal was to be settled by Thanksgiving. Walking through the barn is still risky. Three rooms in the house remain packed with boxes.

It is one thing to move a life-time's accumulation of fly tying stuff, fishing tackle, guns and ammo, books, and boots. It is another to move thirty-five years of old newspapers and newspaper files.

But the chickadees, nuthatches, woodpeckers, and goldfinches have found us. The big dog Nails, Twig the beagle, and the cat Tikki have settled in. That makes it home.

There are lots of places for bluebird houses on the eleven acres. That will make it a castle — if I can just find the saw in the barn to build them.

The Trouble With Deer Hunting
December 5, 1985

The trouble with deer hunting, sometimes, is you have to take the rifle along to convince folks you are making at least a token effort.

Mary Lou likes venison. Comes from a northern Michigan family that hunted nothing but deer. (I'd rather eat parsnips. And Dad loved the bird coverts of the Dead Stream Swamp but scorned deer hunters.)

Since the curse invaded the right shoulder, bow hunting has been impossible — irresponsible. Rifle hunting has become a circus. It is the only time of the year I have to share these drumlins and swales with others. Only the chickadees behave naturally. You no longer "hunt" whitetails. You ambush them. It takes luck or pure mean, dull stubbornness.

Simply put, the fun ain't there any more. It is the least fun thing I do in the outdoors.

Toots, the aging bird dog, especially hates it. She can't understand why I'm leaving the house with hunting boots and gun but not her. Each time I leave a wail starts deep in her gut, sorta warbles around in her belly, rattles through her chest and whines out of pursed lips. Kinda sounds like the lovesick plea of a 100-pound owl.

Anyway, in these boondock precincts the ladies sorta retain their respect by being able to tell the others their husbands have been hunting their bucks. (They'd never admit they don't give a diddly about killing one.)

And it is fun sitting in the blind, with all senses attuned to the critters, the sky, and the wind.

The only fascination this evening had been music from a loose strip of birchbark singing in the wind. Sometimes it almost whistled. I was wishing I'd brought along the pocket tape recorder as I fell into an extended doze.

Then, geezus! "King Kong Grouse!" snapped through the groggy brain cells. It was a crashing, thundering roar coming out of the swamp. Second thought: a C-130 with flapping wings, instead of motors.

Turkeys are common in the drumlin country. But, fortunately, they don't often attack a snoozing deer hunter.

The sun was over the ridge. Darkness was fast filling the gray-brown places at the edge of the swamp, beyond the blind and the maze of thumb-size popple saplings.

Just the right time to have a turkey land in your lap as you try to be alert for whitetails spooked by a world gone mad around them.

The six inches of snow earlier in the season had been chased off by fifty to sixty degree days. The leaves were nearly dry.

Sure enough. The snap, crinkle, snap of hooves. Two deer, obviously does, came down the runway at a cautious, but steady gait. Their shapes were almost indistinct, like shifting fog or smoke.

They moved out of sight toward the cornfield.

Figuring I had put in my token's worth, I reached for the rifle and thought about trading boots for slippers and gloves for a handful of tumbler-Scotch, when the leaves cracked.

He was almost impossible to see. Only when he raised his head from the ground was it clear the shape was real, not just a vision. The binoculars put horns on him — maybe. If he hadn't been acting like a buck, with nose down like a trash hound on a rabbit track, I'd have chalked up the spikes to imagination.

The little 6mm's two-power scope settled on his neck, but was blurred by the dense stand of saplings.

I was saved. At around 3100 feet per second, the bullet's path would resemble a roller coaster track when it hit the saplings. (Good thing I didn't bring the .35 Remington; at 2100 feet per second the big slug would probably bulldoze right through the stalks.)

The flashlight helped find the parsnips under the straw.

She wasn't surprised, or disappointed when I proudly presented them to her.

"See anything?"

"Yeah, a small buck, I think ... maybe a turkey just about flew into my head."

"Huh ... uh ... yeah ... that figures."

The Mouse That Roared
November 18, 1987

Geez! What's a guy supposed to do to get some respect in the deer woods between these drumlins?

I lean against a tree, then rest on a Hot Seat with "bait" all around me, the Remington loaded with 6mm rounds, and a deer runway only twenty-five yards to the west. And what do I find staring me in the eyeballs on the stump only a foot away?

A mouse.

It is a bit of a thing, about the size of my thumb with a lot of brownish-gray fur on it. The eyes appear unblinking. One foot is raised under its chin. Only the nose moves. About as frightened of this big time, macho deerslayer as he is of a congressman.

That, sir, is the ultimate contempt.

That, also, makes the opening morning of deer season priceless.

The deer stand — really our picnic place in the woods, complete with a stone fire ring — has been baited with sunflower seeds and stale peanuts (which Sonny Lang supplies after Murdick's Fudge Shop closes in the fall) since Halloween, when we had our last hot dog roast.

It has been improved this year. A four-foot-wide bird feeder was tacked to a brace of basswood trees. Keeping it full has been a daily chore. The stale peanuts disappear overnight.

Opening morning was just under freezing and one of the brightest in weeks. By seven you could see across to the next drumlin, about a mile away. The leaves were brittle and noisy. The bird feeder and sapling beeches and maples were aflutter with chickadees before first light.

The shooting started at 7:03 a.m. Mostly single rounds. Sometimes a double. Then to the southeast, somebody let loose with five fast shots: a certain miss. By 7:30 I'd counted fifty-seven shots, and probably missed a few.

I'd largely forgotten I'd promised Mary Lou to use the doe permit. As many as nine chickadees were in the feeder at once. Nuthatches sorta bombed in, resulting in a blur of fleeing chickadees. Wary bluejays hunkered on the edges.

A bird I'd never heard before turned out to be a bluejay practicing a new song. Do they mimic others?

A red squirrel, distraught with the visitor who provided the cashews and almonds, carried on like a half-ton lion; his bark and roar booming clear down to the lake, his tail snapping like a whip. Damn, he was mad.

I then looked at the stump. The focus at the distance over the bifocals is sorta fuzzy. But as it zeroed in, there was the mouse. Sitting there. Glaring at me. Challenging me to do something. Like what?

The stump, like everything else around me, was baited with peanuts and sunflower seeds. But he seemed more interested in a staring-down with this big oaf in the old mackinaw and silly orange hat.

The Thermos cup filled with coffee wasn't five inches from him. It was getting cold, but it could wait.

A downy woodpecker flapped in from the north. The mouse wasn't distracted. When I looked back at the stump the mouse was gnawing on a stale cashew nut nearly as big as its head.

There's a danger to baiting your deer stand for birds, mice, and squirrels. Makes them vulnerable to predators. So you feel sorta guilty. Selfish. But it makes deer hunting worthwhile.

When the dole dries up after the first heavy snow, they will find the feeders by the house, just a half mile up the drumlin. It will all work out — so you tell yourself.

Woo! There's a clatter in the hardwoods swale to the south.
A small buck — maybe four, six points — comes racing by. Even a young warrior, with his honed M1 eye, wouldn't have had a shot. If he makes it through November 30, he is on his way to being a trophy that may die of old age.

You sense that the woods are now different. Wildlife is learning a lesson; it is adapting. Genetic traits inherited by decades of culling are coming on strong. Those who see Christmas this year will produce even more wary offspring. It is the nature of things.

It is also good and proper.

There are too many whitetails in these, and many other precincts. They are superb creatures. But in many ways, they are in conflict with modern man and his cars — and crops. They do not easily coexist.

These old country roads around Matchett and Skinner lakes lead to nowhere. But they have been host to a constant throng of traffic as town folks cruise them, looking for an easy kill.

If the whitetails were only half as plentiful, we'd be done with the lazy opportunistic hunters. The deer woods would be kinder to those of us who come to visit with chickadees as much as to shoot a deer.

The little mouse's cheeks have swelled up so much from cramming in seeds and peanuts that he looks like he has a bad case of the mumps. (Remember the mumps? Whatever happened to them?)

He starts my way. It is only a short hop from the stump to my knee. I'm hoping he will make it.

Nope. Suddenly he turns and darts down the side of the stump and is lost in the duff.

A noise, again from the cedar bottom to the south, has startled him. Out of the corner of my eye an average-size doe appears — slowly, cautiously coming toward me.

The little Remington is handy. A check shows the scope is set on 2 power; just right. Inch by inch it comes to the shoulder. The crosshairs lock on the shoulder, waiting for it to clear some saplings.

Whoa! There is something about forty feet behind the doe. A pair of fawns — looking healthy enough to make it through the winter without mamma.

And if they don't, conservation will be well served. There are too many deer in these parts for the habitat and the crops.

But, ah, you can't do it. The rifle comes down.

The doe sees me. She bleats. The fawns disappear. To where? I have no idea.

Geez, that is neat. Just gone; like a wisp of fog.

I'll be back. Maybe, I will even kill a deer. But that won't be my motivation. No, I want to find out if that mouse will visit again.

Early Winter Hike
December 7, 1983

The puppy burst through the snow, yelping once, and cowered between my legs. A few seconds earlier it hadn't shown the least alarm when the .22 rifle spit six rounds. When the two big dogs snapped and growled at its playfulness it came back for more.

But now, for several seconds, the four-month-old black Lab trembled and tried to climb into a boot — with my foot in it.

I hadn't seen the broad-winged hawk that swooped low over the tangle of blowdown birch as soon as Babe had. Where in that gene pool were the instincts from generations ago that taught her the hawk meant terror? The little hawk was about as much threat to her now as the chipmunk sleeping under a stump.

Babe was on loan to us, sort of, while Bill and Mary Lou VanLoo were downstate for the weekend. It's the next best thing to having your own puppy.

Toots, the aging English setter, doesn't think much of it. Pups aren't her thing. In the house she nips at the "black bomb" when it gets nearer than three feet. But out here, in the season's first real snow, she was more tolerant, letting it romp with her and, even run smack into her when it got too excited.

Bill's Cindy died earlier this year. She'd been too lame the last couple years to go to the duck fields. Next year, Babe's gonna have a big shadow to fill.

And she's going to do it — if she ever learns to quit running into stumps and blowdowns. She's already a "charge 'em" retriever on hand-thrown birds. She doesn't think much of ice, but loves the water.

We had walked down here for Toots' first chance to run since deer season opened. Babe came along for the fun of it. I brought the .22 rifle to make Toots feel better and to test Babe's gun nerves. (She ignored its bark.)

The hawk was gone in moments and the pup was back on Toots' trail, bounding through snow that came halfway up her belly, in places nearly a foot deep.

At the edge of the opening, Toots slammed into an instant point, not even looking back when Babe crashed into her. The grouse thundered out of the popples about the instant I saw them sitting. They went out wild, way out of shotgun range — if I'd had one.

Toots turned her neck. Disgusted, I assumed.

But the danged pup sat there, giving Toots one of those puppy looks that says, "Hey, I love you. Gimme some attention." Toots stalked off in contempt.

Rabbits have already established several runways. It looks like a good season shaping up for the beagles.

Picking up the only deer track to cross the swale, I followed it into the hardwoods along the side of the drumlin and into another swale. Then the dogs took over, making such a maze of tracks nothing made sense.

Before the season ended, two hunters — one from the Pigeon and one from Au Sable country — reported that some bucks had already lost their racks. Strange. But maybe isolated incidents. Last winter, the mildest ever, some bucks didn't lose their racks until March. And rarely do they start coming off before late December.

Though rifle season was the quietest anyone remembers in these parts, the first day of December signals the beginning of the Big Hush in Drumlin Country, and throughout the north woods. Even if the winters become more confining each passing year, this quiet time, with nature's beauty etched in such stark relief, with the creatures that remain active so obvious, is deeply fulfilling.

Yesterday, as a blizzard howled off Lake Michigan, snow drifts had cut us off from the rest of the world. We took inventory: the camp stoves are in their place, the lanterns filled, the candle drawer full, water in the jugs, the cupboard and freezer are filled. There are several bushels of squash keeping cool, a row of parsnips under straw and snow to dig.

We can outlast any storm or power line blowdown, as long as the woodstove draws air.

Being at the end of the road and a mile from anyone, and having no children at home or jobs we have to get to (the *Call* is written in the basement close to the wood stove), the snowplow skippers know they can get to us last. If it is a day or two or even three, they realize their bosses will hear no complaints from the Sheppards.

There's something precious and enriching in being totally isolated and independent in a winter blizzard. The pace slackens. It would be heresy to turn on the radio or TV. Instead you play cribbage and crack the covers of a book you haven't read in several years. Bedtime comes early. And you sure sleep warm, and close.

You crack the window over the bed, let the snow blast in, squeeze closer and feel sorry for the poor folks who are still up watching the tube.

On the side of the drumlin, where the junipers grow like sod, Babe yelped in fear or pain. She looked like a black torpedo being launched. Then Toots, mostly white on white, pounced in a spray of snow. She was after a little critter under the snow.

By the time I got there she had killed it; a weasel, now a white ermine. Damn it!

Babe, apparently had gotten close enough to the action to feel its fangs. Another lesson learned this day.

And yet, it haunted me. It has been several hundred years since a Lab has been a wild creature with survival instincts honed to recognize a bird of prey as a threat to pups.

How long do those wild genes hold on?

Not long enough in the human species!

A Couple Of Fawns
December 16, 1987

Something about the double set of tracks didn't register just right. They were caused by tiny little hooves, punching sharp holes in the fresh two inches of soggy snow.

They'd been made only minutes before I entered the swale beside the lake. I picked them up as they wound through a narrow gully of tags and cedar beside the hardwood ridge and then headed toward the cornfield.

Nails and I were on a late afternoon break. She has been in a tizzy since I started confining her a few days before rifle deer season. Even a short trek through the woods is a treat for both of us. She doesn't seem to know the difference between a little .22 rifle and the double-barrel shotgun. But you have to take a long gun. (She stands by the gun cabinet waiting for me to fetch it.)

Killing ruffed grouse that have survived the tragically long two-month season strikes me as just a tad meaner than beating a friend's ex-mother-in-law. So, I just pretend at hunting. Nails, of course, still takes it seriously.

I lost track of her as I trailed the little marks in the snow. After a few yards it dawned on me — there was no doe with the fawns. That's what was missing — there was no doe!

I was too close; melt water oozed into the tracks as I followed them. Suddenly, I was startled by the thought that Nails might be on their heels. Stopping and listening, I heard her coming up behind me. I grabbed her and slipped on a leash; she didn't like it, but sat quietly when I cocked an open palm at her.

Snow clouds hung over the drumlins. Snow had fused with rain since last night. Temperatures were in the low thirties. The pole-size maples in the uplands swayed in mini-gale winds coming off Lake Michigan. If the heavy leather boots (dang, they put on weight every year) hadn't been well-treated, the socks — and feet — would have been soaking wet.

After waiting a good ten minutes, Nails fell into step at heel and we twisted through the swale, to where it ends abruptly in a steep grade which ends at a road that runs between the cornfield and orchards.

Light was fading fast. At home Mary Lou would have turned the lights on so she could see to start supper.

There were little flecks of mud and leaf debris where the fawns had scrambled up the bank to reach the slick muddy road. There wasn't much sense in it, but for some reason I wanted to get close enough to see them.

Archie has left several rows of corn near the edge of the pines, about a quarter mile south of us. I figured the fawns had snuck through the chopped portion of the field and were feeding in the standing corn.

To reach it, we'd have to go north a bit to stay out of sight, then sneak through the hardwoods to the pines. If we went slowly it would be too dark when we got there. So we moved as fast as I felt we could without spooking every living creature in the section.

Nails picked up the drill, after having me squeeze her snout a few times and trudged along, quiet and slow, beside me.

Finally, skulking through the pine plantation, with enough light left in the west to silhouette corn stalks, we spotted our first deer. It was full grown. I couldn't tell if it was a buck or doe.

Moving only a step every two seconds — and with the west wind in our favor — we inched down the corn rows. Four more adult deer. We could be missing the fawns in the poor light.

Then another adult. Oh, and beside her, two fawns.

Squatting to watch, and putting an arm around Nails to keep her from yelping, we stayed for maybe a minute. They were no more than fifty feet from us.

Then at the end of the pines and corn we spooked two adult deer, both with a pair of fawns.

We may have missed the fawns I assumed had been orphaned. But I want to believe the orphan business was my mistake; that mamma took a different route and met them in the field.

That feels good. Maybe irrational. But good.

Hunters need to kill a lot more does on these drumlins. We have more deer than the country can support without handouts from croplands and orchards. Conservation demands pragmatism in managing wildlife.

But tonight, pragmatism got lost as I silently cheered for those Bambis spending winter with mamma.

Back home, the first thing I noticed was the cribbage board on the coffee table between our two chairs. That meant a showdown after supper.

Supper was a favorite; stuffed peppers, cooked and frozen in late summer, plus squash. Then hot, strong, honey-laced tea.

"See anything?" she asked.

"Quite a few deer in Archie's corn. I think Nails flushed a grouse, but was too far away to be sure."

"You wouldn't shoot it anyway."

"Your crib."

Wasn't about to admit to being an old softie who was out there cowering in the snow worrying about a couple of fawns.

"It's your lay down. What else was out there? You're pretty smug about something."

"Oh, just a couple of fawns and a doe."

"Yeah? You were worried about them, weren't you?"

"Play your cards."

(Think I'll start lacing my boots different and see if she notices.)

Stone Boat Ridge
November 9, 1983

We had happened on it by chance. Toots, the aging setter, should get the credit. She was scouting the abandoned apple orchard without picking up a scent when she careened to a stop and gingerly tip-toed around it.

Two other hunters were with us, but they were deep in the old orchard, filling their game bags with apples.

Until a few years ago, we'd hunted this abused and neglected land often. Fifty or so years ago someone had misused the land, had taken from it without giving in return. Now only the gnarled apple trees seem alive. as their ancient limbs intertwine. The remaining land, which once produced crops, was so drained of its energy, it supports only a thin carpet of sod.

The homestead has collapsed. Huge piles of stones stand as a monument to a family's sweat, hopes, and frustrations.

Narrow streaks of wetlands run north and south, supporting a thick web of dogwood and tags. In a good year, grouse and woodcock can be found in the wet places and in the orchard. Deer cross, bedding down on the ridges and under the apple trees, and move to the hardwoods across the railroad tracks into the next section.

What caught Toots' attention was a big buck scrape. The largest I'd seen in two years. A good three- to four-feet wide, under the outside limb of the uppermost apple tree.

Five or six years ago, I had stalked a big buck in this tract. He eluded me, and all other hunters, during the gun season. Several days after the calendar turned to December, he had walked haughtily across my path, probably not more than fifty feet away. He dragged a leg, but managed to survive with it.

Though this is private land, no one seems to claim it. For what? Thus, it is heavily hunted. So heavily hunted that the chances of taking a wise old buck are about zero. If it does happen, it is luck, not skill. And that's no fun.

About the only time to see the buck that made this scrape is during the rut before November 15. So Toots and I returned to the scrape for several evenings, sitting downwind, hidden under the sagging limbs of the orchard.

The evening he appeared, the chill of a misty sunset had just about convinced me to give up. Several whitetails had moved over the ridge. With the binoculars I could put horns on one — four, maybe six, points. He moved toward the scrape, but held back.

Just as I was thinking about seeing if my legs still worked, Toots, the little buck, and a couple of the does I could see turned their heads south, toward a swale maybe fifty yards from the orchard. Even with the glasses I could see nothing.

It was well over a minute before he moved close enough to become a shape in the gloom. The light was so low that everything merged into gray.

Slowly and deliberately, he walked past several does. The little buck stood his ground, well away from the does and the scrape.

Finally, with head up, the big buck turned so I could get a sense of the rack's size. It looked as wide as the little side-by-side bird gun in my lap. Too dark to count the points, but surely more than eight. Could be ten, twelve, or more, who knows?

He came directly toward the scrape and Toots and me. Turning, I realized the smaller buck had disappeared.

There seemed to be no wind, but thirty feet from the scrape he stopped, turned south and seemed to float in the mist out of sight.

For a moment I wished I had the new bow. When arthritis in the shoulders made me give up the recurve some years ago, I swore I'd end it rather than get involved with one of those mechanical, high-tech compounds. I was wrong. With the fifty percent let-off, I can hold the 55-pound compound steady enough to shoot again. But it needs a few more hours in front of the straw before an arrow is sent at anything alive.

Maybe in December we'll be ready. And odds are the big buck will still be around.

Not that it matters. Bow hunting is a complication that October and early November really don't need. Rifle season always comes before you have finished the fall agenda. There has never been enough time for grouse, woodcock, bluegills, trout, perch and ducks. The sunrises and sunsets are too close together.

Bill VanLoo put it in perspective a couple weeks ago. We were standing in a corn field, waiting for ducks. As the sun's rays slid over the drumlin to the east, the fields were bathed in a soft white glow of frost. The first waves of mallards came over the horizon from the south, barely visible through binoculars. For long minutes we concentrated on them and ignored all else.

"Geezus!" Bill stammered. "Will you look at that!"

To the east, a bright orange ball seemed perched on the ridge. It looked about a quarter mile away and about half as big around as a football field.

On the ridge to the west sat the Hunter's Moon, a glimmering yellow-red, like another huge platter you could walk to in a couple of minutes.

"That's mine," he said, eyes wide, mouth open, as he looked from one to the other. "No matter what happens, this is mine forever."

If we'd killed every one of the hundred — or more — ducks circling the field it wouldn't have meant a thing. Hunters who haven't learned that killing is only a minor by-product of fall have some real magic to discover in the years ahead.

Not A Bad Day
September 26, 1984

The edges of the soggy places have sprouted hundreds of nearly fist-size gobs of flaming red jack-in-the-pulpit seed pods this late summer. They look like Christmas tree ornaments blazing where the bracken thins and the turf drops away to cedar and tag alders.

Here in the drumlin country, jack-in-the-pulpits grow in patches. During the right kind of spring and summer there may be a hundred, more or less, in one stand. And this year seems to have been the best ever.

These are humid, dark, mysterious places, the kind that are just right for those old vampire and werewolf movies we remember from the forties. Even on a summer day, with the sun straight overhead, they are murky. The air is thick and tangy.

They held a surprise for this guide and my brother's sixteen-year-old son.

Even at ten feet, Toots was invisible under the bracken. So we retreated to the cedars, hoping some birds had holed up there on this hot early season hunt.

Young Jon didn't have his license, so he tagged along to be with his oldest uncle and see what this bird dog business was all about. Though he has been hunting and shooting with his dad for several years, bird dogs are something he only hears about.

Toots had made several points under the bracken. The birds had held tight and flushed close, but most of the action was out of Jon's sight.

I knew that down in the cedars where ground cover is thinner, he'd get a better look at the dog work, if not the birds.

Although Mary Lou and I had visited the jack-in-the-pulpit patch during spring and summer, I'd forgotten it until I saw the gaudy seed pods at the bracken's edge. Thought I'd show Jon what it was all about.

Toots saw us turn and rushed in ahead of us. At the edge of the pulpits she tightened onto point. Jon was about to get several lessons.

Moving ahead of her, I explained to Jon that the bird would be somewhere within a ninety-degree reach of her nose. But no bird flushed. Calling Toots ahead to pin the bird down tighter, I noticed she was unsure. She was obviously certain there were birds, but not where.

Then Jon spotted them; two grouse sitting on a low popple limb, maybe twenty-five feet away. "There they are, Uncle Glen!" He added, pointing, "in the tree."

When I looked at them and then lowered the old double, he became instantly exasperated: "Shoot them!"

As they flew away their wings carried with them his image of an uncle who lives in the north woods and doesn't do anything but hunt and fish. The old man of the outdoors was a phony; he doesn't even know how to shoot a grouse when it is sitting a few feet away.

He was, as they say, crestfallen. The outdoorsman who took him fishing and frogging as a tad had become a wimp.

In a demanding tone, he asked, "Why didn't you shoot them?"

It was hot and time for a break anyway.

"Let's squat here and pick the burrs out of Toots, Jon. You know what they are?" as I pulled a pulpit seedpod to take to Mary Lou. "They're jack-in-the-pulpit seedpods. Those grouse were feeding on them. I learned something today ... I didn't know they did that."

"But," half angry and half sad, "why didn't you shoot them?"

"Jon, we're not out here to shoot grouse. We're out here to hunt grouse ... to see the dog work, the birds fly, to learn about jack-in-the-pulpits, hear the leaves crunch under our boots, and wonder at the woods.

"Do you understand that?"

He nodded. I was getting through.

"And," forcefully now, I added, "you don't shoot birds that are sitting on the ground — or in trees. You don't shoot birds that flush wildly, that the dog hasn't pointed. That's only killing. It shows no respect for the bird, the dog, yourself, or the magic that puts it all together. It shows no hope for the future."

We sat there. I was plucking and cutting burrs from Toots' feathers. Jon was thinking and looking, from the dog and I to the seedpods and the bush. He's a damn good kid. And I felt good, knowing he wouldn't forget.

We made a swing through the cedars. A couple of birds flushed wild at the edge of the upland, well ahead of the three of us.

Moving back to the edge, Toots' bell went silent, maybe a hundred feet ahead of us.

"She's on point ... know where she is?"

"Over there, I think," Jon replied, pointing. We headed the way he indicated. After some searching, I found Toots on point. The grouse flushed close and relatively easy.

I didn't wait for him to ask. "I'm the only one who hunts in here with a good dog, Jon. The few others who pass through won't even know there are birds here. So they'll be here until I am ready to shoot them. It would be dumb to kill them this early. The hunting would be over. All I'd have left is the killing."

You could see in his eyes and on his face, that the logic made perfect sense to him. Given a chance, the lad will become one helluva sportsman and conservationist.

A few seconds later, Toots was on point. When we found her, a woodcock flushed about five feet ahead of her nose. I shot it.

"They'll be leaving soon, Jon, so I shoot them now."

He nodded, like, "Hey, I knew that."

Not a bad day for an old bird hunter and dog. We did good, Toots.

Sixty Minutes
October 23, 1985

Three squirrels — two blacks and a fox — scurried across the maple and beech leaves as I stepped into the hardwoods from the cornfield, walking as slow and quiet as possible.

Two stopped, turned, and watched before scampering off again. Thirty years ago I might have hit all three with the .22 rifle before they reached safety. Twenty years ago I might have got a couple.

Now it was futile to even humor myself into taking a shot. Besides, a decision to hunt or kill hasn't been made. Mary Lou, who relishes most game and fish, won't touch squirrel. Says it looks like a rat, which I guess it is.

Settling down on a stump with a maple for a backrest, I noticed the trails the little varmints had made dragging ears of corn to their hideouts. The tops of several larger maple stumps, including the one I sat on, were covered with shucked corn. They'd been using them as a table. Or maybe the coons had.

A faint movement to the east turned into a fox squirrel when I cranked the Redfield up to seven power. It kept coming, crossing into the corn not fifteen yards from my stump. Soon I had watched at least a half dozen make their way into or out of the corn.

Then the big, heavily furred, gray showed up. He came down a snarly old beech tree. His tail looked about two feet long in the scope. It would dress hundreds of streamer flies.

Who could I give the meat to? Sure as heck someone would enjoy it.

He stopped, head down, about two feet up the trunk. The safety was off and the finger reaching for the trigger.

Ah, hell. Couldn't kill him just for his tail.

He sauntered right by me a few seconds later.

As I watched him duck behind the beech, dragging an ear of corn, something moved down the hill, near the swale. Biggest darn fox squirrel in the woods, for sure.

It moved slowly, but steadily, up the slope, and as it came close it became a simply elegant fox (not squirrel). Red, mahogany, white, and black. At maybe fifty feet, he saw or smelled me. He crouched, seemed to think about ignoring me, then faded into the underbrush.

Chickadees and woodpeckers were on the move. Blue jays were on the muscle. Overhead to the northwest, a flock of several hundred (from the sound) geese flew low. (We've never had so many Canadas around the drumlins.)

The sun was still well above the horizon, but a chill moved up the hill.

The leaves crackled in the direction the fox had taken. Five deer were heading for their evening feast. No racks.

A chainsaw growled in the next section. The spell was over.

Reaching for the tobacco pouch, I noticed it had only lasted an hour. Amazing what you can squeeze from an hour in the north woods, aye?

A Keeper
September 24, 1986

She had taken to swimming and retrieving twigs in a puddle on Beaver Island at five weeks old. That was in mid-July. At six weeks she was stalking butterflies, moths, and grasshoppers — and, oh yes, the cat.

At two months she was swimming into five feet of water — as far as I'd dare throw her retrieving dummy. About that time she took aggressively to afternoon hikes in the thicket that is the woods in mid-summer.

I deliberately led her to haunts of several grouse broods and the uncommon number of woodcock between these drumlins this summer. Often she scented them at twenty or thirty feet and went into her crouching stalk. The flush was, and is, frustrating for her. Under a roof of fern, she can't see more than a blur, then nothing.

She's a lovable, frisky rascal approaching four months. Proud and strutting, with tail cocked at about 145 degrees. Ready to take on anything that enters her world. Strong-willed and strong-headed, but easy to tame. She'll learn anything in seconds, then dares you to make her remember it, unless she wants to.

Thimbo is solid brown: chocolate, they call her. Our first Lab. Not a bird dog.

(Thumper decided to go back to John, share his bedroom, living room, and dining room. Just couldn't get all the way into birds and shotguns. Just as well. A happy ending.)

The first two days of bird season were as soggy as a Central American jungle. Not fit for dog, gun, or man.

So we took our time getting the season underway. (I am always reluctant to start gunning before October. Doesn't seem right to the birds and isn't right for man or dog. Birds should be hunted when the leaves are lavender, or down, and ferns are brown.)

At the edge of the old orchard Thimbo started exploring; coursing ahead and on the flanks twenty to fifty feet. She came back often, as puppies do, to check in with her security.

The late afternoon sun was bright, but the air was barely in the fifties. The ground cover was wet, soaking boots and pants.

Several times a brood of grouse had been flushed under a big old tree near a swale bottom. Hoped she'd jump them there. Nothing, though we went through the cover three times.

Climbing a low ridge to drop over into another bottom edged by popple, she suddenly went into high gear under a big beech — tail out, circling, and sort of whimpering at a dizzy pace. Like she was chasing a chipmunk.

Nothing wrong with a pup having puppy fun.

Then a grouse went out, barreling over the slope. Be damned.

But, whoa! Two young birds flushed and landed in the beech. She ignored them and kept diving and dashing. At least three more birds dove into the tree. I saw two clearly exposed on limbs. Probably could have picked out others.

It was an easy limb-swatting double. But this department doesn't own a gun that shoots a bird on the ground or on a limb. Yeah, but wouldn't it be good for the pup? Bend your principles — just this once.

Hey, only a damn fool shoots grouse this early in the year. They'll be around a long time, provide a lot of sport, if you hold your fire.

Well — what about the pup's first taste of blood?

Nope. Couldn't do it.

Toots would agree.

Time to squat and do some petting and talking. Tell her about the big setter up there on the drumlin, under the varnished mahogany bird house. Time for some wet eyes and lots of rubbing of the little double. Time to reach in the pocket and ring the old bell I carry just to be sure Toots is still with me.

Damn, I still miss you, old lady!

There will never be another Toots. So, why kid yourself. Another bird dog will never take her place. You'll just choke up when you see feathers flying on a tail stiff to the wind behind a point. So why not try a Lab?

After a lot of ear and chin licks, we left the beech and stumbled into the popple. Ferns were up to my belly. Had to keep crouching and beating them down with the shotgun to find her, when she wasn't stumbling over my boots.

A woodcock went out maybe ten yards ahead. Hadn't expected it and I didn't have time to move the gun before it was gone.

Dropping to all fours, I found her slowly, deliberately pacing around where it had flushed. Then turning, she cautiously crept forward in a crouch, tail curving up. Never looking back.

Got myself up just in time to catch the second of two doodles with the right barrel.

Down again in squat position. Thimbo didn't seem to have heard the gun, as she fanned out, then darted straight ahead. When I got there, she had the bird in her mouth and was shaking it. She spit it out, then grabbed it again.

"Sit!" She looked disgusted, but held the bird.

"Fetch!" Not a move. "Fetch! ... Dammit ... fetch!"

She strutted right to me, there on my butt in the ferns. She stood there, opened her mouth on "Deliver!" and gave up the bird. Then reached up and licked my nose.

Be a damn lie to tell you I almost cried.

Whatta ya think Toots? A keeper?

Ghost
November 7, 1984

About two-thirds of the way up a steep drumlin, at the breakline between planted Scotch pine bordering the cornfield on top and the hardwoods, Toots went on her first point. Had to be a bird — most of the doodles have left — and probably a wild one. The gimpy leg was already throbbing and dragging. It would never pump this tattered carcass up there in time to get a shot. But up it started, protesting every inch of elevation.

If Toots hadn't stood at the door rolling her eyes, her tail beating like a banner in a Lake Michigan gale, and sounding off in that deep-throated yowl of excitement, she wouldn't have been invited along. (A coupla days before, she'd behaved like a spoiled brat. She was protesting someone else hunting with us. So she took off and I just sorta ignored her.)

To make amends, today she'd never been out of sight. And every few seconds she'd come by for a fast pat. It was almost as though she was saying, "Look, you and I aren't supposed to hunt with strangers. OK?"

(Frank Ruswick may be a little strange, but I didn't figure he was a stranger. No sense trying to reason with a ten-year-old setter, though. She's gonna do it her way. And, guess I am too.)

The bird was going to hold. Toots hadn't moved and I was only twenty-five feet downhill.

Then she sat down and looked back at me.

"Damn, old lady, you playin' games with me?" I blurted.

She got up and walked sorta stiff-legged around something, sat on the uphill side, and kept looking down.

Wasn't a bird, after all. A good-sized buck scrape. Damn. That's what I'd abandoned the typewriter to find. The bird hunting was only a second thought because Toots begged to come along.

There's been talk — always is — of a really big buck in this drumlin-land. Estimates run from eight points to sixteen. Eight to ten points would be a pretty good bet.

Several rubs were down in the hardwoods, along the swale. One had the bark bare in patches bigger than a man's hand. Three small scrapes were at the edge of the cornfield, two drumlins over.

Calling Toots away, we plopped down on a fallen fence post just through the pines. A substantial post of cedar, about a foot in diameter, it was almost black, with deep veins. Probably virgin stuff, cut in the late 1800s? And used here ever since? .

The old farmhouse's foundation stood at the other end of the eighty until a coupla years ago when Arch cleared the site to enlarge the cornfield. A tractor, worth more than the original farm ever earned in ten years, now tills and chops corn where kids and grand-kids played for three generations.

And the double shotgun resting on the ancient fence post would sell for more than any possession the mother, grandmother, and great grandmother ever owned. The big white setter sitting nearby is worth as much as the draft horses that worked the land and sustained the family.

Funny thoughts? Yeah, maybe.

It bothered me that the well was gone. Gnawed at me as I thumped the pipe out on the post.

A chain saw growled in the gully along the road, where the young fellas cutting firewood show up most evenings after work. The sun danced on the next drumlin to the west, a mile off.

My left arm had been draped over Toots' shoulders and I was about to use them to push the leg under me when I felt her stiffen. She was looking south. Almost pointing.

To the south, beyond the pines and the hardwoods at the crown of the drumlin, to the edge of a grove of young apple trees, a form finally took shape.

A deer. No, by god, a BIG buck. Looking our way, but past us toward the sound of the saw. In the sunlight, the horns glistened like polished bones as he turned his head to the south.

Pressing down to hold Toots still, I picked up the silhouettes of two, maybe three, whitetails at the edge of the orchard, heading toward the hayfield across the road.

Then he looked back. The chainsaw had him nervous. He wanted to join the does, but didn't want to reveal himself.

Squinting hard, I was sure of eight points. At that distance, there had to be more I couldn't see.

He held his ground. Toots didn't move.

Then as though a cloud of ink had dropped from the sky, he became invisible.

The watch said we'd been sitting there just over a half hour. At home the lights would be on and Mary Lou would be listening to "All Things Considered" on public radio.

Toots' head snapped up as the sky started to whistle. A dozen or so mallards circled the chopped corn three times, set their wings, and dropped in.

Low-base 7-1/2s in skeet-bored barrels aren't the tools for ducks.

I briefly thought about trying to shoulder the fence post and take it home. The grain is probably so fine it runs together like tightly rolled writing paper.

Instead, we stepped back into the pines and quietly skirted the field. I didn't want to disturb their evening meal.

The New Dog
September 23, 1987

Yesterday had been clear and dry, and the first day the new bird dog pup, Nails, could have hunted. She'd had a zipper in her tummy from being spayed until then. However, with the weather so perfect, the typewriter and telephone wouldn't let us go.

So it was now; her first hunt under the gun. I don't know how many birds she's pointed since she was about two months old. But today we might try to shoot one.

The bracken was chest-high and soaking wet. Even the old Filson tin pants, usually impregnable, were soggy by the time we reached the popples. Nails was invisible under the ferns. But she checked in every few seconds; afraid the old man would leave her, I suppose.

The first grouse went out wild, far out of sight, seconds after we reached bird country. A few minutes later, I found her on point where the popple and bracken break into the alders. Cutting across and in front of her, the bird went out from a clump of cedars. Not a chance for a shot.

But geez, she'd had that bird nailed at a good forty feet.

She points sorta classy — for me. One paw up, back stretched out, nose reaching, tail at more than half mast, yet sorta relaxed, lifting one paw then the other, nose well off the ground. (Toots would be proud of this precious puppy.)

She also chases butterflies, red squirrels, and chickadees. Lots of stuff like that. Fine with me. We're in this to have fun.

Moving to the swamp edge — no one can figure birds out at this time of year — I found her on point near one of the massive fire-charred cedar stumps I've never been able to explain. Two birds went out about thirty feet from her.

I'm sure I could have dropped one of them. Maybe two. (Man, that's a big brag!) But it isn't time to kill grouse, yet. The killing season on them shouldn't open until October. Here, where the chances of anyone else hunting or killing are so slim, we'll save 'em until October.

The tangle under the dogwood berries was so thick and high that my eye glasses were running water as I walked through it.

After drying them, I found her on point where the jungle starts uphill and breaks into birch and cedar.

Another grouse. Easy shot. Some would argue that I should have taken it — for the pup. Nuts. She isn't here for dead birds. She's here because we enjoy this. Like being where birds live.

Then I lost her. She was somewhere to the southwest, on a knoll of high ground under an unexaggerated blanket of fern leaves. So thick you couldn't see your feet if you stopped to look.

I almost stumbled over her. She was on point and gave me a disgusted look.

A woodcock whistled out from under the bracken not more than four feet from her nose. It just barely cleared the top of the ferns and leveled out.

The little stub-stocked, 12-gauge side-by-side slammed into my shoulder. The bird disappeared. I wasn't sure if it was down.

"Fetch! Nails! Fetch!"

She was a tornado going through the ferns, going crazy. Not looking for the dead bird. Looking for another live bird to point.

"Stop! Stay!"

With some petting she cooled off. Ready to think again.

"Fetch!"

Seconds later she was standing over the doodle. Pawing it, gently. Not willing to pick it up.

She'll learn in due time. Right now it didn't matter.

She sat there with nose high, tail swishing the ground. Shoulders sorta shaking with excitement, asking: "Hey, old man, not bad, aye?"

Yeah, kid. Not bad.

For a second I thought I was gonna have to reach for a handkerchief. Instead I crouched down and grabbed her. Kissed her square on that big cold, wet nose. Then on the ears and neck.

(Aww, geez, Toots, it is good to be back. You'd love her, old lady — and I miss you still.)

One Good Turn ...
November 6, 1985

The pickup truck at the northwest corner of the cornfield, under the rangy beech, meant there would be no duck shooting this evening. The truck's owner has a tree stand in the hardwoods on the west side of the field. Duck shooting would foul up his bow hunting. And he was here first.

Don't know if he'd do the same for me. Seems like a pretty decent guy, though.

Yet, I didn't want to leave. It promised to be a grand evening for just looking and listening. And duck shooting isn't what it used to be. Tired eyes are a plague; can't see whether shooting hen or drake, so can only take one at a time.

The cornfield is on the top of a drumlin, as so many of them are, because that's where the glacier left the best soil. It reaches way out to the south, toward Torch Lake. On the east it drops down to the house and barns. The hardwoods slope down on the west and off, maybe three miles, is Lake Michigan. To the north is a swale and then cedar swamp.

The corn had been picked a few days earlier, with an unchopped strip near the center, at the peak of the drumlin. Standing in it, hidden, you can see off to the horizon in all directions.

Overhead it was clear. Above the lake, faint clouds looked like gray lace over the water.

The first movement came from the north, as a string of deer confidently moved into the field. The binoculars picked up one small rack. They spread out slowly, does and fawns staying together in small groups.

Then to the south, a movement turned into four more deer, already feeding in the corn. Just after 5:00 p.m., but getting dark — the cursed daylight savings.

Glassing whitetails as more came to feed, I didn't realize the sky was full of ducks until I heard their wings. Wow! Must have been 150 to 200, probably all mallards.

They circled, broke into three flocks, and one bunch, maybe fifty or more, and dropped into the corn near me. The others disappeared to the south, probably going into the end of the field.

The big bunch near me was soon marching down the rows of bent stalks like soldiers, gabbling, and picking up corn.

With a rush of wings, they then lifted off to join a new flight coming in from the southwest. Ten guys could easily have limited out.

I mumbled a curse and remembered we already had plenty of ducks in the freezer. Whistling wings sounded better than roaring 12-gauges, anyway. At least tonight.

When they settled into the field, they were so near I could hear them picking up corn. Probably imagined it, but thought I could hear their feet shuffling.

As the light started to fade rapidly, I got to wondering why the bow hunter was on the west side of the field. All of the deer had come in from the north and south. He seemed savvy enough. Must know something I didn't.

Minutes later I picked out a patch of gray in a small clump of Scotch pine at the edge of the hardwoods. The glasses hinted at it being a whitetail, but not much could be seen. It didn't move for at least a minute. Then like a seeping shadow it stepped out of the pines and under a low hanging maple.

Found the rack when I saw movement in the limb above his head. Nice. A certain eight points, maybe more. Wide and high. Heavy shoulders. He pawed at the ground slowly, with determination.

Expected an arrow any moment. The hunter must have found the scrape and have his stand within range.

Nothing. Suddenly the buck disappeared. That was it. Gone.

Over the lake the sky blazed in long willowy curtains of orange and red. In the field it was dark and starting to get cold. Couldn't move for fear of spooking the buck and thereby ruining the archer's chances. So I waited until darkness and trudged back to the truck.

The bow hunter beat me back. He was stashing his gear. He saw that I didn't have the shotgun.

"Not hunting?"

"Nope. Just came to look. Lots of ducks, maybe come back tomorrow morning. See anything?"

"Lots of does and a coupla small bucks. There's a big one in there. I'm waiting for a shot at him."

I opened the thermos offered him a cup of tea. He took it, rubbing cold hands around the cup.

"Geez, that hits the spot. Tastes different. Sorta sweet but not really sweet."

"Yeah, it has honey in it."

We stood there a few minutes, harvesting the last of the sunset.

Thought about telling him where the scrape is and suggesting he move his stand to it. But decided it was something he should figure out for himself.

Getting into his truck he paused briefly with the door open: "I appreciate your not hunting. Saw the shotgun (in my truck) and know you didn't want to ruin my hunting. Damn good of you."

Well worth it if he'll do the same for someone else someday.

Waiting For A Drumlin Christmas
December 14, 1988

Nails was celebrating her escape from the confinement of deer season. She roared through four inches of snow in the swale bordering the railroad right-of-way south of Phelps Station. The powdery flakes whirled in her wake as she galloped in loops through the willows and cedars that border them.

Still a pup at eighteen months. Let it be. This was not a serious hunting venture. The only gun was a hefty Colt match target model Woodsman. John Robertson had said he'd eat all of the squirrels we could put in the freezer (Mary Lou won't eat them). No squirrels here, but maybe a rabbit. Then again, there would be squirrels in the hardwoods on the drumlin coming back to our old bivouac at Phelps Station.

Nails disappeared into the willows and dogwoods. Not to worry; she always checks back when she realizes the old man is out of sight.

She must have kicked up the rabbit without knowing it. If she'd seen it she would give chase — something to fetch, you know.

It was no more than a momentary blur of movement at first. Maybe just a windblown swirl of snow. Then it took form as it headed southeast.

Moving slowly, the pistol came out of the shoulder holster, the left hand clamped onto and cocked it as the right arm shoved it forward. Eyes that haven't seen a clear pattern in iron sights in years squinted and found the barrel — well, sorta.

Tracking the hare over the foggy outline of the barrel, the pistol came to a wobbly rest as it halted beside the roots of a cedar. The .22 long rifle round barked. A fluff of snow spread sparkling dust two feet from the target.

The pistol came back to shoulder level. The hare hadn't moved.

This time with the left hand supporting the right, the trigger was about to send a second round at the target when a wisp of white came through the corner of the right eye. It was Nails, hot to check out what was going on.

The pistol went down. The rabbit took off. Nails never noticed. I snapped the clip out of the autoloader and cleared the chamber (loaded pistols scare me if they aren't aimed at something I think I want to shoot).

Nails does not, of course, see the ghosts that haunt this place between Lake 26 and County Line. She can't hear the wail of the big redbone, Call, as he brings a fox out of the drumlins and down into the swamp. As he circles and turns the fox toward me, waiting to hear the sound of the .225 Winchester.

Those were glorious years. They ended more than a decade ago; wiped out first by snowmobiles, second by home development, and finally, when the big hound died that winter day under my desk.

The time and place could not endure. Progress left no place for a solitary man on snowshoes tracking a hound through the winter boondocks.

I still hear that throaty bellow when I return on winter mornings. He's out there yet, the scent of a red fox forever sweetening his nostrils as he swallows deep for another trumpet call.

The legs that once kept the snowshoes flailing from dawn to dusk in the wake of his glorious music now stumble and plod. But the time and place live on, if only in a memory.

Nor does Nails have any memory of Toots, the bird dog who grew up in these drumlins around Lake 26. She left us more than three years ago. I'll refinish the mahogany bird house that marks her grave again this winter. More than any other hunting pal, she continues to haunt me.

Thanks to Mary Lou's constant reminders, Nails was not raised in Toots' image. There can be no more eight-hour days behind a bird dog. The old fool is paying the piper for a young fool's immortality. A couple hours, with numerous stump-sitting breaks, is the best we can do.

Not that Nails couldn't rival Toots. She has the talent and spunk for it. I am the one that lacks the mettle. So we just sorta play at it.

Someday the public will recognize the tragic blunder when the government let the railroad pull the tracks from this right-of-way and sell it. That will come, I assured myself, as we moved east into the thick of the cedars.

Nails had disappeared. Her tracks blended with those of a packed deer trail. I need not worry, she isn't interested in the deer. Deer have used this precise route since I started hunting here more than twenty years ago. Nature has its own secrets. I followed the trail, just as I have many times in the past.

At the edge of the drumlin, where the trail turns south to skirt the drumlin, close to the cover of the cedars, Nails' tracks skirt up the slope.

A third of the way up where the cedars begin to blend with popple, she was motionless — ghostly dull white with spotty orange. On
point under three spruce trees.

She must have been there a while. She'd become bored. Her
fanny was plunked in the snow, while her back and nose were still
straight, aimed at the upper branches of the trees. Her tail had
wagged a fan shape in the snow.

At least three grouse were perched in the trees, about fifteen to
twenty feet up. Even I could have hit one with the pistol.

It would have made her day. It would have ruined mine. Grouse
that have made it to December deserve better than the gun.

Turning back, we skirted the cornfield. Where the popples border
the cornfield and the railroad, Toots once held point while I shot
three grouse; one of them a long, angling, shot that dropped the bird
almost squarely between the rails — rails that are no longer there,
like memories that swirl into a winter night.

Back at the car, Nails gnawed at the snowballs on her paws as I
poured steaming tea from the thermos. Inviting her into the front
seat I clasped her two front paws in my hands to help thaw the snow
between her toes, then squeezed her neck as she slurped at my ear.

Even after starting the car there was no rush to leave.

Christmas in this drumlin country has always been magical.

As the first swallow of honey-sweetened tea warmed my throat,
the windshield filled with the vision of a cherub-faced infantryman
hunkering in a foxhole at twenty below, a lifetime ago.

*The brass had promised we could go to the Bob Hope USO show that
Christmas. They then decided we were needed elsewhere.*

*"Sir," he said, cold and as disgusted with his Christmas prospects as we
all were, "I got some water boiling, and three or four C-ration packets of
instant coffee. How about a Christmas drink with me?"*

I suppose I didn't. But damn well knew I should.

*He talked about his mom, how hard she'd worked since his dad died, and
how he had this girl (he pulled out some letters, but the light was bad, and
the cold made them watery) back home in North Dakota.*

*And he'd been sending all of his money (fifty some bucks a month I
think it was then) home so they'd have a good Christmas.*

*Oh, and he had this picture of his older sister's first baby. But, geez, I
couldn't see anything by then. (Probably the rancid taste of that C-ration
coffee?)*

As the heat started to pour from the car heater, Nails sorta collapsed on the seat.

Mary Lou's been pushing me to get the tree up. I don't want to rush this Christmas thing too fast — just try to savor it for all it is worth. Maybe tomorrow morning, when a flurry of goldfinches attack the thistle feeders at dawn, I'll see if I can find the tree stand.

A Perfect Day
October 21, 1987

The bamboo sinews of the Paul Young Parabolic stretched into the back cast, sending the number 8, 4X-long Mickey Finn streamer fly whistling past my ear.

This rod, crafted by Bob Summers, is slow. It takes time to become accustomed to its cadence after a summer of casting faster, shorter, much lighter dry fly cane rods. It is a powerful beast, though. What it lacks in grace it makes up for in thrust.

The loop straightened out far over my shoulder and the corks leaned into the fore cast. Like a mighty spring, the cane almost groaned as it lurched forward, firing the streamer fly far out over the river into the swirl just above the bend of the current. Slack line played out as the fly twisted and sank in the heart of the water.

Huge, muscled, salmon — some dark, some silver — cavorted in the river, from its wide slack water ending at the lake to its gnarled, shallow beginning in the hills. The inch-and-a-half-long fly was not aimed at them. A profane thought.

In reality it was targeted at nothing. An electro-shocking survey a few weeks earlier had confirmed what we've told the biologists for more than a decade; salmon, lampricide, and sand have wiped out the resident trout, except in the very uppermost headwaters, where a remnant population survives. Down here, where the season lingers year around, the chances of catching a real trout are about as good as an old editor's chances of walking on water.

On shore under the overhanging cedars and tamaracks, the bird dog pup's tail swept the needles and grasses like a broom, as her head followed the rod and line. She knew the little double gun and shell vest were in the car.

She's learned to like the game we play in the woods. With the cover mostly down and the season half-finished, she's had her gums on several grouse and her paws on more woodcock. She's figured out this is what she's all about.

So why are we puttering around in the river? There are no good smells there. The action is at the edge of the conifers, where the birches, popples, and alders hold sway. Where the berry patches grab at her feathers and puffballs draw October-fat grouse.

Well, she'd have to be patient. This is a part of the annual rhythm; one last moment to make love with the river — to feel the

current hug and tug at us. To feel the magic of the rod and the wonder of a perfect cast. To be near running water. To turn over in your
hand the beauty of fur and feathers twisted on a shank of iron. To
resurrect a pledge to spend more hours this winter squinting over
the tying vise.

As ancient and perfect as the grouse woods are, there is something more intoxicating about fly fishing. It draws deeper of the soul.
It is more of a commitment. It is where life begins. And ends.

It isn't catching fish. It is being there. Being a part of something
that is harder to identify, to understand. It is a lot of things you really
can't put on paper; that this typewriter hasn't learned to quantify. It
is meditation and beauty.

Beautiful stuff that you fear would disappear if it could be
explained in print.

Nails didn't care about that business. But she seemed happy to
just be there.

The nearly sixty-degree water wasn't much colder than it had
been in August. But the air barely nipped fifty degrees. Even in the
waders it turned cool darn fast.

Reluctantly, but also happily, the time came to snip the fly off the
3X tippet, wind the line and leader onto the reel, and call it a day,
and a season.

Clamoring up the bank and shuffling through the woods toward
the car, I tried to remember if there had ever been a bad trout season.
Probably, in the mid years, say from age seventeen to thirty, when
the pursuit of trout in the creel had been so intense I didn't find time
to idly marvel at the stunning wonder of a tiny mayfly's wings and
to fall victim to the current's spell.

The thought brought a chuckle. Those years are long behind us.
Surviving them is what earned us the privilege of fishing where
brook trout live — or at least used to live.

At the car, the waders came off and the boots went on. The fly
vest was replaced by the shell vest and the rod by the shotgun. I
would at least give Nails a few minutes to vacuum the bracken in
search of bird scent.

Not 200 yards from the trail, she started twisting and darting,
around and around, in an ever tighter circle. Under a rotting blowdown elm she finally froze — on point.

I've learned that at seven months she knows her trade, and there
would be a bird, or more than one, within easy range of the 7-1/2

bird shot.

The hard decision was whether I wanted to kill anything on this last day of trout fishing.

Thumb on the safety, I moved, slowly, in front of her.

Egads! She was perfect, by my standards. (So much so, I was overwhelmed that this had happened to me again. More than two years ago, when Toots left me, I'd been sure it never would.)

A bird went off to the left. A wild shot, at best. He'd been under some blackberry brambles. How she'd scented him was baffling.

Then a bird went out from under the blowdown, not twenty feet from Nails. She stiffened. I shot. The bird crumbled. She cagily shifted four or five feet to the right and stiffened.

A bird, then another, flushed at the edge of the blowdown.

The gun never came up.

A guy can only handle so many riches in one day.

As tea water simmered over the little gas stove on the tailgate of the Suburban, she sat there, tail swishing, big eyes gaping, first at the tired guy with the bent legs and then at the bird I'd dropped in front of her to boast over.

Who was that jerk who said life is never perfect?

Old Ivory Horns
November 4, 1987

In the 1940s, the top of the drumlin was planted with Scotch pines. They now stand there like thirty-foot high, paralyzed soldiers on a bleak parade field. In closed ranks. Rigid. Symbolic, but of little or no practical purpose.

Only the uppermost limbs survive, due to lack of sunlight penetrating the overstory. You can look through this hostile tree plantation as if it were an orchard of telephone poles, except that in the interior it gets dark. On summer days it is suffocating.

The best thing that could happen here, you conclude on every visit, is an Army engineers bulldozer training drill.

The drumlin falls off fast to the west. Beside the pines are the narrow remains of an old two-track. Beyond is a swath of popples and birches which bow to alders and then swale — tangled and boggy.

Puppies being puppies, Nails had disappeared into the swale after she pointed, then wildly flushed two woodcock far from the shotgun. Like kids, puppies need to do their own exploring, make their own mistakes, to find their way in the world. (Accept that truth, try to keep them from fatal blunders, and life will go better for puppies, kids, and you.)

Taking the easier path, I plodded along the old two-track, waiting for her to extract herself from the mire. She'd be back soon, with tangled and matted fur, pickers, and weed sticks. Mary Lou would holler at the door: "Keep her out there until you've brushed her." But she'd relent after I make a token effort.

Since there wasn't a bundle of white and amber to watch, my eyes focussed on a three-foot-square patch of scuffed bare ground. In the middle of it, under the supplicating limbs of a Scotch pine, was the biggest deer track I've seen in several years — larger than half the size of my hand.

Serious deer hunting hasn't interested me in several years. (Too many hunters interfering in the quest.) But geez, that did it. Forget Nails. She'll find her way back.

In the next half mile along the side of the drumlin were eleven more buck scrapes. About half of them showed the big track around them. All were fresh, from yesterday or today.

Eleven — in about a half mile.

Nails came dashing back. Panting and sitting to stare into my eyes, expecting praise for her misadventure. The impulse to scold was easily overcome, as was the impulse to continue the pursuit of birds.

From our wanderings, I surmised that hunters had not entered this secluded part of the section since Archie or Jim cut the corn to the south of the drumlin. (Archie doesn't welcome bow hunters. Right or wrong, he figures they wound too many of the deer he feeds.)

Cutting around the end of the swale, we started along the side of the drumlin to the west. There they were again: buck scrape after buck scrape. And the big track in many of them.

I lost count. But maybe two dozen in the course of a mile and a half.

They disappeared as we went into the hardwoods and then the cedar along the lake.

Three or four dozen geese sat honking on the lake about twenty-five yards from the jungle of cedars. A fast grab on the collar kept Nails from vaulting into the lake after them.

The lake has never been developed. The cedars may be virgin. Many are huge old trees, with layers of still bright green moss on their trunks. Many are blown down. Walking is almost impossible. Instead you climb over and through them, careful not to slip into the potholes at their base.

Truly a wild place. Yet it is just over the drumlin from a cornfield and county road.

Still holding onto her collar, Nails and I sat at the base of one of the larger fallen cedars. The geese were unaware of us. If the shotgun were armed with high base number 2s or 4s, I could have easily killed a giant Canada with each barrel; like shooting fence posts. (But it would have been a darn cold swim to retrieve them.)

I don't know how long we'd been there. Long enough that Nails lay down and, constantly watching me, started gnawing at the burrs in her tail and fanny.

The sun was down behind the drumlins between us and home when the cold started seeping through the sweatshirt and shell vest.

We hadn't walked ten feet when the buck came out of a gnarl of blowdown cedars maybe fifty feet from us. He was a blur of bone white and deep gray with shoulders that looked as wide as one of Archie's Belgium draft horses (but, of course, weren't). He went straight up the slope, through the pole-size maples, beech, and basswood, and then disappeared — in seconds.

With a rifle it is doubtful I would have had a shot.

Jim and Archie still talk, in awe, of a legendary old buck they call Ivory Horns. He hasn't been seen in years. His rack size varied from twelve to twenty points. Wide as a crosscut saw, by some accounts. No one is known to have killed him. Just expired of old age, the legend has it. He'd be fifteen to twenty years old now.

They tell how, when chopping corn, they'd see him in October and early November. He'd be at the end of the field, ignoring and tantalizing them. Strutting that picture-window-size rack.

Hunting seasons must have been tense back then, with every rustle along the deer runs thought to be old Ivory Horns. But he never presented himself for a shot.

They say that he would retreat to the farthest, deepest reaches of the swamps and bogs that flank these drumlins the night of November fourteenth.

The throat-choking, near elk-size beast that erupted within bird shot range of us very probably is one of old Ivory Horns' senior progeny. A noble and rare creature. An ultimate specimen of one of wildlife's most admirable species.

For many years I stalked and dreamed of standing over a magnificent buck like him. No longer. The lust for trophies has vanished. Where it has gone I cannot fathom (youth, maybe). But gone it is.

Old Ivory Horns, Jr. belongs to Archie or to Jim or to story tellers. He is the passion that fires younger breasts.

But he is for real. That's good enough for me. Call it a sacrilege, but I'll settle for a fat, corn-fed doe and dreams of mice, squirrels, and porcupines gnawing on discarded racks come January.

Thumper's Fire
December 18, 1985

It was Thumper's first campfire. Since being liberated from the oblivion of a kennel he's had many new experiences. He kind of grows into them.

Not nearly as bright as Toots, the bird dog whose pillow he now claims, he has learned to mellow, slowly but warmly, overcoming the beatings he's suffered at a trainer's hands. Our first bird season was a mixture of rain, rain, and more rain. There were few birds.

By the end of the season he was reliable. Big. Handsome. Staunch. Never flicking an ear when the 12-gauge roared. Leaping to the retrieve — but putting too much tooth into it.

There weren't a lot of birds. But enough. The little double, with the twelve and a half-inch stock, never fired unless it was a sure thing. Not a bird was missed!

He's grown so you can trust him not to leap over the seat into your lap in the car. At home he sits quietly at the end of the desk or beside the easy chair, his tail throbbing slowly, but no longer desperately seeking assurance he won't be pitched out.

This afternoon was something new. He'd been on picnics, seen fires, sat begging beside them for a scrap of steak or hamburger. But this was the real thing.

There was nearly two feet of snow in the drumlin, where the wind howled, and more down in the swamp. After a month of dragging a lame leg, things were working again. I was desperate to get down into the woods, and away from the light switches, typewriter, and telephone.

There was no other purpose. Within a quarter mile of the top of the drumlin we could be in wilderness. The road is closed for the winter beyond Box 193. So there is no vehicle traffic. In the Lake Michigan blizzard there would be no airplanes. Just blessed peace and — a muted silence!

I'd stuffed a wad of newspaper and an empty bread bag with a couple fistfuls of wood chips in it into the cargo pocket of the old Mackinaw.

When we reached the swamp, it took about three minutes to break up a pile of dead birch twigs and branches. A few kicks in the snow beside the tangle of blowdown cedar produced a wind-free crater.

Thumper had taken it all in stride. Prancing, then watching.

It took only seconds to kindle the blaze. In five minutes we had a warm, but fast, fire. Not much heat. But lots of character.

A pocketful of sunflower seed cast on the snow and the hot seat made it a much-needed refuge after a month of unrelenting confinement.

Thumper started ranging in ever widening circles plowing through snow over his chest. (He stands high, one of the tallest English setters I've known.) I had forgotten him in the magic of the flames when he returned, plopping that big head on my lap, almost tipping over the cup of tea poured from the thermos.

As they always will, the chickadees had found the sunflower seed. The little downy woodpeckers, always curious, had also arrived. For a moment I wondered if a rabbit would come out of the swamp and join us.

Thumper's tail beat a funnel-shaped groove in the snow. He too, became mesmerized by the flames, as I fed them with a steady stream of dead birch limbs. He seemed to even forget I was with him.

Familiar figures began flirting through the flames. At first, there was Dad and his pals at trout and bird camps a half century ago. Then there were hunched-over, hollow-eyed guys, always with an M1 over their shoulder, always asking why we hadn't been pulled back for Christmas. Comrades with tired, grey faces who never talked about the next Christmas; only the old ones — "old" ones for seventeen, eighteen, and nineteen-year-olds.

Mac came out of the haze, talked to Sergeant Campbell and sat down beside Thumper. Wanted to know how disappointed the men were in spending another Christmas here. Wanted to know about their morale? His eyes dreamed of the beautiful Mississippi girl he'd married right out of West Point and the son she'd written him about.

Thumper bolted upright, spun about. Snow flakes the size of two thumbs drifted through the spruce and cedar.

Thumper's tail straightened, then relaxed.

The spell was broken. The fire only embers.

But not the memories. They come strong at Christmas. I hope you have a campfire, chickadees, a bird dog, and a lover this Christmas.

Livable Places
November 1, 1989

Nails, the little bird dog, went nuts. It made no sense. Less so to her than me. She ran in circles, then keyed off in long dashes with her nose obviously in frantic tension.

This pup can smell a woodcock at fifty feet. What was she searching for?

I've hunted this cover along the former C&O railroad tracks for twenty-five years. It has grown too old and sparse in some places, and too thick in others. But it is still fun country. A full three miles of wildness from our former bivouac at Phelps to little Ellsworth.

Finally reining her in, I plopped on a blowdown and hugged her until she started to calm down. Snapping the piece of frayed cord I carry in my shell vest onto her collar, we headed up the drumlin, planning to cross the cornfield to hunt the cedar and popple edges beyond it.

Clearing the hardwoods on the drumlin, my nostrils snorted. They'd just spread liquid — ah — fertilizer on the field. Ripe! Must have blown Nails' smeller into orbit!

So we dropped into the swale to the south. With the wind blowing from the north toward the field, I figured that she'd settle down to business. But no, she was done for the day. Wanted to be a pal. Like, "let's go for a walk in the woods, buddy." Not a hunter.

Fair enough. There are days when I'd rather sit in the sun and read poetry than sit behind a typewriter and try to tell what is happening in the north woods. She gets her days, too. So should you.

The weather was right out of a fairy tale for late October. The temperature at 4 p.m. was in the mid 70s, with a clear, bright sky. As we started into the remnants of an apple orchard near where we parked the car, a squirrel hunter emerged, sweat soaking his shirt.

Too nice to pack up and leave. We rested again at a place along a creek that is the uppermost drainage of the Elk River (Torch Lake) watershed (where once Toots held steady, despite my protests, until I killed a mixed double — woodcock and grouse).

The little Dutch community of Ellsworth was about a mile due south of us. It is a quiet, sorta battered little place on the upper chain of lakes. There's a fair hardware store, probably one too many groceries, a bar, a working man's diner, and two of the most celebrated restaurants in Michigan. You can launch a boat here and travel miles in pretty much unspoiled lakes and the connecting river channel.

Just a few days before, Mary Lou and I had hitched up the old (1964) fourteen-foot "tin" boat and journeyed to Ellsworth through the St. Clair swamp channel, connecting St. Clair Lake and Six Mile Lake. Took us about an hour up and back. We didn't see a person. It was wild, and quiet. Paradise.

We had fled the house with the phone ringing at 4:30 p.m. Back at six p.m. Totally purged of deadline pressures and the meanness that comes from dealing with Lansing politicians and bureaucrats.

Now the sun was closing in on its date with Lake Michigan as Nails and I headed back for the car. A newspaper story I'd read a day or two before gnawed at me. Seems somebody decided Seattle was the best place in the country to live. I could only read the first two or three paragraphs.

Now, admittedly, I don't know much about Seattle. The only time I've been there was to get on a troop ship. That, in itself, is one of life's lousiest prospects. The air was so humid that smoke from the coal stoves in the army barracks was suffocating.

Sure, that ain't an objective comparison. But I suspect that Ellsworth is one helluva lot better place to live than Seattle. And what about Bellaire, just down the crick?

Now I know the article was comparing only well-known places, and probably those in metropolitan areas. But Seattle settles into the murk when you start considering Norwood (not a store or condo in the township). Miles of Lake Michigan frontage and vistas.

Ponder it for a few seconds. How many hundreds of places in Michigan would you rather call home than those rated tops in this poll? The top finishers were Seattle, San Francisco, Pittsburg, Washington, D.C., San Diego, Boston, New York.

Consider dusky, but honest, Alpena, Rogers City, Cedarville, DeTour, Grand Marais, Crystal Falls, Frankfort. The list is endless. Northern Michigan is loaded with treasures.

It is best they not be discovered. When they are, their charm fades under a quagmire of tinsel, as proven by Charlevoix, Gaylord, Traverse City, Harbor Springs, Leland, Mackinaw City, and Northport.

And, I hope the last troop ship has sailed out of Seattle.

Deer Hunting
December 3, 1986

I don't know why it popped into mind after all these years. But it was a vexing thing almost fifty years ago.

Dad didn't deer hunt. Everyone else's dad took off in mid-November to hunt deer — except mine. Made me worry. Geez, real men went deer hunting.

Dad was sorta nuts about hunting birds — ruffed grouse and woodcock. He thought that duck hunting was pretty good, too. Once in a while he'd go rabbit or squirrel hunting. But we knew that was just to humor brother Mike and me.

Until the canoes drove him from the Au Sable, he was into trout fishing. Smallmouth bass fishing in the Huron River — down by Dexter — was, maybe, his favorite.   All with a fly rod. (Far as I know he never owned anything else.)

But deer hunting? It didn't even exist as far as he was concerned.

I dared to ask him about it a couple of times. The answer was something like it was too popular to have any class. Those weren't his words. But it came out like that.

Dad and Mom made the long journey up Thanksgiving. I now don't have to ask his reasons for scorning deer hunting. The pickup truck lights that shine in our windows after we've gone to bed night after night in November, the slobs who trespass, the nerds who drive the roads during the day thinking they're gonna catch a twenty-point buck standing there waiting to be blown away tell me all I need to know about the class of what I fear to be the majority of deer hunters.

There ain't much class left in anything anymore. Fly fishing and bird hunting seem to have been commercialized into status symbols by Trout Unlimited and the Ruffed Grouse Society. They line up along the Au Sable and in grouse coverts like boy scouts in uniform. They talk a pattering language that makes Dad's fears nauseatingly true — that anything that becomes so popular loses class.

Coming down the south end of the drumlin, where the junipers make walking near-impossible, where the spring bubbles out of the ground turning the leaves and soil into a blackish mire, I stopped to ponder these musings. Maybe seven or eight feet down the slope, just beyond where the eight-inch-wide trickle splits, with one flowing down the south slope and the other north, there were tracks nearly as wide as my palm.

If you'd been there, I'd have proclaimed: "Buck, big darn buck."

But, since you weren't, the truth is I'm no smarter about those things than DNR chief Gordon Guyer or any of the PhD wildlife folks from his beloved Michigan State University. I don't know a buck track from a doe track — any more than they do.

It was one darn big deer track, heading right down the drumlin and into the hump of hardwoods in the swale where my hunting blind is. It might have been one of the two eight-pointers we've been seeing since September. Or even the ten-pointer. No one had shot them.

That wouldn't turn Dad on. But forty-five minutes later, down on the blind, he might have taken a liking for deer hunting.

The dried beech leaves on the saplings kept up a constant din in the light wind. A small herd of cows might have passed a few yards away without being heard. So you really didn't have to worry about shooting a deer, and then gutting it, and dragging it up the drumlin to the house. You could relax and not concern yourself about the possibility of all that hard work.

With the season nearing an end, I'd been overly generous with the bait — sunflower seeds and stale peanuts, but mostly cashews, no less, from Sonny Lang's fudge shop in town. One or more chickadee had grown brave enough to perch on my knee for the seeds balanced there. Others scampered along a log covered with seeds not five feet away.

But the most interesting were the mice. At least a half dozen. Gnawing on and carrying off the big cashews. Two of them worked as a pair. They'd sorta nuzzle up against each other now and then. Next they'd be nose to nose, each chewing on a different end of a big peanut. With winter coming on, it seems like an unfavorable time to be so friendly. But shucks, what do I know about mice?

Makes you envy those college folks who make a living studying one-track stuff — like mice, or birds, or wild grasses. Butterflies and mayflies would turn me on, too. (But Dad never told us kids people made a living doing those kinds of things. I always thought you had to make something. You know — like cars, heating ducts, newspapers, stuff like that.)

Two of the mice discovered the fist-size pile of nuts I'd dropped by my right boot. They dashed in and started grabbing. One became alarmed and spurted away sending cashews half the size of its head flying.

Dang, man, this is living.

Somebody sneezed. What? Somebody sneezed?

One of the mice dashed behind my pant leg. I wondered if he was gonna be in my shorts in a second.

The somebody was a small buck. I finally picked out the rack; two points on one side. Maybe two on the other side. There were a bunch of saplings in the way.

The buck seemed to sense something was wrong. Just stood there. Maybe the nuthatches and mice were sending him a message. But why would they think a guy who had been feeding them for nearly a month would do anyone harm?

Dumb thought. But true. A guy who is wacky enough to bait his deer blind for songbirds and mice doesn't want to blow away a deer. The little fella turned southeast and ambled into the swamp along the lake.

Deer season was over. The little folks are gonna have to find the feeders by the house to enjoy handouts over the next few months. The mice are welcome; Sonny loaded me up with plenty of peanuts.

If it doesn't snow too hard in the next few days, think I'll bring Mary Lou down and show her all the bird nests that are visible since the leaves fell. (Damn, wish I knew which birds made them. It's tempting to think about making a living studying bird nests.)

You see, Dad, there can be some class in deer hunting — even if there isn't much in deer killing.

A Great Opening Day
September 25, 1985

The bracken was waist-high. Popple leaves helped wipe the mosquitoes and sweat off my neck. Only a ruddy fool would be out here pretending to hunt birds. But Thumper, the four-year-old, gunshy setter needs the experience and confidence.

And confidence he lacks. Every time he felt he lost me, he panicked; leaping high above the bracken, neck craning frantically, yelping in distress.

Egads, John, what a burden you've dumped on this old fool.

Then, where the cedars blend into popple, the bell went silent. Moving fast, I got there on time. He was locked onto something; standing tall and tight, tail stiff, left front paw raised. Paying no attention, not even looking, as I moved in through the ferns.

The woodcock flushed wild. The little double swung, picked the bird up easily, just dodging into the cedar and tags. Thumper didn't move. I held off the trigger. Too soon to test him on the roar of a 12-gauge.

Enough! He'll make it. Now he was dripping white, foamy saliva from the unbearable temperature and stifling humidity at the swamp's edge. My shirt had soaked through into the shell vest. Britches were heavy with sweat. Dumb time to open bird season.

Less than a minute later at the creek, I longed to join him as he bellied down and sunk his muzzle deep into the current. Still afraid, though, that he'd lose the first real pal he'd ever known; he constantly looked up, plaintively wanting reassurance that he hadn't been deserted.

Ah, it will take time. Maybe a coupla years, to turn him into the bird dog he should be. A challenge worth accepting; worth proving to yourself you can handle.

If you've been in this bird and fish chasing and conservation game long, you've learned that time should not, cannot be crowded. There is no perfection. But you keep striving for it, and you are haunted by the understanding that time is not a factor in a perfect work.

And there is no conclusion, no finality. A near-perfect point, a near-perfect shot, or a near-perfect cast one day can turn into abject clumsiness the next. No conservation battle is permanently won. You will never write a story that you couldn't have written better.

If you can turn a stumbling puppy, or a cringing, beaten older setter into a happy, secure pal who lives to hunt, find, and point birds for you, you have accomplished something rare.

Thumper would have sat forever by the creek with me, I think, tail swishing in the tall grass, if I'd kept rubbing his neck and chattering.

Instead, we headed around the other side of the hill, back toward trail and truck. At first, he hung beside me. Then the spirit hit him again, and he swung out, getting brave enough to hunt.

Coming up the hill, the bell went silent again. There by a blowdown, he was on point. Stretched out, tail stiff, leg up, ignoring me. Damn! (My lovely old Toots would sorta half-sit when she pointed; "not gonna get too serious about this business ... too much fun, you know.")

The grouse held tight, flushing maybe thirty feet from me. A young bird, flying uphill in the open. An easy shot. I didn't touch the trigger.

Thumper moved forward, stiff-legged, sure of himself. He then clicked back on point not ten feet further. Moving slightly ahead of him, two more little birds flushed. Might have been an easy double. Then a third.

Thumper moved cautiously, slowly; then faster, as he swept the area smelling for sign of more birds. There were none.

The truck was less than a quarter mile away. I checked the gun to make sure I hadn't put any shells in it.

Opening the back of the Suburban, I poured his dish full from the gallon jug of water. He lapped at it furiously for three or four seconds and then look up, asking, I think, if we were gonna make it.

Back home, I visited Toots' grave, just down the drumlin from the swing. Thanked her for a great opening day — and for her help with the new mutt.

Thought I'd get away without crying. Didn't make it.

Northern Michigan Fall
October 18, 1989

A mean frost had settled into the Au Sable Valley during the night. About one-eighth inch of the nasty stuff glazed the windshield.

Nails was eager. A morning for birds — for sure.

The fireplace in Tom Symons' 86-year-old family sanctuary, located on a high bank upstream from Kelloggs Bridge, was tough to leave. After chipping the frost off the windshield, the fire, a cup of coffee, and Rudyard Kipling's 1899 "Soldiers Three" seemed more important than charging into the grouse and woodcock woods.

Tom's grandfather built this place in 1903. It has hosted legions of sportsmen and conservationists. A few years ago Tom replaced some rotting logs, installed a new roof, and had other rescue work done. If those pioneer outdoorsmen from the turn of the century returned today, they'd be at home.

It is a grand place.

About dawn, the National Guard let loose to the west. The cabin seemed to pulsate. Windows and china rattled. Were they dropping 500-pound bombs? But the cabin survived. Again.

The Guard and their defenders say they've been doing their thing in the Au Sable Country long before the fishermen and other recreationists arrived. Not so. This cabin was here when the Au Sable was the cathedral of conservation, long before the military moved to the Hanson cutover on Lake Margrethe.

The bombs stopped in a few minutes. No damage done. Mary Lou slept through the attack without even turning over in bed.

As the sun began to sparkle on McMasters Bridge, Nails and I pulled off the trail just south of Dog Town in the Mason Tract and skirted the edge of a recent popple clearcut. The young popples are thicker than corn stalks in a September field, and about ten feet tall. Impossible to walk in them. But the birds should be out on the edge.

It wasn't so.

Nails made her first sortie into the jungle of dense stems and was on point not four feet from the edge. Within the next fifteen minutes, the little bird dog pointed and flushed well over a dozen woodcock. She went wild. She'd never experienced anything like this. With every other step, she was onto another bird.

I remained "outside." I could have shot some of the birds, but never raised the shotgun. I couldn't have found them, and she was too out of control to fetch.

I finally called her out and sat down beside her. It took five minutes to calm her down enough to quit shaking. Good for a young dog? I don't know.

There were probably several hundred doodles in the thicket. Most likely, the flight had dropped in late the night before.

I've seen it happen a coupla times before. Once Jack Lockwood and I both filled our limit in about fifteen minutes up near Pellston in much thinner cover. Jack's young Lab, Toby (now long departed), wasn't keen on retrieving woodcock. Jack was keen on her fetching woodcock. It was a glorious adventure.

Much has changed in northern Michigan. Jack is now retired and hiding out near Escanaba. The map of this north country in those twenty some years has been redrawn. Condos now blot out the sunsets. Homes and cabins fill the wetlands.

For example, Drummond Island is experiencing a building boom. During a recent four-day visit, construction crews fanned out across the countryside every morning. A sign proclaimed: "My Land, Not Wetland!" at an obvious wetland.

Many of us have hopefully predicted that the epidemic mutilating northwestern Lower Michigan would stop at the Straits. Maybe we were wrong. Some people who arrived in the northwestern Lower decades ago are now jumping ship for the U.P.

And the truth is it isn't my land, or their land. It is, or should be, no one's. Most of the undeveloped land from St Martin Bay east is wetland.

Despite the building boom, Drummond Island remains a jewel. An autumn picnic in your boat anchored in Harbor Island will renew anyone's spirit (especially if Pete and Jill Petro's tupperware Whaler is anchored a few feet away). The sunsets and sunrises over the islands in Potagannissing Bay will knock your eyes out.

Frost has come early and hard to the north woods this year. The down jacket was just right the other night as we grilled hotdogs on the beach off Fisherman's Island. The crowds were gone. The color has been awesome, but is retreating fast. Mary Lou has harvested hundreds of pounds (true!) of squash, bushels of tomatoes, and other precious things from the garden — which is now ready for next spring's planting. A bounty of parsnips is sweetening.

If it gets any better than fall in northern Michigan I couldn't stand it.

Deer Opener—1985
November 20, 1985

The pre-dawn hush was so intense you could hear the frost snapping in the twenty-degree chill that hung between the hardwoods and the swamp on opening morning.

No reason to be here for another half hour. I could barely see the rifle. Couldn't see my boots. It was black!

Then: Swoooompsh thud!

Something had hurtled through the darkness, aiming at my skull and landing not ten feet away. I didn't move. After years of this, you learn nothing out there wants to harm you. Stick tight, listen and look, and you'll learn something every time.

Silence. For long minutes.

Had to be a good-sized bird. It wasn't something that fell like a tree limb. It had come flying through the air. But why didn't it move? Maybe afraid to.

Fifteen minutes later the bird's shape assumed a misty gray focus. Ruffed grouse. Standing there on the ground, it was looking away from me. Not budging. Not even turning its neck.

As dawn neared and it took sharp form, the bird slowly sauntered a few feet into the hardwoods, then again stood poised, neck upright.

The chickadees found me and began chattering in the small maples a few feet over my head. A fox squirrel clattered across the leaf mat. Binoculars sighted the grouse, now digging under a fallen birch.

One, then two more grouse flew in. The first now joined them in browsing. Somewhere to the north a woodpecker started battering at a tree.

To the west over the swamp, geese were milling around in the sky, shaping their formation as they lifted off the lake and turned east toward one of Archie's fields. This country has been filled with increasing numbers of Canada's and the hunting has been miserable, due to politically-biased federal regulations. This morning the majestic flight of geese quickened the blood pressure, making whatever was still working behind the numb nose think about flying south.

The grouse were still there, maybe thirty feet away, totally unaware of the critter with the orange hat beside the maple — as the first rifle shot thundered to the northeast.

It startled me. Had forgotten the business of the morning was supposed to be looking for bucks. Just one shot. Probably Archie taking that buck he's been watching in his home fields.

Seconds later two more rounds to the southeast. Probably one of Archie's family filling his tag in the cornfield north of the pine plantation. Better get serious about this, Shep.

Wham — wham. Then five more.

Boy, he sure missed that one good.

Next there were three shots to the west. Somebody in Jack's party.

The wind had come up, rustling the hold-out beech leaves.

Now a shot just north, where Mel and his guys had been stalking and making blinds since last weekend. I figured that my buck had been spooked by then. It probably caught their scent and will bed down for all daylight hours until at least December.

The grouse fluttered farther into the hardwoods. I could still hear them as they picked away under the crunchy leaves. A red squirrel chattered overhead and to the south. Pesky little devils.

Figured it was time to report to the typewriter. If I didn't, a blasted buck might show up and ruin the whole morning.

A Bad Winter's Start
December 4, 1985

No matter what you hear elsewhere, the 1985 rifle deer hunt was the worst in at least a half century. The only possible exceptions could be the Novembers spent in World War II, Korea, or Vietnam.

In fact, it occurred to this department to ask the DNR to extend the season into December. Then, on December 1, a roaring, raging, snarling blizzard came smashing in off Lake Michigan and buried the old Oldsmobile and Suburban and left us stranded. As this is written, you can barely see the chickadees and downy and hairy woodpeckers in the feeder three feet from the window.

We are completely snowed in.

So? Maybe we should ask for a refund on our deer license. Except for a few minutes opening morning and evening, my hunting was confined to what I could see hunched over this typewriter, in a pain-racked daze, looking occasionally out the window.

Three times, in the half to full hour of clarity I could muster at a time, a buck — one spike and twice a four pointer — crossed the field below the drumlin. Even if I could have hoisted the rifle, I wouldn't have considered shooting at them.

What for? I could barely hobble to the heating pad.

The wrenched hip finally fell back into place this morning, allowing me to sit without half fainting. Good timing, aye?

Of course, that being the nature of things, it gets worse.

Mary Lou is just now recovering — but completely — from a wretched cold. So bad that at times I worried I'd have to drag her to the hospital. Yeah, drag; back too bad to carry her.

Whatta helluva way to start winter, aye? Maybe not. Things can't get worse.

The new typewriter is finally getting tamed. And it is really pretty neat, the first in over thirty years that can actually keep up with these rantings. Well, that is if I don't hit one of those keys that sends the paper spewing out of the thing.

The ice fishing rods are strung with fresh two- and four-pound-test line. The hooks are honed on the jigs and the spud is sharpened. There's a nearly-new .22 rimfire pistol built on a Colt .45 Government frame in the gun cabinet that should poke some dandy holes in the snow behind snowshoe hares in the next couple of months.

The steaks in the woodstove tonight were perfect — pink but

warm through. There are bushels of parsnips under the straw and snow, and dozens of squash keeping ripe in the cellar.

There's a 1959 Lyman 18-footer in the garage that needs hundreds of hours of care this winter. And there are hundreds of trout flies that need tying.

Heck. Not bad to start winter knowing it has to be upbeat from here on.

Deer Opener—1986
November 19, 1986

The bait was really working. There were tracks everywhere in the glow of the flashlight. The area around the hunting blind looked like a woods convention the night before opening morning.

The six inches, or so, of snow at 6:45 a.m. on opening morning lent a sorta eerie dusky glow to the hardwoods and surrounding swamp. Setting the little 6mm auto-loader beside the seat that Dave Marshall had constructed gave me confidence it would be an interesting morning.

For several days I'd been baiting the blind with suet (hung from a branch of a beech tree), stale nuts, and sunflower seeds.

That's the way to hunt deer.

A gentle breeze rustled dried leaves still clinging to beech saplings. The woods reveal many secrets when early winter leaves them naked. Like bird nests. Within view were at least a dozen — mostly in beech, maple, and basswood saplings — that had been hidden until the leaves fell. Ten feet from the blind, an eager young buck had rubbed barren a young maple's bark — about eighteen inches — two feet from the ground. In the top of the hardwoods were four squirrel nests.

Mice, squirrels, and songbirds had discovered the bait and left a dizzying maze of tracks in the snow.

The first flicker of activity occurred on the beech tree baited with suet. It took some squinting, but finally a nuthatch came into focus, head down on the smooth bark. Two minutes later it squawked. Opening morning's first creature sound.

As if on cue, the chickadees picked up the chorus. Within seconds they were chattering from every direction. Silly, you say, but I wondered if they were sharing the morning gossip. Seemed like a friendly, everyday conversation.

The first rifle shattered the serenity of the thirty-degree morning. Maybe Archie, son Jim, or one of the sons-in-law had scored. They always do. They bag their buck just at dawn, then hang him, and get back to cleaning the barn.

The chickadees were oblivious. There were at least six coming into the sunflower seeds now. Flitting here and there. Grabbing a beakful. Jabbering. Happy little beggars. Just about as perfect a creature as anyone could conceive.

Two nuthatches were on the suet beech tree. Another on the old stump where some sunflower seeds had been scattered.

The shooting really opened up around 7:20 a.m. By 7:30 at least a dozen rifles were heard. A few seconds later some guy to the north jerked (yeah, jerked) off a dozen rounds; five fast ones, a pause to reload and five more, reload again and two more. Don't ever remember hearing anything like that before in the deer woods. (He must have been killing a stump.)

All of the commotion set the crows to clamoring over near Skinner Lake. Reckon they were pretty peeved at all these city folks invading their turf.

A downy woodpecker swooshed in, landing on the suet. Always wonder if those guys really fly or just sorta tumble through the air. One of the nuthatches bounced up the beech tree and delivered a throaty protest.

A red squirrel suddenly declared his intention to drive the intruder (me) away from his winter hoard of cashew nuts. I finally spotted him on the limb of a basswood; tail flicking and mouth half open, eyes blazing. Another answered. He wasn't twenty feet away, on the snow, equally aggressive. Maybe he was gonna dash in and bite off my ear.

Reaching for the thermos, I saw the blurred outline of a snow-shoe rabbit about thirty feet away. He sat there — like a rock. When the coffee was poured, the hare had melted away.

Overhead, a flock of mallards circled the lake. They probably were chased out of a cornfield by hunters.

Then came the damndest "rurrr" sound. I knew I'd heard it before but couldn't put a tag on it right away. It grew louder and then more so. The cold neurons fell into place: a pair of mute swans coming into the lake. I've never seen them, but I'm sure that's what they were.

The bluejays were getting bold enough to figure it was safe since the chickadees, nuthatches, and woodpeckers hadn't been evicted. One, then in an instant, three or four, were squalling and screeching from every direction. (Remembering how much sunflower seed they've squandered at the feeders by the house, I briefly thought about grabbing the rifle and blowing one of them away. But damn you, Sheppard, they're invited guests. And it is fun to watch the cardinals drive them away from the feeders. And you must admit they are handsome devils.)

It wasn't going to get any better than this. How could it? So around 9:00 a.m., I returned the thermos to the big back cargo pocket of the ancient Mackinaw, hitched the rifle on my shoulder, and started checking things out.

Just a little over a hundred feet south of the blind were fresh tracks of three deer. Sneaky critters. I hadn't heard a thing.

I'm grateful they hadn't spoiled a perfect opening morning. Gutting and dragging a deer up the drumlin to the garage would have ruined everything.

The Deer Blind
November 17, 1984

The stars and the remainder of the moon had an electric charge. The twenty-eight degree temperatures spiked the pre-dawn zing as I briskly hiked to the blind.

There was no need for a flashlight. You could pick your way through the hardwoods by starlight.

The blind on the little knoll is a lousy place for killing deer. It is mostly natural. Cedar boughs were added to widen and deepen the hideout that looks down on the swale to the west, along the edge of the little lake.

The small swale, really a puny cedar swamp, is a true wilderness. Blowdown cedars, toppled because high water in recent years has left their roots with little to cling to, are stacked in tangled webs the size of houses, suited only for the passage of snowshoe hares and savvy whitetail bucks.

But here, at the edge, rut-crazed bucks follow ancestral runways in November. They are more often smoky images than solid shapes, as they nod and bob down the trail, their noses vacuuming the scent that has made their kind one of nature's most prolific species.

Every few minutes a car could be heard on the county road about three miles to the east. Other than that, not even — as my grandchildren will soon be saying — a mouse could be heard stirring.

Dawn flowed down through the maples, beech, basswood, and popple in muted silver streaks. Deceptive. Enchanting. Light would appear along a narrow band, then disappear. Then return with brightness more than fifty feet away.

The woods awoke slowly, but in unison. First a hairy woodpecker's shrill cheep, cheep, as he forged into a dead popple stalk.

I may have moved. The woodpecker froze on the trunk of the tree. After a couple of minutes, he jerkily pranced around the trunk, seeming to watch out of one eye as he banged at the bark, probing for insects.

In a wave, several chickadees moved in. They fluttered and gossiped overhead briefly before the first descended on the sunflower seed at the edge of the blind.

Though the temperature was still below freezing, the tattered old Mackinaw, with high collar pulled up over ears, was as snug as a sleeping bag. When the first leaf crackled, it took a stubborn determination to fight through the stupor to listen and look.

Three deer — none fawns — moved at a confident pace along the runway, just inside the cedars. The glasses found only does. Within seconds, a doe with two fawns followed.

A red squirrel hollered to the east, behind the blind. He was up there, in a tree somewhere, his tail snapping.

The sun topped the drumlin west of Skinner Lake. For a fleeting second it glimmered red on something in the swamp — probably fresh-frozen water at the base of a downed cedar or birch.

Another shape, then another, eased into the swamp. The glasses found racks on both of them. Nothing special. Their noses seemed to sweep the leaves off the trail. If I'd ever legitimately qualified with my .45, I could have nailed them like Matt Dillon.

Inside the Mackinaw it was still cozy warm. Outside, there was a suspicion the nose was brittle enough to snap off if a twig fell on it.

The procession continued. Eleven more does and fawns. Two more young bucks.

It was a full day, and time to pour a cup of the coffee that had been made two hours earlier and fill the pipe. It was then he came out of the swamp. Not the biggest buck by far. But at least nine points and probably sixteen to eighteen inches across with maybe a three-inch beam.

The rack looked heavy, like a burden, as his nose broomed up the doe smell — systematically weaving from left to right. An exaggerated guess put his dressed weight at 150 pounds.

Damn nice buck. And an easy shot.

He melted back into the blowdown. Steam rose like chimney smoke from the thermos cup. A chainsaw growled to the south. A truck clamored up the dirt trail to the north.

The best morning of my deer season was over. It was November 14. Not until mid or late December will the wild critters return to doing their natural thing.

Robins, Thumper, And Bambi
November 23, 1983

Last Tuesday was about as unpromising a day for the rifle deer opener as we've ever greeted between these drumlins.

A soggy snow the evening before had left over an inch plastered to the trees. By 6:30 a.m. mixed snow and rain started. The heavy mounds of snow then fell from trees onto the crackling bed of leaves under them.

It sounded like a whole army coming through. A hundred deer could have walked within fifty feet of the blind unseen. Each splat of snow aroused my interest. Peering from under the orange cap, however, drew a slap of snow or rain on eyeglasses.

An owl wailed out toward the edge of the lake, across the swamp, as I settled into the blind, clumsily stumbling to find the seat in the darkness.

The blind is an isolated, gnarled, twisted clump of cedar, with a few small birches poking through at the edge of the opening between the hardwoods and cedar-balsam swamp. It is in that transition zone where everything from red squirrels and chickadees to whitetails and bobcats show up.

On just about any other kind of morning you're guaranteed to see and hear plenty of interesting little natural skits played out. But this morning it was just wet, cold, and noisy. To pretend to be seriously hunting deer was ridiculous. Instead, I pondered on our last bird hunt of the season two days before.

We had hunted mixed cedar and hardwood at the edge of a cornfield — a place we'd hunted dozens of times before, but not in the last two or three years. It was sorta like coming home. And what a homecoming!

In a half hour we had three birds. The last one flushed wild, just when Toots started going birdy. When it blasted through the cedars it was almost out of range. The little side-by-side was on target but didn't bring it down.

By the time the bird reentered the cedars it was wobbling. I marked the spot where I was certain it went down. But Toots paid me no mind, running back into a dense cedar swamp every time I called her back.

I had damned her rather abusively before it dawned on me she's right more often than I. Sure enough, about 150 feet south, she was sitting beside the dead bird, rightly too indignant to bring it to me. I admitted who the fool was and crouched down to take my licks.

Things really perked up two days later. It was cool, but clear and still, at 4:00 p.m. A quick check showed the buck scrape at the edge of the little gully that connects the swamp and hardwoods to the south had been used recently. Chickadees, nuthatches, hairy and downy woodpeckers, red squirrels, and bluejays were having a glorious time.

Within fifteen minutes, chickadees had discovered the sunflower seeds spread on the popple log at the edge of the blind. Some were landing in the cedars a foot from me.

Then things went quiet. Straining to see the buck that was sure to emerge from the swamp, I heard a noise to the north, behind me. Twisting as far as possible, nothing appeared, but the noise came closer.

Damn! A snowshoe hare, apparently out for a leisurely stroll. In front of the blind, about twenty-five feet away, it stopped. First it looked right at me, as though it could see me through the cedars. But then it turned half way around and looked behind.

Geezus! There was a small buck, its nose to the ground like it was trailing a doe. Maybe it didn't yet understand what this mating business was all about. Three points were visible and there was probably another one on the side away from me. Too small — no more than a hundred pounds.

Just like Bambi. The Thumper started down the trail again and the little buck followed.

It would have been an easy shot for the 6mm, but for what? And maybe the big buck would come out to defend its scrape.

As the little fella and his hopping pal disappeared into the tags and dogwood, the chickadees, nuthatches, and woodpeckers got back in action.

Then of all the crazy things, a robin sang somewhere to the west. The greeting was returned by another robin in the hardwoods.

Robins, Thumper, and Bambi? This is deer hunting?

I wasn't sure Mary Lou would believe me. And I'm still not sure that she does.

WINTER

Christmas Storm
January 4, 1984

For only the second time in memory, whitetails are yarded in this Drumlin Country. In more than two decades of watching wildlife on and between these unique ridges along the Lake Michigan shore, the only other time we saw whitetails locked into our "pocket yards" was during the 1981 winter.

Starved wild turkeys have been showing up for nearly two weeks. Though it is tough to make an accurate count, my guess is that no more than four dozen goldfinches survived the vicious Christmas storm. I'm guessing we lost a couple dozen. There are also fewer chickadees. Hairy and downy woodpeckers seem to have survived, along with the nuthatches and evening grosbeaks.

The broad-winged hawk still glides through the meadow, but his days are numbered unless he vacates this brutalized land. The mice are under three feet of snow. High winds have left it with a concrete-like skin.

After talking to people across the Upper and northern Lower Peninsulas, it appears the six-day Christmas storm concentrated its meanness on the Drumlin Country. Though it was cold and snowy just about everywhere, the wind and snow were far worse here. For the first time ever, a state of emergency was declared. Cars were ordered off the roads.

Grace Truax's folks made it over from Oscoda Saturday afternoon — Christmas Eve. When they got to Charlevoix they found the six miles of road to Phelps Station closed. Christmas Eve and Christmas night were spent in a motel, six miles from Grace, Doug and Stephie. Christmas dinner was a hot dog in the 7-11 store — standing up.

Fish biologist Ron Rybicki's son made the 800 miles to Charlevoix from Dallas. He couldn't make the six miles from town to his folks' Black Road home and spent the holiday holed up in the fish hatchery in town.

May Lou and Shep were snowed in for five days. The turkey and trimmings planned for eight for Christmas Day were cooked and may keep us in sandwiches and sweet potatoes until trout season opens.

Only desperate humans venture outside in such weather. Visibility was less than fifty feet. The three daily trips to keep the bird feeders full and clear of snow — though short and brief — were torture. Eyeglasses were useless. In two or three minutes, eyebrows and mustache were coated with ice.

There was nothing to see. Even at arm's length it was difficult to see the feeders as the wind filled eye sockets with snow. The only sound was the fury of the wind. It kept raging for three days. Though it then slacked off for a few hours the storm picked up its tempo for three more days.

Blessedly, the full fury of the storm was localized; it concentrated on a narrow belt here in the Drumlins, just off Lake Michigan, from about Atwood north to Petoskey. Inland and north and south a few miles there was far less snow and, more important, far less wind.

At Grayling, Bill Lehtinen reported easy going — just winter. The same reports came from Roscommon, Gaylord, the Soo, Marquette and Copper Harbor. At Alpena they were reporting only six to eight inches of snow.

Brook trout eggs in the Cedar River and Monroe Creek may have been mauled. It seems likely, however, that all is well with mayfly larva and trout eggs in the gravel of the Jordan, Black and Au Sable.

Being snowbound is not troublesome. The wood stove has plenty of fodder. The freezer is full of vegetables and soup stock. The workshop in the garage is only a minute away; it keeps boredom from winning — and it produced a new five-foot long bird feeder. There were a couple of new books for Christmas, lots of Christmas Scotch and the holes in the cribbage board never wear out.

New Year's Eve afternoon, Archie brought his eight-foot-wide snow blower down and cleared the drive and road. The county followed with its big plow. The wind and snow quit. We celebrated our freedom with a shrimp dinner at Duffy's, a drink with Doug and Grace Truax, and got home about 8:30 p.m. to take up where we'd left off with the books and cribbage board.

New Year's day was cloudy, but bright. There wasn't even a hare's track in the swamp. Nothing was moving — not even a mouse!

If Old Man Winter is out to prove he can make up for last year's record mildness and unprecedented summer heat, the wild folks that survive are gonna be lonely come spring.

Remembering Trees
March 11, 1987

There is a beech tree not far from here that I've become particular friends with over the years.

If you gawk at trees and things a lot you decide that beech trees are probably the most original and creative. Their limbs and trunks conform to no rules. They twist and turn, wrinkle and squiggle in individual patterns. I once met one with a hollow trunk big enough for two full-sized men to stand in — one on the other's shoulders. It had been that way for thirty years. Some brain-dreary home builder cut it down.

Well, this beech I've been keeping company with stands alone in a field. There are weeds and some blueberry bushes in the summer. Popple are trying to invade from one corner. But my beech buddy is far and away the dominant life in the meadow.

It is a stubby sorta pal. Some time ago, more than twenty years, and maybe forty to fifty years, a lightning bolt smacked it on the crown. Though its trunk is the girth of one of Archie's Belgian draft horses, it reaches only twenty to twenty-five feet out of the ground. Its limbs are a maze of contorted, gnarled arms — thin and long.

I sometimes watch the moonlight shimmer through its limbs and imagine a ghostly aberration silhouetted between those out-reaching arms and the moon. If the director of a Hollywood horror film discovered it, the old beech might be a candidate for an Oscar.

But fortunately, no one else worships the beech. Most people would pass it without noticing its singular character. That makes it a private treasure — even though I don't "own" it. (Right or wrong, I despise people who think they "own" natural resources.)

Not more than a quarter mile from the beech is a cedar that I've spent hours staring and wondering at. For no apparent reason, it is nearly without limbs on all but the west side. There it balloons like a lass about to endow the world with sextuplets. (We need more cedars in our forests.)

I've sat in a deer blind, in a spring trance, and on a stump getting my breath from following a bird, trying to figure out why the cedar assumes a peculiar shape. No answer has presented itself.

On a high bank above the South Branch of the Au Sable there is a spindly jack pine contorted into the shape of an *L*, with the base of the *L* about two feet above the ground. It has been that way since the

1930s at least. Until George Mason's will closed the area to camping
in the mid-1950s, Dad and I used to set up a tent nearby. The old
fence line between Mason's property and the meadow ran just
beyond the jack pine.

Dad's stories about how the tree got that way changed from time
to time. As I recall, sometimes it was Indians who bent the tree to
give others directions to a fallen brave's grave. Other times it was a
pioneer grayling fisherman who bent it, as a sapling, to tell his pal
how to reach a hot fishing hole. It doesn't matter. The truth wouldn't
be near as much fun as the mystery and the wonder that nature can
hold such tantalizing secrets.

Downstream from the bent jack pine there was a sweeper that
stretched half across the river, swaying in the current, but still alive.
Many's the night a raccoon perched on it as this then much-younger
man cast giant Hexagenia mayfly imitations to the trophy trout that
lurked beneath. Once, I even landed — and released — such a trout.
The hole under the sweeper was far too deep for even a strong-
legged young man to wade.

Like Charlie Welch, who helped land that biggest-ever brown
trout, the sweeper is gone. With it went the hole — filled in with silt
— and the brown trout. A DNR stream improvement crew decided
the sweeper didn't belong there. I will forever believe the sweeper
was the guardian of the hole and big trout. (Ah, the canoes it tormented on that curve below Falling's meadow.)

Over a long-abandoned railroad grade and beside a nearly century-old cedar stump there stands a stately hemlock — tall and privately graceful and proud. It takes a bit of walking to get there. Only
a dozen or so fishermen, plus some lost deer hunting slobs, probably
get there each year. I may be the only one who stops to pay homage
to the hemlock.

Before sand from Antrim County roads, lamprey poison, and chinook salmon got the better of it, the hollow cedar stump harbored a
giant trout. The current would seep mayflies into the base of the
stump's cave-like opening and the fish would slurp them down.

Just try to float a fly in there so it appeared like a natural drift! It
couldn't be done. I spent hours mumbling to myself and the hemlock. Sometimes I'd tote in a couple of beers and rotate from casting
to squatting and chuckling to myself for my failure.

It was the hemlock that kept my sense of humor percolating. In
the fall I'd return, with bird dog and gun, to celebrate its goldenness

and offer my verbal pledge to be back in the spring.

Down in a swamp west of Houghton Lake there is a massive old white pine trunk that blew down in a storm maybe a hundred years ago. It is covered with green moss and bright red British soldiers. On it some forty years ago I saw my first drumming grouse.

It is a wild, secluded place. Not many people go there. Few of those who do would be of a mind to stop and ponder the drumming log.

When I stumbled on it many years ago, most of the swamp was young shintangle. The last time I returned it was dense and grown with mature aspen and cedar. But the log was still there. Toots and I shot a grouse and two woodcock within a hundred yards of it. I sat on the log — nearly as big as an imported car — and cleaned the birds while Toots sat at my feet.

Which reminds me of this blow-down cedar across a miniature trout crick. Years ago, I could hop over the crick. For the last ten or so years, it has been too wide. Or my hop has been too short. So I walk at least a quarter mile to use the cedar as a bridge.

There are really too few trout in the crick to feel good about killing any of them. In the fall Toots and I would visit to watch the brook trout glisten as they swayed over spawning gravel just below the log. But the blow-down cedar was a good luck charm; several times we killed a bird within shotgun range of it.

In the spring we'd come and just sit. Listen to the gurgle of the crick and convince ourselves that some things won't betray us.

Toots has been gone since April 1985. But maybe, I'll find her there in a week or so. If you pay attention, trees have a way of enriching your life. And, mister, we're not talking about stumpage.

The Bird Nest Hike
January 16, 1985

Though about a foot deep, the snow was fluffy. Snowshoes were not needed. Stepping forward with kicks created puffs of clouds. White. Clean. Quiet.

Toots romped ahead, and then every few hundred feet she would roll over and over. Like a kid making angels. The snow seems to scour her long white hair, making it glisten. She's never as clean as she is when taking snow baths.

This was a bird nest hike. Bird nests reveal themselves at this time of year, if you take the time to look for them.

Most are six to ten feet up in hardwood saplings. Others are in dense brush, like tag alders along a stream bed. Some are about the size of two thumbs. Others larger than two fists. A few are so flimsy that they are already falling apart. Others are tough and durable.

Every year Mary Lou wants one fetched for the Christmas tree. Says it means good luck or happiness, or something friendly like that.

They intrigue me. I'm tempted to photograph them and ask someone wiser what species made them.

That leads to wishing you had the time to learn more yourself — that you could have the luxury of maybe taking a year off just to study things like who makes what bird nests. You might learn why they make them as they do and where they do.

Such thinking can make a guy want to kick himself for being in such a hurry to learn to make a living, instead of taking the time to learn just for the learning of it. Kids do it now. But things were different back then. Which isn't saying they were better — or that we were wiser.

There's a quarter-mile-long swale that snakes along the edge of the upland like a thread. Never more than 200 feet wide. Thick like a brush pile. Tangled and impassable, if you're in a hurry.

But if time is not a factor, and you're willing to accept a few scratches on your beard, there is lots to see. At one point, entangled in vines and brush so tight it took a half minute or so to take another step, five nests were spotted. Only two looked the same.

Imagine what this secret place was like last spring and summer. Adult birds coming and going. Babies chirping and squawking. All colors, some bright, some reddish, some yellowish, some drab brown

— endless variations.

Then ponder the complexity of the ecosystem that makes it happen. An awesome, staggering mental exercise for an uneducated typewriter slave. (And there are people playing *Trivial Pursuit* on this winter weekend afternoon.)

The trance was broken with the realization Toots hadn't been around for several minutes. It took a while, but her tracks turned up. Following them led me to where the swale ends at the edge of the cedars.

She was on point, and impatient; her tail flagging slowly as I came up behind her. Two grouse could be seen about ten to twelve feet up in a cedar.

There was only one thing to do.

I saluted these survivors of a three-month hunting season, than slapped my hands together. They bolted from their perches, almost silently. There were four birds. One was a magnificent creature in red phase. Hope the rest of winter is kind to them.

The walking was easy under the cedars. Toots' joints were aching and she was limping as arthritis, or whatever dogs get with time, gnawed at her right hip. The day was ending.

I think I saw the snowshoe's eyes before Toots sensed it. It looked like a small mound of snow. Toots stopped with me, as I unsnapped the holster and started to draw the old Colt Woodsman.

Then let the barrel slide back into the leather.

Dumb? Who needs a dead rabbit today? (Besides, at fifty to sixty feet I'd probably miss.)

We'd bagged a limit of bird nests. And, just maybe, we're richer for not having all the answers. If we did, the magic might be gone.

The Northland Farmer
January 29, 1986

Then every star shall sing to me
Its song of liberty;
And every morn will bring to me
Its mandate to be free.
In every throbbing vein of me
I'll feel the vast Earth-call ...

Robert Service

Several score or so ago, I believed the only way to find the freedom I craved, with the ties to the land I considered the essence of life, was to work the family farm.

It wasn't to be. Now, in retrospect, it is clear it never could have been. But for a while, in those youthful years, it seemed there could be no other calling that would keep my veins throbbing.

So, minus a plow, but with a snoot full of belligerence, a gut full of romanticism and patriotism, a pair of fists, and a typewriter, I went to places farmers never visit.

Now, settled in this drumlin country, where the uplands are fertile farmland, those childish dreams often are haunting. Archie and Louise Potter, our nearest neighbors, who live about a mile up the road, bring them to life.

There have been four generations of Potters on these hills and in these swales.

They wouldn't want it written in the public press, but the other folks who toil the earth in these precincts envy Archie — and now their son Jimmy. They say, somewhat reluctantly, that what Archie puts in the ground produces a good crop, be there drought or flood, scorching heat or cold. They insist that Archie's cows always, no matter the curves Nature may throw, produce the finest grade milk.

We've heard it said that his good fortune is due only to his plowing the churchyard — where several generations of Potters have wed and worshipped — on blustery wintry mornings, or some other such quackery. (And, sadly, the little church at Barnard seems to be dying. New generations don't have as many youngsters to keep the traditions, and farms alive. Further, Vietnam showed some that the church really isn't what they were taught.)

But, if you've supped deep on the earth you know there is no magic in Archie's crops and his milk isn't peerless. It is hard — damn awful hard — work when mixed with a deep respect and love for the land that makes a good farmer — the best farmer.

Though they'll tell you the way to successful farming is a degree from Michigan State University, you know right off that Archie, and his kin, aren't handicapped one iota without it. There are fancy farmers around these parts, with degrees and computers, who bring in hired hands in the morning to do their milking. They survive on tax breaks, government subsidies, and big city financing.

The Archie Potters do it on grit, muscle, and a dust-to-dust closeness to the land. There is a kind of instinctive feel for what the land needs and how to provide that need. This was never learned in a classroom or an extension service bulletin.

On spring mornings, when the warmth starts returning to the land and the wind blows from the south, it is as though the big man stands out there with flaring nostrils breathing in the scents of his fields, letting them tell him what they want this season before he puts the seed in.

You see the big hands and hear the gentle voice guiding the massive Belgian draft horses as though they were wee puppies.

On late summer and early fall evenings you watch the big tractor hum down the cornfields and feel an enchanting fulfillment as you sense the contentment and satisfaction in the eyes of the quiet, grandchild-loving giant in the cab.

Often, there's a little tyke — not more than five — in the cab with him. With a tractorin' man's hat drooping down over his ears, and chattering away at grandpa, this future farmer learns about the secrets of the earth, of the soul-enriching rewards of loving and respecting that land — and of the need and rewards of hard work.

Oh, it isn't all work. He takes three or four, probably never more than five, hours off each opening day of deer season to shoot a nice buck. But, yeah, that's part of the land. He wouldn't consider shooting a buck on other land any more than he would torch the church.

The land doesn't belong to people; the people belong to the land. The Archie Potters belong to the north*land*. There aren't many left.

A Christmas Dream
December 21, 1983

"The functions of a jet-propelled plane or a computing machine have become a greater wonder and a greater interest to the average boy today than the sprouting of a kernel of grain."

Ernie Swift

A giant amaryllis plant has been blossoming about three feet from this typewriter. Once the pods were positioned and the buds started opening, the eight-inch-wide red flower spread its beauty so fast you could almost see the magic.

This afternoon its backdrop is the two feet of fresh snow that covers everything in Drumlin Country. The radio reports only a couple of inches fell a few miles north and south of us. But here, on this drumlin, we've been snowed in for the second day. Might get out tomorrow, if the wind quits howling and the plows get off the main roads.

Outside, the wind and snow are in complete control. Swarms of goldfinches and grosbeaks dominate the feeders, which now must be filled twice a day.

Memories of Christmas past mixed with fantasies inspired by being snowbound encourages imagination. A vision begins to focus as I gaze into the swirling storm.

There is a long stretch of river; it is the Black, the South Branch, the Mainstream, the Fox, the Jordan, the Cedar. The best of all of them. Gentle, but swift, it has gravel in midstream, but is dark and thick under the sweepers. A bright moon shimmers off the snow that covers the cedars and pines. The river's currents flow in diamond-bright serpentine light.

The air is cool, maybe thirty degrees, but the river is warm, about sixty, as the feet of your waders dangle in it. Hendricksons, blue-winged olives and tricorythodes mayflies are hatching at once into spinning clouds.

In the moonlight, you can watch all the trout in the stream, on station, an inch or so under the water, leaving an almost imperceptible eddy as they open their mouths to suck in spent flies.

It is paradise. A star is now overhead. The rod is strung — a tiny 18 olive on a 6X leader — but I can't lift myself off the bank. I've stumbled into a fly fisherman's Holy Grail.

The big hat comes into focus. Hub! His rod works like fluid. Then Charlie Welch! He's not as serious about it, but that long rod is still with him. Omar Jabara's rod bows as he salutes Cal Gates; never have two men been more expert, but more gentle, at their lovemaking to the trout and the mayfly.

Fish are caught. Dozens. Each cast is like the flow of the Northern Lights — smooth, bending, twisting, in rhythm with the heavens. Always the fly dances over the eddies and the largest, most difficult trout take it readily. And all of the trout are brook trout, the natives that belong here.

Never is a fish touched by hand. It swims off after a couple of minutes on the line, as though the hook were made of moonbeams.

There are no canoes! That's right, no canoes!

"You guys always had it this good?" Cal asks.

Arnold Hubbell's rod hesitates for an instant, as star dust seems to fall from the line. He says nothing.

Charlie Welch tucks the over nine-foot rod under his arm. With a courtly bow, he smiles: "Haven't seen a canoe since 1969. They outlawed 'em *down* here! But, if you brought your own, we have some big, quiet places where they let one a day pass ... did you want to go canoeing?"

"You kidding? Ah, what do they call this place ... I think I've been here, but it wasn't quite the same, not nearly the same ... you guys are doing a good job of it. Glad you let me join you."

Omar bows, with the grace of a great blue heron, as his cast flows out over the riffles like a gentle breeze. A sixteen-inch brook trout takes the little fly. Seconds later his wrist twists and the square tail flicks free.

Hub, who was never one for words, unless he was talking about snaggers, dams, canoes or poachers, asks: "You've been coming here a long time? Haven't seen you before, but I somehow know you've been here before. You'll be right at home."

On his way by, Hub flashes that big "got 'em hooked now" smile and waves — "Merry Christmas, Shep!"

Uh, huh!

It was so real, I have to look to make sure it is Toots' head on my knee; she wants to go out. Geezus.

Merry Christmas to you, too, Hub, and to Cal, Omar and Charlie. And to everyone else who shares these ramblings and our fascination with nature.

A Wild And Quiet Place
January 18, 1984

The snow snapped and glittered in the bright midday sun like a sea of diamonds. Under the snowshoes it squeaked sharply in the five-degree temperature.

The leafless maples, beech, and popples threw long, gray shadows reaching deep into the meadow. On the west side of the drumlin the tangle of man-high old junipers under their white blanket looked like an Army encampment in the Arctic. The scene flashed a memory cell: for an instant I expected a GI in overwhites to emerge from one of the "tents," his M-1 also wrapped in white cloth.

Once across the field, and into the hardwoods, snow seemed to flow in a smooth, shapeless contour. The first animal tracks appeared — mostly red squirrels. Wing marks, however, suggested a blue jay had swooped down to snatch a fallen popple bud. Two downy woodpeckers clacked and smacked at the trunk of an old decayed beech. I've eyed the tree many times for firewood, but decided it had a higher value for the insects it provides wild things.

Nearing the break between the hardwoods and the swamp the pace quickened. In a few feet there would be deer sign if whitetails are getting out of the nearly three feet of snow piled in the swamp. The runway is the most used between the swamp and the old Skiel farm cornfield.

The wind pounds the drumlin top at the now gone and forgotten homestead. Most of the snow is swept clear, exposing the corn Archie always seems to allocate to the wild critters instead of his milkers. (He also makes the more than mile-long run almost daily with the "honey wagon" to spread undigested remains of corn harvested for his cows.)

The combination of frozen corn kernels and cobs and manure seem to attract everything that moves in these parts in winter. Fox squirrels, big fluffed-up guys and gals, are most obvious, but the skim of snow untouched by the wind between the bent and twisted stalks reveals tracks of all sizes — from the size of a pencil head to those of whitetails. Even the grouse come to peck.

Skirting the tangle of blowdown popple and birch, the deer trail looked like a trench in more than two feet of snow. It snakes up into the maples, beech, and basswood, then down into the gully, through the cut in the dogwood, and up into the cornfield.

The days are short and the typewriter demanding. The days with decent weather have come when the typewriter is most demanding, leaving us to fret about how things were going in the swamp. Were the deer still locked in, as they had been earlier?

There may be, probably are, a fawn, or two or three — born late — that normally wouldn't have survived birth, but did last spring due to the extremely mild winter, and then died during the holiday storms. But if winter behaves normally from now on, whitetail losses should be minimal in Drumlin Country.

Following the deep-packed deer trail into the heart of the swamp was tempting. But the feeling that invading the yarding area will only add stress was more powerful.

Turning south and west, the snowshoes picked a path through the cedars to the maze of wind-ravaged cedars that lay intertwined in all directions at about a ten- to thirty-degree angle above the snow, their root clumps forming small hills. Only hunter-pushed whitetails and snowshoe hares enter.

It is a quiet, wild place. A kind of place meant for pouring honey-laced tea from the little thermos and listening to the roar of the hush.

Setting the thermos cup in the snow to cool the tea, I lit my pipe; the steam and smoke rose slowly, as straight as a sentry pine. The click of the old Zippo lighter as it snapped shut was like an explosion — a violation.

So loud; it must have made the hare blink or move, because that's when I saw it under the cave created by fallen cedars knitted together about thirty feet away.

The little Colt Woodsman .22 pistol was along. I briefly thought of using it, but sluffed that off as ridiculous. For a guy who could never qualify with his service handgun to be shooting at rabbits is like trying to shoot down a B-52 with a hunting bow. But, worse yet, what if I hit him? Egads, I'd ten times rather eat broccoli and parsnips than snowshoe hare.

The first cup of tea was gone. The second was too much, half was poured on the snow. I felt guilty. It left such an ugly stain I decided to keep the ashes in the pipe until I could dump them out in an ashtray.

The rabbit was still there, hunkered under the cedars, eye blinking about once a minute, as the snowshoes pointed back for the drumlin.

Fighting For A River
February 10, 1988

We'd been called together at the DNR's Gaylord district office by Steve Swan, district fish chief and a guy whose environmental integrity I'd go to the bridge with on a moment's notice. The subject was a river. Not any river. The Jordan River; once one of the world's finest brook trout streams. Still one of its coldest, purest and most charming. Now, however, in many ways, the Jordan is critically wounded. It continues to breathe, but its life has been sapped by sand, lampreys, chemicals and salmon.

After many agonizing years for those of us who truly know and love the river, Swan and other professionals now recognize the Jordan's agony, and its need for resurrection. They were gathered around the table to discuss how we could and would restore its dignity — and return it to life.

It is a big job — one that has never been fully achieved before. But biologists like Swan, Mason Shouder and Jan Fenske are fired up. They know the technology is there. They know how to scour out the sand, to stop lamprey-killing chemicals, and to block salmon with weirs.

Gaylord Alexander was at the end of the table. Gaylord has to be considered the godfather of trout stream technology. He has spent thirty-one years romancing trout at Hunt Creek Trout Research Station near Lewiston. If there is anyone who knows — or cares — more about trout than Gaylord he ain't crossed my path.

No boring academic, Gaylord is a wizard. A genius who can look at a stream and tell you in seconds what it is, what it was and what it should be. He knows its ills and its promise.

Sitting next to Gaylord was Bud Jones. A "simple" country boy from Alba who has been tramping the Jordan since he could toddle. He knows where its owls, hawks, and warblers nest. He can show you where oldtimers caught eighteen-inch brook trout.

Bud is a guy with the patience to climb a tree and sit for hours, day after day, to catch a glimpse of a nesting Bristles hawk. He can also bear the mediocrity, dullness, and excuses of bureaucrats with a quiet and calm constraint, while holding his fury in check.

Gordon Guyer was off in Lansing. But all of us knew he was in the room. Gordon has made it clear that restoring the Jordan has his top priority. That it must be a model for what can be done for the dozens of other Michigan rivers suffering the same wounds.

The talk was of sand traps, bank stabilization, a road that had bled suffocating sand into the river, of lampreys, electric weirs, the ravages of salmon, and the young steelhead that gang up on trout.

It was pragmatic stuff. Like how much rock is needed to stop an eroded bank from pouring its sand into the river. And about how much that rock will cost.

The drive home, in a snow squall, was anything but pragmatic. The heater in the big Suburban made the heavy jacket a cocoon that nourished memories from a younger and healthier Jordan.

Jan Fenske, a gal with a degree in fish biology who truly has a feel and a passion for the job, had asked where sand traps ought to be located. One spot came to mind, downstream from a survey line that old cobber Bill Mittig and I once parried over. It had the last surviving gravel as the river was being buried under several feet of sand. For many years, when the river fought its last gasps in the suffocating sand, the only truly good Hendrickson mayfly hatches were found here.

Through the blur of the snow on the windshield, I could picture Craig — then a toddler — with waders that could have reached over his head if we hadn't bundled them under his chin, trying desperately to cast to rising brook trout.

I remembered an eighteen-inch brook that once was fooled by my ginger quill on this stretch. Several — well over a dozen — twelve- to fifteen-inch brook trout came to the fly here over the years. Many to big Red Hex imitations.

Oh, what a hatch that was when the Jordan was alive and well. Twenty years ago not more than a handful of oldtimers knew about the Hexagenia recurvata hatch. It is a fly as big as the famed limbata, but with a rusty color and not nearly as plentiful. It comes off — or did when the river was well — in late afternoon to mid-evening. No waiting for dusk.

As the nymph hits the surface, the big flies struggle to emerge. Literally every trout in the river becomes a glutton. To have experienced it is to have known a kind of magnificent delight beyond the ability of this typewriter to describe.

You picked your fish carefully. The hatch would last only for a few minutes — unlike the Hexagenia limbata hatch which can go on for hours and days. So you cast only to the biggest fish. You knew they would strike with abandon. In doing so they would put down other fish in the area.

Then there were the times when the little — 22s and 24s — Tricorythodes would splatter the river just upstream (below Stevens Creek) in such numbers it looked like a blizzard of salt and pepper.

This was small trout water — brook trout of six to nine inches. You need fine leaders, and fine casts.

Landing a nine-incher was ecstasy.

On the south bank there was — still was last summer — a berry patch. Two bear cubs once visited while I decided whether to leave the river or stay; I left rather than invite an encounter with their momma.

There's also a little spot just upstream of the berry patch where Mary Lou and I used to build a tiny fire and cook a hot dog, or a fresh-caught trout. A spot where Toots, the finest bird dog to grace this old dreamer, once dumped me in my waders.

Yeah, the berry patch is still there. The blackened coals from the fires remain under several years of vegetation. Woodcock and grouse still come to the beaver-barren popples.

Brook trout? Miniature white-winged black mayflies?

They are gone. Only memories.

But not abandoned memories. As the gale off Lake Michigan caterwauls outside this window tonight, there is the hope that if we do our job, our grandchildren and great grandchildren can bring those memories back to life. They can be real again — forever.

That is conservation. Hardcore conservation.

Some of us may not be around to see the Hendricksons, Red Hex, Tricorythodes and brook trout return. But we know it can happen. And we're gonna make it happen.

Not only on the Jordan. But on the dozens of Michigan streams deserving redemption.

The old cane rods on the wall over this desk, the fly-tying vice, and the feathers and furs in the bench upstairs are not meant for the scrap heap. If we do our job, someone will be casting over Michigan brook trout when these pages are long withered.

And you know, it would be nice if one of them squatted on the bank, with waders dangling in the river, or leaned against that old hemlock where I've buried under the moss the ashes from many a pipe, and promised that if anyone messed with "his stream" he'd go to bat for it just like those oldtimers did when it needed them back in the late 1900s.

The Dusky Sparrow
March 14, 1984

I have never seen nor heard a dusky (seaside) sparrow. Odds are pretty good that not many people have. And odds are something like ten jillion to zero that those of us who haven't will.

By all accounts in the bird books, we haven't missed much. The dusky sparrow is described as a rather drab fellow, a notch bigger than a chickadee with a rather so-what song.

Not a very flexible creature, either. It requires mucky saltwater marshlands, flitting around in the grass — eating little crabs and snails.

Too bad for it. Folks down in Florida don't think much of marshlands getting in the way of highways, condos, farming, and other profitable endeavors. And they don't think much of little creatures that flit around in them. So, as the story goes, dusky sparrows have just about disappeared. And there ain't ever gonna be any more.

Those folks in Florida saw to that.

We have folks like that in Michigan. Like the former Grayling Chamber of Commerce boss who was quoted as demanding that we quit coddling Kirtland's warblers so the National Guard could get on with the business of spending more money with local merchants.

But in Michigan — it seems to me — that kind of folks don't have much clout. What happened to the dusky sparrow could not happen in Michigan; at least this department likes to believe that.

I'd even venture that if the Kirtland's had enough sense to stay in Michigan year around — instead of slipping off to the Bahamas — there wouldn't be thousands of people walking around with a knot in their gut every spring waiting to see if the species met its doom over winter. Michigan folks would make sure the little birds of the jack pines — which aren't worth any more than saltwater marshes — had everything they needed right here.

It is difficult to describe the value you put on things like the Kirtland's, which many of us have seen and heard, and dusky sparrows, which we haven't and won't. It is even more difficult to describe the sinking sorrow that gnaws at us when we contemplate their extinction.

We can, certainly, live without them. Just as we live without the thousands of other species that have disappeared over the eons. But, somehow, we know that the human species is a cheaper, less likeable creature because it's contributed to the extinction of this small creature, if not being the primary cause.

This isn't just sentimental trash. If dusky sparrows were about twenty times bigger, lived in wild, lonely places, and were plentiful many of us would hunt them. A diet of crabs, snails, and such should make them fine eating. If they held for a pointing dog they'd likely have organizations dedicated to their prosperity.

Wherein lies the point of these ramblings: If dusky sparrows had been game birds they wouldn't be on their last thousandth of a blink from disappearing. Conservationists (read sportsmen) would have seen to their welfare. They — and their salt marshes — would be flourishing. Just as ruffed grouse, wild turkeys, quail, woodcock, mourning doves, giant Canada geese, and wood ducks are flourishing.

The spoilers would have been turned back at the edges of the Florida marshes when they started closing in on the dusky sparrow if there were guys with double barrels and setters on the bird's side. Members of the Dusky Sparrow Benevolent Society would be raffling off a shotgun and wildlife prints in honor of their favorite autumn targets. Artists would make big bucks drawing pictures of them. Outdoor writers would bore readers to tedium with tributes to dusky sparrows. And wildlife biologists would be checking on the spring nesting success — instead of checking to see if any of the last four on earth croaked in their cage last night.

Of late there's been a lot of tripe in the papers in these parts about the meanness of hunters. If they could, I'd urge the writers to check with the Dusky Sparrow Board of Directors in bird heaven on whether they'd prefer that their race were dusky sparrows or woodcock.

The Sluice Hole
March 16, 1983

The river here is pinched through a narrow, and often churning channel. Upstream and down it flares like a funnel. But here, where a logging railroad grade once crossed, an agile young man could leap across.

It is a good place to come when the spring thaw has left other banks soft and squishy in early April. Even so, there are usually piles of snow under the dark cedars. But not now. At least a month early, the snow was gone.

Downstream, where the river again flares, and a jumble of rock and logs create a wide, quiet pool, a hen steelhead is usually on station by mid-to-late April. Sometimes the same nest will be used by several fish as late as June, if trout fishermen don't drive them off.

In some colder years, the first steelhead don't make it this far upstream until after the trout opener. Several times I've felt the corks on a tiny five- or four-weight cane rod nearly explode as the bamboo bent into a fly-hooked steelhead. (Only once was one landed — a four-pound cock fish that became confused. He had silly genes, so we ate him.)

Though over a month early, I expected to find fresh-run steelhead in the breeding water in the second week of March. It has been that kind of winter. The horned larks have been back for two weeks. Geese dropped into the lake last week. Mute swans are staking out their mating territories. Mary Lou (Sharp-Ear Lou, we call her) heard the first frogs March 8. Sparrows have been flitting in and out of the bluebird boxes.

We are going to have to start Toots and Twig on their heartworm pills soon. And I expect Mary Lou to complain about her first black fly bite any day now.

Standing in the shadows of the cedars, my mind flitted back to a summer evening picnic here. Sister Anne and Mary Lou, patiently sipping at a bottle of prepared, chilled margaritas, waited for me to get food on the blanket. The salt shaker was nearly empty, and the bottle drained, by the time food was cooked.

Handling a giggling grandmother and sister on a trout stream was different. But fun.

No fish showed for fifteen or twenty minutes. Then a shadow moved from under the grass and fern-matted bank. It was a big fish

— maybe twelve pounds. Still bright silver. It hovered over the nest, which showed no evidence of having been tail fanned yet.

Just staking out her territory?

Two, then three, smaller fish darted nervously over the nest and around the big female. They dropped back, like a miniature swarm, and singly would flash around her, never closer than a foot or so.

The time for breeding had not arrived — but they were anxious.

The female steelhead, it seems, is sadly vulnerable to hoodlums with spears. I worried that someone with less intrinsic interest would follow my tracks to her. And hoped that conservation officers John Crane or Tom Sweet would see my tracks and stake the place out.

Maybe this early spring will be good for the steelhead, giving them a chance to spawn before the fishermen arrive.

Maybe the little brook trout will do better — and the mayflies and caddisflies. And the woodcock and grouse chicks. And the hemlocks and adder tongues.

It is all maybe's. No one can remember such a gentle winter. Its impact on natural things is a total unknown even to the most veteran outdoorsmen. We guess, but don't know. So we ponder, but don't really worry.

Give her a chance to do it her way, however she decides that is, and Nature will get it right.

Riding home I felt as giddy as Anne and Mary Lou did after their liquid picnic. Nature does that to some of us.

Getting Ready For The Keys
January 11, 1989

It takes a sense of humor and a defiance — or ignorance — of pro-
portion for a guy who is a lifelong slave to number 14 through 24
dry flies to crank out a Lefty's Deceiver.

It also takes a gob of feathers as long as your hand and as big
around as the neck of a Coke bottle, and a hook almost big enough to
gaff a chinook salmon. The Lefty's Deceiver, you see, is named after
that giant of saltwater fly fishing, Lefty Kreh.

It is big enough to send just about every brook trout I ever caught
into shock. In fact, it is probably big enough to eat most of the trout
my friend Ed catches in the Au Sable's Holy Water. The darn things
are so hefty that a couple decades or so ago, I talked Dad into having
one of his guys build me a special fly tying vise from a design con-
ceived by the late and great Jack Schweigert of Jack's Rod and Fly
Shop in Roscommon. You could anchor a canoe in a fair current with
this vise.

But that ain't the worst of it. To lash your Lefty's Deceiver to
your fly line you have to tie this perverted thing called a Bimini twist
into your leader. Before you're done with that, you've got monofila-
ment twisted around your ears, toes and anything hanging out
between. I mean it is mean.

So how did a normal brain-warped brook trout fly fisherman get
involved in such demented doings. Blame it on Gary Schnicke and
the late, still beloved, Arnold Hubbell.

Hub and Gary came back from the Florida Keys sometime in the
late 1960s or early 1970s with these tales and pictures of hundred-
pound tarpon on fly rods. Geez! The impact was almost as powerful
as the first time Mary Lou held my hand. I went bonkers.

Ordered enough torpedo-length saddle hackle to make a feather
bed for King Kong and started tying Lefty's Deceivers and other saltwater flies. Got Schnicke to teach me how to double haul a twelve-
weight fly rod for sixty-yard casts.

(Well, that ain't the truth. I got him to try to teach me how. He
was a lousy teacher; Gary spent most of his time rolling on the
ground trying to catch his breath while I unwound the line from
around my ankles and neck.)

Anyhow, it never worked out — that is, I never got to Florida. I
tried 'em for pike and muskies. Never got a strike. And never had a

chance to go to tarpon — or bonefish — country. So I gave most of them away over the years.

You know, this guy would say, "Hey, Shep, I'm going to the Keys (or Mexico, or Caribbean) for tarpon. What kind of flies do you use?"

I'd say, "Here have a handful," and reach in this bulging cardboard box and hand him a dozen or more Lefty's Deceivers and other expensive salt-water flies.

Then the other night, when the wind was howling at fifty plus m.p.h. and you couldn't find the bird feeders, Bev Rogers called from her winter home in the lower Keys. Bev's the feisty little gal who, with her Mountain Man-size husband Jim, has been spearheading the unfortunate drive to ban bear hounds.

Despite our disagreement on outlawing bear hounds (but agreement on effectively outlawing trespass), Bev is one of the most honorable, fun to be with, beautiful gals I've ever met. Jim, of course, is anything but beautiful. Except for a perversion about junk car dealing, he is honorable. He has some other characteristics that the Marine Corps PFC school might have corrected, but we try to overlook those.

And both are tough and stubborn. Our kind of folks.

Anyway, Bev called to tell us that while the wind chill just a bit inland from Lake Michigan was thirty or more degrees below zero, she'd been swimming twice that day. Water temperature in the high seventies. She said she had the air conditioner on in the afternoon.

They have a really fine place less than an hour north of Key West — right on the water. You can get to the genuine wilderness of the flats within a half hour using the little sixteen-foot aluminum outboard skiff. The utter shame man has brought to the land is forgotten. The water is clear and calm. The fishing magnificent. In fact, last year we caught so many strange fish we had to buy a fish book — you know, like a bird book.

Aside from joshing about the warm, sunny weather, Bev and Jim invited us down again early this spring.

Mary Lou's gonna check on the plane tickets. If we can afford them, we'll go. Last year our round-trip tickets from Grand Rapids to Key West cost us $200 each.

We had a grand time down there last spring. Never went out for supper. Ate fresh fish and shrimp almost every night. Managed to avoid going to towns. We met some great people and escaped having to fly in Jim's World War II Grumman Widgeon airplane.

Also, I have to admit I was taken with what that country must have been when the first pirates landed. It sickened me to realize that they are trying to destroy northern Michigan just like they have the land (not water) there.

We caught fish — beautiful, delicious fish. All on spinning rods. Many with live bait and bobbers. I'd sit on the dock until midnight — often sipping too many Scotches — teasing fish with tiny shrimp. It was kinda hypnotic.

But the three fly rods and all the flies and fly gear I'd brought only came out once.

When I came home, Bruce Richards, the guy who runs Scientific Anglers — the fly line company out of Midland — and who had helped me gear up, asked how the fly fishing had been.

I explained to him that I'd pulled that bolt in my back the day before we left, barely managed to crawl on and off the airplane. Our friends met us with a wheelchair at Key West airport. When I tried to fly cast I ended up on the deck of the skiff whimpering in agony.

Alarmed, and genuinely sympathetic, he asked, "Oh Shep, how'd you do that?"

Like a damn fool I told him the truth: "Putting my underwear on."

"Oh s__t man," he blurted, "that would cure me right then from wearing underwear."

So forgive me, Bev, if I show up without shorts under my shorts. But I'll have enough Lefty's Deceivers to sink the skiff.

New Year Thaw
January 2, 1985

A flock of — maybe — two dozen goldfinches browsed on seeds whose stalks had been bent under snow a day before. The little rivulet that had been stilled by ice and lack of runoff ran swiftly through the dogwood and cedars to the swamp.

The thermometer back at the house was hanging just over fifty degrees. (The radio said it was up to sixty in some places.) Rain had fallen for nearly twenty-four hours. Only a patch of snow remained here and there. Hayfields and meadow openings showed splashes of green.

If you bent low and listened intently, the little furrow of running water chattered and chuckled like a full grown crick. Maybe it was bragging about an unseasonal spring to life down the drumlin and through the swale.

Tonight, the weatherman said, the warm weather would end. This post-Christmas spring would disappear in a rush back to winter. The New Year would come in on a flurry of snow.

A friend in town, during yesterday's downpour, commented that it was all baffling — that such things don't happen in the frigid northland in late December. Well, he's only been prowling these lakes and streams and hills and condominiums for fifteen or twenty years. So what does he know?

Sure, a year ago we were snowed in (and our Christmas family out) for six straight days. There were ten foot drifts across the road. Lawmen had the roads out of town blocked. Mary Lou and I finished a turkey intended for eight, but shared by two, in March.

This year the turkey, shared by eight, is only a few sandwich scraps as this is written. The road to town is greasy slick; a muddy mess. Not a shred of snow or ice.

But unexpected, no. Such is the way of the north country. You learn not to expect the expected. The weather up here is unpredictable. There is no pattern, regardless of what the long-term records say.

And despite some short-lived disappointment for the businessmen who rely on ice fishermen and snowmobilers, it is good. This almost tropical turn in the weather means a few days' edge for wild things — like the canaries, who were dependent on bird feeders a year ago, and who now have hundreds of acres of weeds to prowl.

Turkeys, fawns, young foxes, and many other creatures are thriving, at least momentarily. Grouse hunters worry about "their" birds; afraid that without deep snow too few will survive to provide them with targets next fall.

Bah, humbug! Deep snow and cold surely provide some protection during mean winter months, but warm open weather means protection isn't as necessary. (And, besides, the problem isn't too few birds; it is too many hunters.)

The canaries suddenly bolted, in a dozen directions, then turned as one for the thick popples nearby. A young broad-winged hawk — probably the same one that stalks the bird feeders — swooped over the field. We're glad to see he is also savoring a kindly winter.

A whitetail, maybe a buck, tried to cross the lake this morning. His tracks stretched to within fifty yards of where open water was obvious from the mushy shore. Then south — then north. Then angling back to shore. Confused by the loss of an easy path he'd been using to reach the chopped cornfield on the west side? Not to worry; there is food everywhere.

Deep in the swamp, the jackrabbits stand out in their white coats. The fox and great horned owl must find them easy, succulent targets. But that is the way Nature set the stage. It will all work out.

Winter may, almost certainly will, rage back with a vengeance. But it will be futile. These places, these creatures, are programmed for four months of fury. They're now assured of no more than three.

No greater gift could they receive.

Happy New Year, friends.

The Real World
February 22, 1989

Full daylight was only a promise. A promise that the brightening orangish-pink light creeping up the drumlin to the east told us would be kept.

Two to three inches of feathery snow during the night was too much to resist. With a couple cups of coffee for nourishment, I struck out with Nails as soon as it was light enough to read the new story in the snow.

Fresh snow is like having the morning paper to read. Everything that happened the night before will be reported in its own language. You just have to be patient to read it.

How clear that story reads depends on wind and, I soon remembered, a young bird dog's enthusiasm for a new day and the wonders of a morning romp. Within a few feet of the door, Nails disappeared in a cloud of flying snow. You could see the puffs of snow, but rarely the dog inside them.

It had been a busy night for creatures in the yard. Lots of mice. At least three rabbits — a cottontail and two snowshoes. We've been lucky this year with the red squirrels — not many around. Fox squirrels had come from the northeast and west, but not a single red squirrel track. Darn house cat had been poking around, though. The top of the picnic table had a ruffed grouse's signature.

No deer had been to the salt block. Curious sign just beyond it: wing marks in the blown snow. Not big enough for a hawk. Maybe a small owl? They seemed about the size a blue jay would leave. Couldn't read what else had happened.

Nails came roaring back to check in. She slammed on the brakes just long enough for a couple of pats and confirmation that she wasn't going to be told this was serious business. Then off in another burst of snow.

Thought about ordering her on heel. That way she wouldn't erase the drama in the snow. But heck, this was her fun.

Deer, lots of them, had been moving along the edge of the swale. Way too many. Hunters didn't take half enough last fall. With a relatively mild winter, they are still being killed on the road. Orchards are a maze of tracks. Farmers are going to continue paying a high price this spring.

Wildlife managers are going to have to learn new tricks. We must trim the deer herd down to no more than half. Drivers, farmers and, yep, hunters will be rewarded if the herd is halved. The quality of hunting will soar if whitetails again become so scarce you truly have to hunt and stalk them. With enough natural food they cannot easily be duped into becoming victims of baiting.

The swale bottoms out in a rim of cattails. Here and there, springs seep to the surface, blotting out the snow.

Nature had written a rich chapter there. Mink. A weasel, his tail signing his name in the snow. A fox track came in to the edge of a boggy area from the southwest, then angled off to the west.

Following these tracks, there was sign where another fox had stood watching, then left paralleling the first arrival at a few feet. Then I saw a churned maze of snow, like they'd discovered a nest of mice and had joined each other in the feast.

Suddenly aware that Nails hadn't paid a call in a while, I headed north, where I'd last seen her. Picking up the tracks, I followed to the northeast, then north, then back south.

The sun had climbed over the drumlins now. It was almost blinding on the glistening snow. Wished I'd brought sun glasses. But who would have thought of that in the dim pre-dawn glow when we left the house?

At first Nails was just a shapeless blur in the shadow of a cedar. Darn, she was on point. As I hurried toward her, her tail started to swish little fluffs of snow.

The grouse exploded in a miniature tornado of snow not more than five feet from her nose. She sorta lurched into reverse, then almost fell on her nose recovering.

Now she was serious about this business she was born to. Within the next fifteen minutes she pointed three more grouse. Better than she'd done all October. The combination of the swale's warmth and the mature popples on its flanks offer an ideal winter haven for the birds.

Turning in the wet britches for a dry pair and the boots for slippers, the typewriter seemed far friendlier than it had in several mornings. Even the two-hour-old coffee had a somehow sweeter taste than when fresh brewed.

The phone rang. To hell with it. A nuthatch was tipping upside down on the beech tree to get at the suet. The real world could wait.

The real world? Isn't that what we abandoned when we closed the door?

Anticipation Of Spring
March 13, 1985

What a difference a month makes in this land of trout and grouse, snow and mud.

A month ago there was four foot of powdery snow between the drumlins. Where the wind was especially clear it was stacked, maybe, eight feet deep. Snowshoes sank eighteen to twenty-four inches. Even a walk to the garage was a Herculean task. When the road was open, which was only sometimes, the pass between the drifts was so narrow it took careful guidance to keep the mirrors from clipping them.

The birds were going through four to five three-pound coffee cans of seed a day. They looked so wretchedly miserable holding on in a screaming gale while they tried to get enough calories to survive the night you thought about inviting them indoors.

The cover never went on the typewriter before the sun had set. Now it goes on an hour earlier (even if it has to come back off after sunset) and there's still a couple hours of daylight left. The sunsets seem to have moved north about a quarter mile.

City folks may find it hard to like mud, but by mid-March we just about worship it. The cars and boots are a muddy mess; anyone who complains is regarded as unbalanced.

Sure, at this writing, there is still plenty of snow; better than a foot or more down in the swamp. Snowshoes glide over it almost like skis.

No matter what the calendar says, or what the people in southern Michigan see, hear, and smell, spring doesn't come to these precincts until early or mid-May. So we cherish our late winter and wring every possible joy out of it.

Bud Jones has been trying to call the mating owls, by imitating their mournful pleas for lady friends. He's getting them in close, but not close enough to see. So far he's talked to a saw-whet, barred, and great horned owl. (I take his word that he can identify them by their call.)

One of late winter's grandest observation posts is the deer blind between the swamp and lake and the hardwoods. Each visitation requires a pocketful of sunflower seeds and another of stale peanuts (donated by Sonny Lang from Murdick's Fudge in town).

It only takes one donation to bring the chickadees in. They're at the seeds within minutes after you plop down on the Hot Seat. It is like they are trained to spot them on the snow.

The goldfinches also catch on by the second day. If you sit still for fifteen minutes after throwing out the seeds, they flutter in; at least two dozen of them the last time.

The peanuts disappear, too. But the snow is too hard one day and too mushy the next to pick up tracks. Blue jays, certainly, are taking many. I've seen downy woodpeckers clumsily take them. Almost surely, red squirrels and mice are heavy into the peanuts. Several holes have appeared around the peanut pile. I've been hoping to catch a mouse poking his nose out after hearing fresh supper plunk on the snow. No luck yet.

Mice probably need the handout more than any of the creatures. In addition to the owls, there's a couple hawks and at least two foxes stalking them.

Up on the slope where the junipers thrive, you could read sign where a pair of foxes were hunting and catching mice for a few days back, when the snow conditions were right. Across the trail, in Archie's newly cleared land, one made a dive for a snowshoe hare a while back. It looked like he lost the race. Couldn't figure out what a hare was doing in that jumble of hardwood stumps. It was more than a quarter mile from the swamp or the pines.

An otter, or maybe more, has been traveling between the lakes. As I interpret the sign, he makes the trek about every fourth to sixth day. Always on the same route. You can tell because he slides down every slope, leaving a neat furrow in the hard-packed snow.

By late afternoon, water is starting to seep over the edges of the ice in the pond. Spring will come when the frogs and peepers sing their first chorus and the woodcock join them with their exciting display.

In the meantime, there's plenty to see and hear as Nature tunes up for her annual renewal.

Winter Walk With Toots
February 16, 1983

We hadn't been in this direction since bird season; there was no other reason.

Toots and I have this complicated formula: we strike out this way one day, that way another day and another way another day. Our winter walk begins about the time the sun bunches up over the drumlin to the west. We then say to heck with the telephone and typewriter, and check what's been happening out there.

The winter has been irresponsibly wondrous for irresponsible editors and curious bird dogs, both fascinated by what goes on in the swales between drumlins. With less than a foot of thickly-crusted snow, the snowshoes really aren't needed in the hardwoods and fields, where they behave more like skis. But in the swamps they're the only thing that keeps you from plunging through to mud and water.

A tiny highway of tracks led from a brush pile to one of the most remote bluebird houses. A mouse has taken up the nest since it was cleaned last fall. As we approach, a twitching nose appears below out-size ears and eyes in the entry hole.

When we stare back, the nose quit dancing and the ears flick. Maybe trying to hear if anything is coming up behind?

No reason to oust it now. Wait until just before the bluebirds are due and then plug the hole after cleaning it.

On the little lake a black splotch moves far down the east shore. A crow, probably. But what would it be eating there? Drawing closer it becomes an otter. Walking slowly, and only when it seemed to dip below the snow rim of a small depression, and keeping Toots on heel with hand signals, we get within seventy-five feet of it before it disappears.

It had kept open a hole made by an ice fisherman and was sliding in and out of it — according to the evidence. A spring keeps the ice open along shore, so it could swim the distance without being exposed on the open ice.

It has been a funny winter. The road to the lake is always closed by the end of December. This year the guys with four wheelers are still driving it.

There are several otters that seem to move between the five small lakes tucked in the drumlins here. So many that one guy we know blames them for the perhaps imagined decline of his perch fishing.

Deer trails weave up the drumlins and through the swamps. Yet a rabbit track is rare this winter. Swamps that commonly have a maze of well-packed snowshoe hare trails have only an occasional single rabbit's track.

As I collect dead twigs from a blowdown maple beside an impenetrable snarl of wind-killed birch and cedar, more than a half dozen chickadees gather before a match is lit. As the fire snaps and larger sticks are added, more continue arriving, jabbering and flitting about, sometimes no more than inches from my head.

The little blaze, no larger than a hand, is sending a faint wisp of smoke almost chimney true into the air when Toots leaps, poking her nose deep into a hummock of snow at the base of the matted roots of a cedar. About five feet to the north, a mouse squirts from the snow and streaks across it to dive into another hole in the crust. I'm reminded of a lemming that became friendly enough to sleep in my parka pocket at an Arctic camp.

Toots comes up, shakes snow from her head and pretends nothing happened.

A red squirrel, now two, *chrrr chrr* somewhere in the branches of a small spruce. You can imagine their tails snapping as they order the intruders out. Toots ambles up to the tree and lays in the snow. The racket grows louder, but the chickadees ignore it.

One of them has become brave enough to sit on the trunk of the fallen birch, no more than two feet from my shoulder. When it finds and snaps up the first of the sunflower seeds spread there from my pocket another joins it. The others hold back.

If I stay long enough at least one of them would become tame enough to eat from my hand. But what good is a tame chickadee? As the fire dies to a fist-size mound of gray ashes, I kick snow on it and leave the rest of the seeds.

The crust on the drumlin is too slick for the snowshoes. Carrying them, I find myself chuckling over a phone call a couple hours earlier from a former colleague who still slaves over a typewriter (computer, I guess) in the city. Before he hung up he said he hoped to get up in May, when winter's over and "there's something to do up there."

Guess he's not into quiet afternoon campfires in the swamp with mice and chickadees. Just as well. Grown men are supposed to have more serious things to do. Poor blokes.

Red Squirrels And .22s
January 25, 1989

If you live in the north woods, you've been here many times.

It is two or three o'clock in the morning. You are as numb to the world as a white pine stump that felt the saw's bit in 1878. You don't have to get up for two or three hours. When you went to bed the moon and stars were glistening on sparkling new snow.

I mean, hey, everything is jack perfect. You know where you've been and where you are going in the morning. You've got it down pat.

Then: Wham! Wham! Wham!

A jackhammer is going off on your ribs. Your eyes snap open. Your head, sorta, slides around on the pillow and in the mist.

This creature next to you, the one with the delicious God-given curves and padding and *BLOODY ELBOW* is snorting: "You hear that? They're playing football up there. Get 'em out of the attic!"

Ah, geez, woman. So there's a couple (or half ..., maybe a dozen) red squirrels ripping around in the attic. What are you going to do about it in the middle of the night?

This growl starts somewhere beyond her toenails and rages up (through all that neat padding) and out her nostrils. No way she's gonna let you go back to sleep.

There are two solutions. One, get up and make a couple of cups of tea or hot chocolate. Most times that will soothe her back to sleep.

Two, go shoot hell outta the attic with a shotgun. At least that will quiet the pesky little so-and-sos until tomorrow night.

But you'll still end up making tea, or coffee, for the Sheriff's deputy who then shows up a few minutes later in response to the neighbor's call that the Sheppards are shooting hell out of their house at 2:00 a.m.

Next to senior whitetail bucks, red squirrels have to be about the most crafty critters in the woods. But, like trophy bucks, they sometimes stumble on their own noses.

My solution to bloody ribs — and elbows — in the early morning is to try to shoot every red squirrel I see around the house. I detest baiting as a hunting technique. But killing red squirrels isn't hunting. It is war.

I put nuts, cereal and cat food out on the picnic table to lure them in. I may have killed a dozen or more so far this year.

The best was some ten days ago. When I slid the door open, he (she?) darted off the picnic table like a streak of fire. Went up a maple about fifty yards out. A few seconds later it poked its head (that's just about the size of a half dollar) out from around the tree's trunk.

The post in the Redfield scope locked on that devilish little eye. The little bolt action Ruger .22 rimfire rifle barked. Ha! The tormentor dropped flat-out dead.

This old grunt was pretty proud of his shooting. By the time I rounded Mary Lou up to brag, something had carted the trophy off. Tracks in the snow (including blood) would have proven my point to anyone but her. (You should see the scars on her elbow.)

She didn't believe I'd made the shot.

When she went to town a couple of days later she came home with something in a bag she wouldn't let me see. Fearing it was a file to work her elbow into a sharper point, I was desperate to prove I'd been eradicating the woods of red squirrels.

Wow! It couldn't have happened to a more deserving guy. A red squirrel parked itself on the picnic table, wolfing down peanuts, not twenty yards away. He didn't even hear the door slide open.

Mary Lou is all but salivating as I raise the little rifle.

Pow!

The little s-o-b gawks around, trying to figure out what the noise was.

Then he hears the bolt slam a new round into the chamber and zips down into the snow, stopping about fifteen feet away, in clear view.

Pow!

To make a miserable story as miserable as it can get, that happened seven times. Never more than thirty-five yards away. Always with the full body exposed. Always dead still. Never any blood.

And, wouldn't you know, always with Mary Lou standing there watching — and sorta chuckling or gasping to catch her breath. (Oh yeah, she hooted when I accused her of messing with the scope. Then she got her file and tourniquet and went to work on her elbow.)

Having spent nearly all of the past twenty-five years where I can step out on the porch and plink away with my .22s, I fire several thousand rounds a year. Love the little rifles. I have an almost decadent number of them.

If you didn't know, frozen apples and potatoes make delightful targets. Beat the blazes out of today's aluminum cans, which don't even shudder when you plow a forty-grain slug through them. The thing to do is collect feral apples — the kind that never get ripe — in the fall and store them in a cellar for shooting all winter.

I've been playing this childish game since before Mom and Dad would let me. A pal and I went together and had his big brother buy us a single shot, bolt action, Winchester .22 rifle. I think we paid ten or twelve dollars for it. We kept it hidden in his barn.

Most of the time we'd buy shorts. They were cheaper.

My recollection is that shorts cost twelve to eighteen cents for a fifty-round box. Long rifles were around two bits for a box of fifty.

With my memory about as wobbly as my shooting, I checked with Harv Jacobitz. Now Harv used to own two of the world's largest cartridge equipment reloading manufacturing companies. So he's been in the business for a while. (And he's no more reliable than I am.)

He says he was paying eleven to seventeen cents for a box of shorts as a kid. When he was flush, he bought long rifles for twenty-six cents a box.

Hey, if you don't remember it, those were big bucks back then. A box of .22 shells meant a whole weekend's fun. (Movie tickets were cheaper. A coke at the drug store was two cents. And, oh geezus, we hadn't even learned how to fight wars we didn't win back then.)

What's all this got to do with red squirrels in the attic and elbows in the ribs?

Heck, I don't know. Wish I had the guts to put a dead red squirrel under her pillow.

Winter Hawk
January 15, 1986

T he Sun!

People all over the northland were talking about it. They were trying to recall the last day without snow. It was difficult to remember when the sun had appeared for more than a peek through a snow cloud. Most decided it had been since about the middle of deer season.

Though the temperature was snappy (twenty-two below zero, they say, at Pigeon River Country State Forest headquarters), staying indoors was impossible.

Not that an excuse was needed, but why not dream one up that's really whimsical? Like, how about tracking down a hawk? You ever try tracking a hawk?

Well, we've had a hawk flitting by the bird feeder windows and, several times, we spotted it hunting over the cornfield above Archie's lake. The glimpses we've caught suggest it is one of the marsh hawks that rear youngsters in these precincts every year. But that doesn't make a lot of sense. And I can't rely on these tired eyes.

So maybe, some time squatting at the edge of the hardwoods and cornfield with the pocket-size binoculars would produce a better look. It didn't sound very probable. But, what the heck, who really cares? Sure as heck not the hawk — or me.

On the top of the drumlin, the wind that has been raging off Lake Michigan since November has the ground nearly bare. The corn stubble sticks up six or eight inches. Just inside the hardwoods, the snow is more than two feet deep; in many places more than three feet deep.

Inland a few miles there is half as much snow. It has settled in basketball-size clumps on tree limbs and stumps. Here, the wind has battered and mauled it into heaps as much as five feet deep around the base of trees.

But, no matter, the snowshoes found it packed enough for easy going. Especially at only a few feet a minute, as I scan the horizon for wings.

Where in summer there is a boulder almost half the size of a one-man ice shanty, the wind-sculptured snow was higher than an arm could reach over your head. A twin row of puncture marks pierced the snow, coming down the field from the north, as though the hawk, or a giant eagle, were carrying a broom handle in its talons and stabbing them into the snow every few inches. As straight as marines on parade.

Fox sign. A pair. The snuggle season for them, you know.

Following them north toward Archie and Louise's led to a crater in the snow. It looked like both had pounced. No blood. I wondered if the pairing ties were strong enough for them to share the mouse, or whatever, they had probably caught.

Turning back to leave the open field, their signs lead me down to the lake where there is a fox den under a blowdown of elm and cedar. I found a fluff in the snow where they had stopped to mate at the base of a knoll.

Fifty or so yards on, one had bolted to the south, dragging its paws in the snow. Maybe it spotted a red squirrel or jack rabbit. The trail led to the base of a big, hollow-trunked beech. No other tracks. Then it cut northeast, to intercept its short-term lover.

They rejoined under the naked tamaracks beside the lake and headed across it. No way was I following. Under the deep snow is slush. If a snowshoe plunged through, that gimpy leg would never drag it back home.

There should have been whitetail tracks leading from the swale up to the cornfield. None could be found. And there hadn't been snow for nearly two days — a record for this winter. Things have to be mean in there. No one has seen turkeys either. If they could only reach the field, Archie has left plenty of corn. Nothing else he can do for them.

Gonna be hell on a lot of wild things if it keeps up.

Shadows were stretching ever so longer as the sun headed over the brow of Fisherman's Island. Trudging slowly up the slope, it became a game to walk on the shadow of one maple tree and then skip to the next.

At the crest of the ridge, the sunset was starting to glow over the big lake. Mary Lou would have water simmering for hot chocolate. There were pork chops to grill in the wood stove, fresh-dug parsnips and a Christmas Siamese kitten, named Tikki, to tickle under the chin.

The hawk? Probably a rough-legged. Maybe we'll find its trail if the sun shines again this winter. Tonight, here's hoping it has a full belly and takes a minute to enjoy the sunset with us.

Living With Winter
January 1, 1986

He must have blinked.

~Suddenly, as if zapped there by Alley Oop's time machine, there was a snowshoe hare (jack rabbit) huddled under the drooping snow-weighted cedar bough about sixty feet away from where I'd been standing for at least two minutes.

Even with the sunglasses it was impossible to see tracks in the snow leading to its perch.

The sun had come out about an hour and a half ago, after a couple inches of fresh snow. The wind had gone down about dawn. First decent weather in almost forever. It seemed unlikely it would last long, so there was a dash to get into the snowshoes and see what the real world still looked like.

There hadn't been any serious intention to use it, but the heavy-frame .22 autoloading pistol had been strapped on, and a couple of ten-shot clips dropped into the Mackinaw's big rear pocket.

Jack rabbit, in my opinion is one of the least desirable wild foods in the north woods. Besides, it would be pretty safe with me shooting at it, even if it held still while I drew, loaded and armed the pistol.

Which it did, even when the slide slammed back to chamber the round and cock the hammer. Maybe it had frozen to death there.

The roar of the little round surprised me. The rabbit jerked, as though it were about to leap away, then sorta crumbled into a heap. That was another shock. (Better not shoot at another one this year; that way can claim never missed a single shot. But, shucks, there's thousands of .22 shells left from that big sale I got in on.)

He was skinned in a minute or so, gutted and wiped out with snow before going into one of the plastic bags that are kept handy for putting anything from a weed to a partridge or duck in. Too cold on the hands to bone him there.

Even with the big shoes, the going was mean. Easily thirty inches of snow on the level — which there's darn little of — and four feet where wind had piled it up. Soft, leg-grabbing stuff. The sun drew snaky shadows, like skeletons, from bleak hardwood limbs and big dark patches beside cedars and spruces.

Blue jays clamored in a thicket. No chickadees or woodpeckers; they were probably all huddled around the feeders up at the house until spring. Life has been a little rough for them since Mary Lou spotted the northern shrike on Christmas day. First we've ever had in the winter. We are also hosting our first cardinal in about five years. Never had so many hairy and downy woodpeckers before. With few grosbeaks and nuthatches, there are no goldfinches this year, after dozens a year ago.

At the edge of a thick, narrow cedar and tag break, a grouse exploded from deep snow not two snowshoe lengths away. The powdery snow glittered in sunlight as it settled.

I wondered if the bird dog would have winded him before he spooked. Good thing he hadn't come along, probably would have drowned in this stuff.

Turning to watch the grouse fly off toward the lake, I stumbled over something under the snow and ended up the color of a fresh snowman; the worst part being the blotted eyeglasses.

Heading up the drumlin, where the junipers cover the hillside, I felt the wind picking up and decided it was making the strange shrill, but sorta warbling, noise. Then a flock of medium-sized birds rose from the junipers and swung north. Through the smudged glasses couldn't tell what they were.

Drying out beside the wood stove with a tumbler of single malt Scotch had become more important than trying to follow and identify them. Besides, there was the rabbit to get into the pot with some onions, spuds, carrots and whatever else I could wrestle up.

Winter. There's more than one way to live with it. But beat it? Never.

Winter Bluegills
February 13, 1985

Hunting winter bluegills in northern Michigan lakes is a young or rich man's pursuit.

That was the obvious conclusion after more than a dozen holes and not a bite. A rich man would have a snowmobile to haul the sled to carry the power auger. A young man wouldn't have arthritis snapping at his shoulders and knees.

Perch, walleye, whitefish, pike, and trout are friendlier, and far less frustrating. If you know where they should be they'll probably be nearby, and they'll either bite or they won't. Simple, right? A half dozen — usually less — holes are enough.

That's not enough for pesky bluegills. There must be a half mile of dropoff along the weed bed where you *might* find a school of bluegills on the feed. The odds, however, are mighty slim.

If you do run into bluegills, chances are they'll ignore your tiny jig and waxworm. With two feet of snow on the lakes between the drumlins, there's only a dribble of oxygen under the ice. Their metabolism has slowed to a trickle.

So, change that to a rich, young, or nutty man's sport. If he's been around long enough to know the way the deck is stacked, he can't have all his parts working if he goes chugging through snow and cold with hopes of finding bluegill.

But then, if he's been around that long he probably doesn't know how else to waste a sunny, windless February afternoon when the thermometer soars just above freezing. (And while he'd never claim total sanity, he considers bluegill-chasing saner than sitting in front of the tube watching basketball and golf.)

The watch under the tattered Mackinaw said just after 5:00 p.m. There was still enough light to tie on a home made, pearl-colored teardrop. But not enough oomph left to drill another hole. The old holes would have to be revisited.

It seemed foolish to plan on sticking around long enough to need it; yet, what the heck, you're sorta hooked on its hum and yellow light, so you fire up the old Coleman two-mantle.

The little jig drops into the hole. The two-pound-test line is invisible; your hands certainly can't feel it. So a magic act is performed stripping line from the unseen coil on the ice down through the water.

The jig hits bottom, then jigged a dozen times, in three to four jerk rhythms. Raise it a foot, or so, and repeat the procedure. Foot after foot, until it is less than two feet under the ice.

Nothing. Do it all over again.

Nothing. You tell yourself you're nuts. Then move to the next hole.

It is fast getting dark. However, it is easier, somehow, to see the delicate line in the lantern's glow than it was in the sunlight.

Three holes later and still — zero! (You old fool.)

But try one more. The teardrop hits bottom. You raise it a few inches. On about the second jig the spring bobber at the end of the wimpy six-foot rod stays down when you lower the rod to let the lure drop. The rod snaps over your head.

Ha! Whoopee!

And it's no perch. You feel the gill turn its side to the hook. The rod bends and throbs. Hot dang!

You release the near seven-incher as fast as you can, excitedly rebait and slide the jig back into the water. Whap. You've got another.

They run from five inches to nearly eight. The action is fast and furious, for what seems an hour. But when you check the watch, it turns out to be only about fifteen minutes.

When it's over you have no idea how many you caught and released. But who cares?

Back home, she asks if you'd like to scorch a couple of small steaks in the wood stove. Sure, but it seems a mundane matter after such a victory. It is worthy of a tumbler of that single malt Scotch Kay gave you for Christmas.

She, finally, asks how the fishing was. You start to babble. She gets up, bends over and presents a dandy smooch — meaning I'm happy for you, but I don't need a blow-by-blow description.

The bird dog slips her nose onto your lap. You rub her ear and tip your glass in a salute.

Hey, old man, you've still got it. Got it all!

Winter Break
February 15, 1984

The snow under the bird feeder looked like the bottom of a coal bin. The black husks of sunflower seeds created a mat several feet wide, causing the bright afternoon sun to melt a hole at least fifteen inches deeper than the snow around it.

Sitting on the swing for the first time in about three months, there was a feeling of glee, of escape, in the realization that the sun was making our cheeks tingle, instead of the wind that had been growling at them since November.

It is a false spring, for certain. The snow banks are dropping fast, but are still five feet high. The snow is slushy and clumpy; snowshoes sort of dig into it and come up as heavy as railroad ties. On the hill, they want to slide, so you roll back on your fanny and swoosh downhill. At the bottom you've got a wet rump — tolerable when it's warm.

There are a dozen to twenty chickadees flitting around the feeder. For the first time since mid-December they are concentrating on fun instead of cramming as much energy into their bodies with as little effort as possible. For a few days survival is forgotten.

Their song has changed. Even a guy with a tin ear hears the happiness in their chatter. Two of them hop up, then down, on some concrete blocks that form a kind of stairway. Pretty soon five are playing the game.

Two downys circle around and around the suet log without probing for rations. Their toe nails sound metallic as they grab the cedar. A hairy woodpecker swoops in and the little downys glide down to the basswood tree.

Toots is on rigid point at the base of the old tree. She's been stalking a fox squirrel — with a tail as big as a real fox — for the past two weeks. It dashes from the hardwoods to the basswood, which stands alone just down the drumlin from the feeder. Then, after long minutes of careful surveillance, it chugs for the feeder.

Toots came within two feet of catching it once. But the squirrel has since kept more distance between itself and the big bird dog.

Now, though I can't see it, odds are the squirrel is trapped in the tree, on the side away from the swing. If it makes a break for the woods, Toots could break a leg chasing it through the heavy snow. I call her back to the swing. She whines and drools, but sits obediently.

Crows are bickering over something down by the lake. They haven't done that in months. Just business-like one- or two-word caraaws. Now what we hear is, plainly, idle gossip.

Three land in the top of a big maple down by the pond. The .22 is only about twenty-five feet away, an easy shot at about 150 yards.

Gee, what a dumb idea. (Besides, I'm learning that 150-yard shots aren't as easy as they used to be.)

There's an urge to do something, to wring some action from this winter respite. But the short trek on the snowshoes quickly showed a hike was pure labor. Ice fishing is no fun; under a foot of wet, heavy snow there are six inches of water on the ice. And the fish aren't biting in our small lakes.

A chickadee lands two feet away, on the frame of the swing. Another joins him. Toots' head swivels, then snaps back, afraid she'll miss the squirrel.

Deer haven't left their tracks across the field since the Christmas storm. They have been moving, sometimes, from the swamp up to the wind-cleared cornfield. This fifty-degree plus day should give them a new charge of energy. If they can keep the trails open, and winter doesn't come back with a vengeance, they are over the hump. Some fawns have died, but the stronger survive.

For the turkeys it is another story. Those that aren't close to a corncrib have already lost. No matter. Though it seems sad to city folks, that's the way it happens.

The sun is low enough that it drives straight into my eyes. A fishing cap is pulled down to shade them.

Rusty has been fly fishing the Holy Water. There are things to be said for living in the flatland of Au Sable Country. Some days, like today, there is the temptation to trade it for these drumlins.

But no, Mary Lou is at the dining room table poring over seed catalogs, selecting this summer's squash, peas, beans, parsnips — and the parsnips are still under two feet of snow. The jack pine plains never grew parsnips like the drumlins do.

Toots lunges. The squirrel is making its break for the woods.

"Whoa!"

The old setter locks into a snow-spraying stop. The squirrel might even raise, or father, a family in a few weeks.

Memory Of Lee Day
February 12, 1986

It was a dozen or so years ago. Like too many readers he'd sent several notes saying he appreciated the way we try to shoot straight at the *Call*. That he would like to stop in someday, if he were in the area.

Then the call came. He was on his way down from the Upper. Could he slide through Charlevoix and visit for just a few minutes?

Multiply that by thousands and this typewriter would never get any attention. But damn it, what is the fun in writing to people you don't know? Besides it was late afternoon and the typewriter had ... well really, you know, it had about as much attention as it deserved for one day.

After the knock on the shed door, I felt the limp wrist and saw the sway-backed old Chrysler; I was surprised he'd made it the six miles from town. He was tall and scrawny with a bent to unassertive cordiality.

Said he was a newspaperman. Then admitted he worked for the mayor of Detroit, whom I felt was presiding over the deliberate strangulation of the city.

Wow! That ticked him off. Not mean and nasty, like the newsmen I'd broken knuckles with when we had both started in the trade. But a deep, and sensitive, hurt. Racist — he felt. And it pained him to feel that.

In turn, my gut churned. No tall and lanky, or short and chunky, giant he-man is gonna get away with that.

But he wasn't the kind of dude you slugged. Or the kind you pitched out. You had to talk to him. He was captivating. In ten minutes he had me signed on as a brother. Not many, if any, can do that to this old codger.

Lee Day came from a similar place in life. No money — no prospects — but with complete confidence that the American system would give them to us. The difference was that he believed a unionized, really socialized, brotherly love system would give him the opportunity to achieve. He was taught that all people were, truly, equal.

It wasn't that way with the minions this guide came from. The toughest, meanest, minority-hatingest would dominate.

The difference was love and hate. Scars and salve.

But as contradictory as they seem, there was a fundamental trust that the individual will — and can — prevail.

So, in those first few minutes, we fell in love. Though he had no scars on his knuckles or legs, they were deep in his soul. He'd hang it out for the resource just as deeply as any would.

No man, no institution, no political party, no bank ever compromised Leland Day. No man — no man — ever stood taller. No man — no man, ever — was more than Lee Day.

They say his heart was on the Au Sable, where he had a place and loved to cast his flies. Those who say that knew only his edges. His true heart was in the wilderness of Canada and Alaska — in the real wild, where he toted his canoe and was forever warmed by his love for Mary. Where there are no bigots — because there is nothing to hate.

Lee was always looking for that perfect world. Unlike me, and most of us, he couldn't accept the idea it will never exist.

And even after he had to leave the *Free Press* copy desk a few years ago, after the cancer started chasing him, he kept prodding us to get the faith, to believe we can make the world in his vision. That's why he loved newspapering as much as he did the wilds and people; he believed they are a critical tool in the evolution to peace and justice.

Hey, cobber, we expect you to have all the best trout hides, hatches and flies figured out if we ever join you. Damn, but you made this a better world, and us better men, Lee Day.

Phelps Station
January 19, 1983

You could easily make the point that tip-up fishing for pike is about as exciting and challenging as swatting balls with a club, or gawking at a pack of walruses wallowing around on the ground brawling over a pointy ball on a TV screen.

You'd get no argument from this department.

Guys who get serious about the tip-up thing are inclined to develop eyes that spin like those twirling circles on pin ball machines, after squatting on an ice-covered lake for hours waiting for thumb-size orange flags to pop out of wooden sticks.

But if you don't get serious about it, there are times when it seems to fit the weather and the need to let the gray matter between the ears go as numb as possible. (And tip-up fishing does not tilt pike and musky populations, like spearing does. Like most fish biologists I know, I'd outlaw spearing.)

It was too early for the bigger bluegills to feed. The temperature was just at freezing; the wind, for once, was well under a gale with the sun sometimes peeping through. The ice was nearly bare, about four inches thick — easy spudding — and the walls at home closing in.

During the long holiday between papers, Toots and I had tramped and re-tramped just about every foot of swamp and drumlin here on the Charlevoix-Antrim County border. She hunted birds and I walked and wondered about the little things starting to grow during the false spring of Christmas. She didn't know the shotgun's barrels were empty, and I kept her out of the pines, where the grouse had retreated, so she was happy.

The bluegills had been hitting before the Christmas thaw. But when ice started forming again, the wind took to howling. It kept up for days. Bluegills aren't that important to me as the years pile up.

So it seemed the right thing to spud a tip-up hole in Lake 26 and half-heartedly explore around for bluegills with a long, limber rod until their dinner bell rang about 4:30 p.m. It was thirty minutes to countdown when the flag went up.

Now it is your guide's theory that the only way to fish tip-ups is to let the pike have a good three to five minutes to play with the minnow. Let him tooth it a while. Then chaw on it a while. Pike, somehow, sense that a minnow with a hook in it isn't going anywhere — that they can spit it out and come back to torment it at will. (Mean devils!) So give 'em plenty of time.

Besides, no one has caught a good pike from this lake in years. The spear fishermen took the last trophies about fifteen to twenty years ago. That upset the balance and it has never recovered.

(Sometimes, I have this delightful but morbid dream. There's a five-foot-wide pit of muck. On one side are the snaggers. On the other the harpooners. At a signal they attack each other. They gouge and gore and tear at each other. In the bleachers are salmon, lake trout, steelhead, brown trout, pike and muskies, all cheering them on without bloodlust in their gills.)

The spring bobber on the little ice rod had started to bounce just before the tip-up flag snapped to attention. Ignoring the flag, I finally hooked a four-inch perch.

Yanking the tip-up out of the ice, the line was slack. After hauling in fifteen or twenty feet, it went tight. Real tight! Either the other end was in weeds or there was a *b-i-g* fish on the other end.

Laying a bit of muscle into it, the line jerked free, but still with solid weight holding it back.

The fresh twelve-pound test line had been put on in early December. No way was there anything in here big enough to break it. But the fish went wild a couple of times and I gave line. Memories of the twenty-one-pounder a spear had killed in the north end of the lake in 1963 or 1964 flooded the memory membranes. Could there be just one left?

No way!

I hauled in line confidently. The big, nasty nose comes into the hole, then the long, serpent-like body thrashed on the ice. About twenty-eight inches — I guessed. Maybe five pounds. Aww, shucks — maybe seven.

The minnow and hook were well down in its belly. With the pliers I pulled the lower jaw down and clipped the line as far back in the gullet as I could. He'd be feeding again by tomorrow afternoon — I thought — as I slid his snout back into the water.

Carrying the tip-up to the hole the perch had come from, I found the ice rod half buried in the wind-drifted snow.

The lousy wind! It was pouring out of the north. The toes on my left foot were snapping and yelping. They wanted blood; I wanted to fish for bluegills.

To the west, out over Fisherman's Island, the sky was glowing. It was too late, too dark, to see the spring bobber if a bluegill hit.

Gathering up the gear, I thought of Bill Lehtinen's Lab, Tara. A great duck and goose retriever, sure. But also a super tip-up dog.

She watches the little wooden sticks. When a flag springs up she follows the fish, somehow sensing from above the ice where it is. Around and around she goes, stopping only when the pike rests to play with the minnow. Then, when the pike gets serious and glides off to the weeds to swallow its meal she tags along, stopping over the fish. When she's sat in one spot long enough, you know the pike has swallowed the bait.

Not bad for a dog that's been palling around with a Finlander and an Irish beauty since she was a pup!

"Did you see the sunset?" Mary Lou asked as I clomped in with the left foot feeling like it was in a foot-thick plaster cast in which Fourth of July fireworks were going off.

"Caught a fair pike ... best one I've seen in five or six years over there ... let it go. Got too cold, with the wind, to stay for bluegills."

"That's OK. Been cooking this chili since last night. It should be ready ... have cauliflower thawed ... wanna cook a couple hot dogs in the (wood) stove?"

Geez, did I ever.

Bird Watching
February 25, 1987

There was a lot of excitement the other morning in the dining room over Matchett Lake. The sun had poked over the drumlin and Archie's cornfield only a half hour or so before. The sunrise has been humbling — a truly soothing, low drama. The kind that makes reporting to the typewriter a struggle of wills.

But I'd been at it for well over an hour. Hearing Mary Lou stumble out of bed (you can't miss it — the two dogs bound off the bed onto the floor with thuds and race for my basement office), I decided it was time for another cup of coffee.

Coming up the stairs I caught her at the dining room window doing all kinds of "oohs" and "Ooh ... look ... what is it?" (She's two-thirds blind until her second cup of coffee.)

The dogs were swishing around the dining and living room. Frantically looking for the source of the commotion.

It was outside. Two purple finches in the bird feeder. A half dozen more under it.

Now, geez, purple finches are about as common as beech leaves in these precincts. Well, not really this winter. The last time we saw finches was sometime in December. It has been a funny winter — for birds and weather.

A little thing like the first purple finch since Christmas is a big thing here and for sixty-two million other Americans, according to the U.S. Fish and Wildlife Service. We are said to spend millions of dollars for 1.2 million pounds of birdseed — at more than $12 per fifty pounds from the co-op in Charlevoix. Another $18 million is reportedly spent every year buying bird guides. How many millions more on binoculars, film, gas, boots, motel rooms, et cetera is beyond my comprehension.

The *North Woods Call* gang is only mildly into bird watching, compared to many fanatics. But as best I can tally, there are six pairs of binoculars, including one in each car, and about a dozen bird guides, including two in one car and one by each of three windows.

Birdseed is an almost crippling financial handicap. Bird appetites are too fickle for our fragile income. The Charlevoix Co-op, as an example, is on hard times — going out of business. A couple months ago the discount rate on everything in the place was twenty percent off.

Last winter our birds went wild on the little black sunflower seeds, ignoring the big striped variety. So we'd stocked up on the black ones and on thistle seeds that last winter's swarms of goldfinches devoured.

Well, early this winter they wouldn't touch the black seeds, demanding the striped ones. And the few canaries around spurned the expensive thistle seeds. So we carried fifty-pound bags of striped seeds from the co-op — at twenty percent off. Good deal, aye?

Yeah. By mid-January the big striped seeds were being rejected even by the chickadees. Only the cardinals wanted them. So there are several bags in the spare bedroom to keep over summer. And now we're investing in black sunflower seeds. And, egads, we're into fifty pounds of suet.

So, why would anyone get this crazy over little feathered creatures that really aren't that rare? Why would an old grunt go to war to assure survival of little blobs of feathers? Why does the Audubon Society have a budget in the tens of millions? Why do thousands of people stumble through snow and risk frostbite at Christmas to count birds?

If you really have to ask, you'd make a lousy neighbor!

Oh, and since the purple finches reported home, sparrows have started arriving. The chickadees and sparrows are getting sorta lovey dovey. We hear owls cooing love songs in the hardwoods. Nuthatches are doing some funny bobbing on the ash tree and also down in the woods on the beeches. Boy crows are becoming sorta reckless and pushy.

The goldfinches are trickling back. It will be a while, but they'll start to show their colors in time. Next month, sometime, we'll hear the first oriole orchestrating for a mate in the big poplar behind the garage.

I've been listening for, but haven't heard, the first drumming grouse down by Matchett or Skinner lakes.

Ah, and sometime in April, or maybe this year in late March, the bluebird and swallow scouts will return to the drumlins. That will tell us for sure that the world is OK — something you'll never learn from the TV news or the daily newspapers.

Stay tuned to the real world; watch your bird feeders.

A Walk With Thimbo
January 14, 1987

Thimbo, the seven-month-old Lab pup (pup? she weighs about sixty pounds) stood stiff-legged with her head cocked quizzically over the hard-packed snow. Then she pounced, springing about three feet all in one bound, and started digging frantically.

Within seconds she was through the crust and two or three inches of snow underneath, throwing dark swamp dirt along her belly and past her tail.

Yep. I got myself a sixty-pound brown mouser. She brings them to the door. Mary Lou shrieks and orders her to take them down the steps and back into the yard.

Just what every guy wants, a hunting dog that specializes in mice.

It must be a horrid winter for mice. Down in the swamp, where I sat watching her burrow along the mouse's tunnel, there isn't more than four inches of snow, except in little windrows here and there around blowdowns.

Being one of those weirdos who thinks mice (outdoor mice) are interesting creatures who add to life's richness, I was starting to feel guilty about turning this over-sized bundle of energy and muscle loose on them. With virtually no snow cover, they must be having a bad enough time with the owls, foxes and other natural enemies.

But if this winter is tough on mice and probably ruffed grouse, it is kind to the rest of us — whether we're winged, two-legged, or four-legged. It has been just cold enough that hiking back in the wettest part of the swamp is possible, even pleasurable. Even if the snow were deep, pleasurable is not descriptive of a swamp hike; the snowshoes hang up in the tangle and you're usually at a forty-five to sixty degree list.

Deer and humans seem to be faring about the same when navigating on the crusted snow; about every other step one foot breaks through, but it only drops three or four inches — awkward but not annoying.

The afternoon Thimbo attacked the mouse there had been a dusting of fresh snow on the old crust. Just enough to read sign — sorta.

Mice and chickadees are still taking a detour from their regular haunts to check for the handouts of seeds and nuts left around November's deer blind. A few of the sour nuts donated by Murdick's

Fudge in town remain; they must be tired of them. Not even the red squirrels are interested. (I'd carry down a supply of sunflower seeds on our late afternoon treks, but fear the little folks could become too dependent.)

One of the forever tantalizing quirks of nature is the deer-hare ratio. Everyone knows that even when snowshoe hare numbers are down, there are still enough to leave a bewildering maze of tracks in the swamp and on its edges. Not this year. Rabbit tracks are rare to nonexistent.

This year there is more deer sign than rabbit sign. The whitetails are still moving into the uplands as freely as in summer. Plenty of corn remains in Archie's harvested fields to keep them fat and warm. The downed corn is so accessible that even the grouse and squirrels are still feeding on it.

Finally beating our way through the thickest maze of the swamp, we got to the little lake. The pup made a wild dash for something she thought she saw on the ice. Almost instantly it looked like she had sixteen legs as her belly burned raw ice and her legs scrambled in all directions — including up — trying to regain footing.

There are spring holes here that an animal her size could break through. But she didn't. She got to her feet. Fell again. Then did the same thing two or three more times, walking almost tippy-toe now, sometimes looking off in the distance, like maybe if she looked the other way she wouldn't fall again.

Someone had been ice fishing several days ago. Must have been after bluegills; there are lots of holes around the lake's deepest weed bed. These were a waste of time. For some reason these bluegills seem to go into a deep slumber at ice-up.

Walking the shoreline led us to fan marks in the sprinkle of snow. Hawk or owl? But no sign of what it dove on — not even mice tracks. Thimbo saw me on my knees taking a closer look. She came up, put her nose down, then very deliberately backed away. I didn't believe she could smell a bird that fluttered in the snow for a brief moment. But what else explains it?

Down the shore, where it rises abruptly to hardwoods, an odd blob of snow hanging under the gray roots of an old blowdown cedar demanded attention. It could be a rabbit, but I didn't believe it.

Moving closer, it turned into an eyed bundle of fur, holding tight against a background of gray and brown. Winter was letting it down too.

Slipped a clip in the service .45 frame's handle and looking over my shoulder to make sure the pup wasn't about to bolt into the line of fire, let off a round. Missed, of course. The rabbit dashed north about four feet, reversed field, and then headed straight up the steep bank.

When it was all over only two rounds remained in the ten-round clip. There wasn't a speck of blood anywhere. Thimbo was standing on top of the bluff, looking down, seeming to ask what the hell that was all about. (Glad she can't talk; I wouldn't have had a very good answer.)

A splotch of green, about the size of a thumb, thrust through the dried grass along the old logging road, where it breaks through a tag and cedar-clogged swale. There is unfrozen water here. My knees were turning numb from the cold water as I knelt to see what could be growing in January.

Thimbo sat on a lump of dry ground. Did she wonder why anyone would get down on his hands and knees in spring water in January?

I could figure only one thing; it was a leek. Decided to pull it to be sure, but stopped just as my fingers closed around the base of the stem. Sorta shuddered to think I almost killed something that valiant.

So instead, I threw it a salute and wished it well. Green things in January rate adulation, not death.

Winter Tackle Boxes
January 27, 1988

They've been there, three of them on the rolled-up boat tarp in the corner, one on the floor in front of the bundle of blue plastic, since late October or early November. Just sitting there — glaring.

It had gone on so long that an acid tingle of hostility had developed. The tension and meanness had become so great that I'd try to pretend I didn't see them. But that was a lie.

One evening, when I announced I was going to the garage after supper but remained seated at the fly tying bench reading George Weeks' excellent book, *The Stewards of Michigan*, Mary Lou asked: "How come you aren't going to the garage?"

I didn't admit those four damn tackle boxes had me intimidated.

The garage is one of those three-car editions. Irv Drost, the reprobate who had it built, had one end partitioned off, insulated, carpeted, and paneled, with a regular house-type door. He put a wood stove in one end of the fancy little room. He furnished it with classy stuff made from salvaged shipwreck timbers.

Irv used the room for drinking. Yeah, that's what he claims. Irv, you see, isn't altogether daft. But, well, you know ... (Hell, he even moved to Florida.)

Irv, who was raised just up the road, grew bushels and bushels of grapes (about seven kinds, I think) — strawberries, raspberries, blueberries, rhubarb and I don't know what all.

Claims he made 500 half-gallons of wine one year. The spiffy room at the end of the garage was where he and his buddies drank the stuff.

Oh, be thankful you weren't invited. It was awful stuff. Several times he talked me into trying "just one swallow." Man, that took guts. I never drank panther-you-know-what, but if it was boiled with vinegar it would have to be better than Drost's best wine. (Of course, you can't trust my taste. I never tasted wine I could stomach — not even Tom Symons' $70-a-bottle stuff.)

The evening I decided to face up to cleaning the tackle boxes I could have used about a half gallon of Irv's "wine."

Dad taught his sons to do the worst part of the job first. So I lunged for the biggest box; jaw locked, shoulders hunched. The showdown was now. It is truly a big box. (I've lived out of rucksacks for weeks with less room in them.) It's the box I use for bass, panfish, perch, walleyes, etc. The other boxes are for inland trout lakes, Great Lakes trolling and for Mary Lou.

When I tried to jerk the big box off the tarp it just stuck there. Mean %@*#%!

So I grabbed Mary Lou's box. Good choice. It is about two feet long and fifteen inches high. She got it last year. The old one was spilling over with lures. That happens every few years.

It isn't that she uses all those lures. She just hoards them. If she sees something at the sport shop, or in my box, that is "cute" she just has to have it.

You know, we're out fishing and she spots this spoon or plug or spinner in my box: "Oh, that's cute; let me use it."

"You don't need it."

"Aww," all whimpery-eyed and wiggly-nosed, "Come on, let me try it."

Whatta ya gonna do? She's the most fun fishing pal I ever had. (The only one I ever cuddled with, too.)

Pull it out of the tackle box and she leans over the middle seat of the boat and snatches it up. Bang — gone. Forever gone.

In her box I found whole assortments of Mepps Lusox and Burke Frogbaits, still in their plastic bubble packages, with the excess cardboard neatly trimmed off so they'd take up less room. Last fall on Bay de Noc we could have used those Lusox lures. She never admitted she had them squirreled away.

She's got the biggest assortment of Loco spoons in Charlevoix or Antrim County. She is deadly with them for lake trout in Torch Lake, Lake Charlevoix and Copper Harbor. But why she needs so many I'll never know. Puts one on and it is there all day.

She also has a passion for Rapalas. There must have been at least a dozen in her box. (Guess they must be "cute" too.)

I chortled as I thought of her stock question when the fish aren't biting: "What should I use now?"

Now, if I knew that, I'd be using it and the fish would be biting. Right?

For a few years I found the question so exasperating I would give her a glib answer: "Put on a purple and green fire plug." She never did. Now I just pretend I can't hear the question.

After filching back the Super Duper spoons she'd relieved me of over the years (you can't buy them anymore, as far as I know, and they are one of the best Great Lakes smallmouth lures I've ever used), and stripping the old line from her spare spin reel spools, I closed the box and made another lunge for the big one.

This time I grabbed the handle with both hands and yanked. It came loose. Oh geez, what a mess. Last summer had been a hard one.

The top two drawers were a tangle of spinner baits, wiggle plastic things and tiny Flatfish and Mepps spinners. Lots of them were soaking in fish lure juice that had been spilled about mid-July. Yuck.

Danny Doherty (at Jack's Sport Shop), a fanatic bass fisherman, swears by the juice. I've tried a half dozen or so varieties. If it works I can't prove it — which doesn't mean it doesn't work. (I only try it when the fish aren't biting.)

But, egads, it can foul up a tackle box. This was gonna be one long and tedious chore. (Which, of course, is why the tackle boxes and I had been glaring at each other for about three months.)

In the two-car part of the garage there is an obstacle course of table and band saws, drill press, sanders, grinder, lathe, etc. In the middle is a five-gallon can of emergency gas. Heading for it I remembered a news release from Bill Cork, who writes for Plano tackle box.

Stumbling through the dark in a foot of snow, a hundred feet to the house, I fetched Bill Cork's words of wisdom from my desk. Aha. Glad I remember it. Scrunching over it back in the garage, the news release proclaimed: "Never, never clean a plastic box with gasoline. No matter how carefully you dry it, the stink will get into your lures."

Instead of gasoline, Cork insists you should use "a soft detergent — your wife's gentlest. Mix it with warm, not hot, water." Oh, dang. Another trip to the house for a bucket of "warm, not hot" water with a few squirts of Ivory dish soap in it.

Cork says use an old toothbrush to "get the gook out of nooks, crannies and corners." Well, being a guy who doesn't have teeth, I ain't got many old toothbrushes around. But I managed to scour out all the little compartments with a rag from an old tee shirt wrapped around the end of a small screwdriver.

Then, one-by-one, I hand scrubbed 22,017 plastic worms and squiggly tails. About a third of the way through I thought about getting the triple G (Gruesome Goose Gun) from the house and blowing the whole business away. (But another hike to the house was unbearable.)

Somehow the Jitterbugs and Hula Poppers, Burke Snakebaits and Frogbaits in the drawers below hadn't been contaminated.

That produced a whirl of nostalgia and reality. Some of those Jitterbugs and Hula Poppers had been purchased in the mid-1950s at a sport shop along the Huron River in Dexter. Seems to me, but don't hold me to it, there was a washed out mill pond there. As a young reporter who didn't make much money — no, make that no money — I'd spend an hour deciding which $1.50 plug to buy.

Many of my finest outdoor memories are of evenings casting Jitterbugs and Hula Poppers, with old Pflueger Summit and Supreme plug reels, to bass on small, quiet lakes where you could hear the dragonflies over the lily pads.

Sometimes, rarely, I even got a strike. Mostly I listened to the quiet and promised myself I wouldn't spend my life beating a typewriter in the city.

Those still much-loved Jitterbugs and Hula Poppers haven't been used since I discovered Bing McClellan's (Burke's) truly weedless topwater plugs and snakebaits. But they will have a place in my tackle box until some grandkid claims it, sorts it out, and throws away that "old fashioned stuff grandpa had."

Cleaning tackle boxes is a lousy job. But it is better to do it in January than June. It gives you time to remember all the good times of the past.